Richard Bednar

No. 1251
$16.95

Playing The Stock & Bond Markets
With Your Personal Computer

by L.R. Schmeltz

TAB BOOKS Inc.
BLUE RIDGE SUMMIT, PA. 17214

FIRST EDITION

FIRST PRINTING

JUNE 1981

Copyright © 1981 by TAB BOOKS Inc.

Printed in the United States of America

Library of Congress Cataloging in Publication Data

Schmeltz, LR
    Playing the stock & bond markets with your personal computer.

    Bibliography: p.
    Includes index.
    1. Investments—Data processing.   2. Mini-
computers.   I. Title.
HG4515.5.S36   332.63'2'0285404   80-28360
ISBN 0-8306-9647-4
ISBN 0-8306-1251-3 (pbk.)

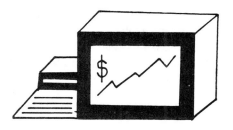

Preface

We've all seen the old western movies where the hero seems disposed to talk in monosyllables, but comes through to save the day at the last minute. Although we may have to deal in a more extensive vocabulary, the whole object of this book is to make you the wearer of the white hat in your investment melodrama.

Few books are available for the unsophisticated beginner in the investment field. Even fewer are published for the amateur interested in using a personal computer as part of an investment program. My own search for information turned up an article here and there in computer oriented magazines and a couple of books geared to programmers of large mainframe computer systems. Although much is being published about personal computers these days, integrating them into an investment program seems to be a rather large void. This book is the result of my efforts to learn something about the field of investments and how to use my personal computer in that field.

The process outlined here is based on the premise that good grounding in the basics on any field will build a solid foundation for later growth. Combining two relatively complex fields can be tedious or titillating, depending on your attitude. As a beginning effort, your purposes will be far better served by a simple process you thoroughly understand than a more complex one you don't.

What we will do, together, is develop an investment philosophy that reflects your interests, emotions, aptitudes and life style. This philosophy, once developed, will form the basis for integrating a personal computer into your investment program. By taking some of the aura of mystery from computers, you will be able to tap the potential of todays electronic state of the art.

I could certainly be remiss in not acknowledging the efforts of many people who had a hand in the preparation of this book. Marketing directors at the computer manufacturers, software supplier and publishers went out of their way to furnish information and photos. Personal correspondents, the editorial staff of TAB Books Inc. and many, many others deserve a heartfelt thank you for all their efforts.

Les Schmeltz

Contents

Chapter 1

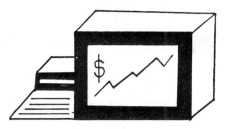

Introduction

Stock exchanges have been part of the American scene for many, many years. From humble beginnings, the major exchanges have grown to the point where millions of shares change hands daily. Investors no longer fit the old stereotype of being exceedingly rich and powerful. Sure, some of the rich and powerful still deal in the stock markets. But so do farmers, retired schoolteachers, blue collar workers, white collar workers and no collar workers. More and more Americans of modest means are turning to stocks and bonds in an attempt to offset the ravages of inflation. Many others participate more indirectly in the markets through mutual funds, pension plans, stock option fringe benefit plans and in numerous other ways.

With the dramatic diversification of stock and bond ownership has come a seemingly unquenchable thirst for information. Thousands of books for, by or about investors have been published over the years—some good, some bad. Many of the "classics" published in the early half of this century contain information surprisingly applicable to current market conditions. More recent offerings, with some notable exceptions, are geared primarily to systems and approaches for "beating the market".

Computerization came early to Wall Street. Increasing market volume generated staggering amounts of paperwork for both the exchanges and brokerage houses, creating a pressing demand for computer services. Collection, analysis and dissemination of statistical data were ideal applications for even the crudest computers. Increasingly sophisticated hardware and software have provided data processing capabilities undreamed of a few short years ago.

Fig. 1-1. The personal computer will very likely become an integral part of American family life in the near future. New applications for units such as this TRS-80 are being introduced almost daily (courtesy of Radio Shack, a division of Tandy Corp.).

Today, virtually every broker has split-second access to information from his company computer and can complete a transaction on the floor of any exchange in a matter of minutes. The next few years may well see all stock and bond transactions handled by computer to computer communications, eliminating the exchange floors entirely.

In addition to streamlining the operations on Wall Street, rapidly advancing computer technology has produced another phenomenon—the personal computer. For roughly the price of a major appliance, the investor can purchase a personal computer with as much capability as many mainframe units of a few years ago. Doubling or tripling that amount will provide the personal computer owner with capabilities unheard of as little as five years ago. Even the smallest computer, properly programmed, is capable of rapidly manipulating sizable amounts of data. Market projections are forecasting computers to be as common as television sets in American homes by the year 2000. A phenomenon? Yes. A passing fad? No! Like it or not, the personal computer will be a significant influence on many aspects of all of our lives in the very near future. See Fig. 1-1.

Virtually every company promoting personal computers lists investment analysis as one of the possible uses. Ads showing nice graphic displays of market trends or portfolio performance are far more common than the programs necessary to accomplish these displays. Even the most elaborate computer is utterly incapable of operating on its own—programs must provide specific instructions for every action taken by the computer. Some of the commercially available programs do justice to the ads, many don't.

As a personal computer owner and small investor, I found a definite lack of printed information when I started investigating possible ways to use my computer for investment purposes. A few magazine articles and books were located, but nothing that started from scratch and provided basic information was to be found. Much of the information contained in this book is the result of my own efforts to better understand the logical link between personal computing and investment management.

Hopefully, both the personal computer owner considering investment applications and the investor considering personal computing applications will find some helpful information in these pages. If you are a crack computer programmer who has stacked up a sizable fortune through astute investment advice obtained from your personal computer—you should be writing this book, not reading it!

This book will provide some basic orientation to both personal computers and the stock market, providing a foundation for further study of more detailed information as listed in the Appendices. If you are stimulated to expend the amount of time and effort necessary to pursue any of the suggestions made, our time will have been well spent.

Every effort has been made to present both the pros and cons associated with the use of a personal computer. Perhaps, after careful consideration of all the alternatives presented, you may decide a personal computer has no place in your investment program. So be it! In that case, the price of this book will save you a great deal of money and effort to reach the same decision on your own.

WHO AM I TO TALK?

Some time ago, I got interested in a method of investment analysis using moving averages to determine both market posture and individual stock recommendations. The majority of this approach was well outlined by M. G. Zahorchak in his book, *The Art Of Low Risk Investing*, Van Nostrand Reinhold Co., 1977. A number of logical steps and calculations used in this approach were ideal candidates for a computer program.

With more nerve than knowledge, I wrote and rewrote programs to capitalize on this application, each program showing a slightly firmer grasp of computerese. Finally, the program was up and running on the time share system at the office. About that time, I decided to purchase my own computer—an Apple II and adapt the stock program for it.

I described the Apple program in the November, 1979 issue of *kilobaud/microcomputing*. As a result of that article, a veritable flood of responses received. It soon became evident that many microcomputer owners were interested in investment applications.

Many of the correspondents offered suggestions for improvements and described their own systems. Others simply wanted a question or two answered, or wondered if the program was for sale. A common thread ran through most of the letters received—a real frustration at the lack of information available.

As in many relatively new fields, much of the practical knowledge available has simply not yet been published. Several of the people named in the Preface shared material and ideas developed in their efforts to integrate personal computers into their own investment programs. Although my name is listed as the author of this book, much of the credit belongs to them.

Although the program I developed has been refined, expanded and adapted for my own investment objectives, you will not find it listed in this volume. Why not? Because it reflects my biases, objectives, life style and market approach—the very same factors that will enable you to develop or modify a program to better suit your own needs.

DISCLAIMERS

In order to make you a more informed consumer of what is to follow, let me explain that I am not:

☐ A 100% successful investor who has accumulated megabucks from the market.

☐ Your personal financial advisor, a registered investment advisor or a stockbroker.

10

☐ About to divulge (if I had any) secrets to guarantee investment success.

On the other hand, I am:

☐ A computer hobbyist, "odd-lot" investor interested in developing a systematic approach to the market.

☐ Excited by the challenge of producing a usable product (program) with tangible results (making money).

☐ Convinced that my personal computer can be a valuable ally in the battle for profitable investing.

PHILOSOPHY

All authors have biases and some sort of a philosophy they are trying to convey to the reader. In the interest of saving time and digging, I would like to devote the next couple of pages to some personal thoughts on this whole business of investing in stocks and bonds, computers and related matters. Some semblence of objectivity will return in the next chapter, so read on or skip to Chapter 2—your choice.

THE NEWS

One of the most consistent producers of news copy, outside of Washington, D.C., is Wall Street. Commentators and writers (especially on slow news days) spend much time and energy telling us not only what the market did, but also offering some sort of explanation of why whatever happened happened.

These little newsy explanations can be downright entertaining at times. For years I have suspected that someone in an obscure little office reaches into a fishbowl filled with noncommittal generalizations of market behavior, inserts the current date and flashes the story to the news wires at the close of each days trading on the stock exchange.

As a small investor myself, I resent the whole world suspecting I unloaded some stock today because of "concern over rising interest rates" or "the market lacking leadership caused some profit taking late in the day". More likely the sale resulted from the fact the stock was a loser, had reached my price goal, or I was just plain tired of owning it. I certainly could live without knowing "leading economists predict a slight drop in the fourth quarter money supply" and "indicators point to a recession sometime in the second half of 1990" when I've just purchased a few shares of General Shoestring because it looks like a good buy right now.

This is not to say, however, that one can afford to ignore all the financial news. One of the strengths of the stock and bond markets is the ready accessability of relevant information. Few, if any, other investment vehicles are required to divulge equivalent amounts of information. Obviously, a lot of chaff accompanies the useful information grains.

Learning to separate the relevant from the ridiculous is an art that takes much time and practice. Once you have learned to study and digest only the information that is pertinent to you, time devoted to reading financial news will become far more productive. See Fig. 1-2.

LOSING THROUGH INTIMIDATION

The small investor is fair game for all sorts of intimidation activities. If you have ever read any of the popular financial newspapers or magazines, the number of ads for advisory services, newsletters, money managers, mutual funds, etc. has probably caught your eye.

You know the type of ads I'm talking about—they inevitably start off with blaring headlines announcing some startling revelation or another like:

—Will you know when Lipshitz calls the next major market move?

—The Dow, is it headed for 1100 or 500 by the end of the year? Dr. Yutz tells all in this special report!

—Special research report on a little known (fill in the blank) stock free to new subscribers.

—Midnight Mutual Fund leads the way to new investment opportunities!

—Etc., etc., etc. . . .

Everything from investment grade diamonds to ranch lands in Alaska are opportunities crying for some smart investor to jump in, so they say. Brokerage houses, professional money managers, and even market statistics are presented in such a fashion that the general public is suitably impressed.

The operating premise common to most of these sources of intimidation is simply that the average investor is utterly incapable of making an intelligent decision. (If history repeats itself, they may not be too far wrong). Better to listen to us or buy our services, they say, than to try to go it alone in this financial jungle.

Well friends, contrary to the hype being presented, an average investor **can** make his own decisions and do just fine without the overpriced "crystal ball". Nobody, but nobody, knows what is going to happen in the future—your guess is every bit as good as anyone elses.

Brokerage houses advertise their prowess in handling transactions involving millions of shares, but very few (if any) turn away the small investor interested in only a few shares at a time. Any broker worth his salt is more than willing to work with you in developing a mutually profitable relationship.

Don't let yourself be intimidated into thinking investments are reserved only for the "pros". There is plenty of room in the market for anyone interested in participating, whether they are dealing in a few million or just a few shares at a time.

THE WHIMPERING HERD

We've all seen the thundering herd advertised on TV, usually during golf tournaments. (Never could figure out why during golf—guess I must belong to the upper crust because I'm interested in picking up a few pointers for my weekly excursions to the public links!) Anyway, "Herd Psychology" is a term often used to describe the group behavior of professional money managers and mutual fund advisors.

This "whimpering herd" has stampeded its way through a lot of investment fads, dealing in numbers of shares that cause tremors through the market with every transaction. Many major market moves are precipitated by the rest of the herd jumping on the bandwagon with one of their fellows who has enough conviction to lead the way. With the overwhelming majority of shares on the New York Stock Exchange controlled by this herd, obviously the market is going to go down when they all decide to sell and up when a buy is in progress.

The secret, of course, for the small investor is to buy when the herd is selling and sell when they are buying. Although this may be easier said than done, many unique opportunities are presented to the perceptive investor. A few shares here and there certainly won't disrupt the orderly market, especially when the herd is looking for buyers or sellers.

THE FACTS OF LIFE

Certain facts must be learned prior to undertaking any activity, others become self-evident along the way. My all time favorite cartoon caption summarizes this best by saying there are certain things you just cannot explain to a virgin!

As a small investor, I make no claims to being an oracle of market advice. Here are a few gems of wisdom, however, I have gathered along the way that may be of some interest to you:

CLEVELAND ELECTRIC NYSE-CVX

RECENT PRICE 16 | **P/E RATIO** 6.8 (Norm 8.6 / Trail'g 7.1) | **DIV'D YIELD** 12.8% (Norm 8.9% / Trail'g 12.3%)

Target Price Range 30 — 1983 1984 1985
25 (+56%) — 25
20 (+25%) — 20

TIMELINESS 3 Average
(Relative Price Performance Next 12 Mos.)
SAFETY 1 Highest
(Scale: 1 Highest to 5 Lowest)
BETA .65

Aug. 22, 1980 Value Line

© Arnold Bernhard & Co. Inc.

1.06 x Dividends p sh divided by Interest Rate

3-for-2 split

Relative Price Strength

Percent 3.0 / 2.0 / 1.0 shares traded

CAPITAL STRUCTURE as of 3/31/80

Total Debt $1191.3 mill. Due in 5 Yrs $240.3 mill.
LT Debt $994.0 mill. LT Interest $74.4 mill.
(LT interest earned: 2.2x)
Pension Liability $10.0 mill. in '79 vs $13.0 mill. in '78

Leases, Uncapitalized Annual rentals $6.0 mill.
Pfd Stock $327.1 mill. Pfd Div'd $25.4 mill.
1,200,000 shs. $7.35 to $7.56 cum. ($100 stated value). call. 105 to 110. 150,000 shs. $75 to $88 cum. ($1000 stated value). call. 1075 to 1088. 57,000 shs. $77.50 cum. preference ($1000 stated value). incl. $232 mill. with sinking fund beginning 6/1/81.
Common Stock 41,551,330 shs.

OPERATING STATISTICS

	1977	1978	1979
% Change Sales (KWH)	---	+ 1.6	+ 3.6
Avg. Resid'l Use (KWH)	6412	6517	6557
Avg. Revs. per KWH (¢)	4.80	5.00	5.48
Capacity at Peak (Mw)	4386	4556	4511
Peak Load, Summer (Mw)	3550	3249	3097
Annual Load Factor (%)	64.5	66.1	67.3
% Change Customers (yr.-end)	+ .5	+ .9	+ .8
Fixed Charge Cov. (%)	145	122	128

Est'd Ann'l Tot'l Return: 16%-21%
% Due to Yield: 12.8% — 16%-15%
% Due to Growth: 2.2% — 15%-15%
% Due to P/E Change: — 1.0%-6.0%

	1970	1971	1972	1973	1974	1975	1976	1977	1978	1979	1980	1981	83-85E
Price range high	26.4	28.5	25.9	25.3	22.2	18.9	23.2	23.4	22.8	19.6	18.5		
Price range low	18.7	22.1	21.2	18.7	13.5	15.6	17.7	21.3	16.6	15.5	13.5		
Revenues per sh	12.08	13.27	14.31	15.95	22.36	21.48	19.16	20.36	19.92	19.97	19.65	20.00	24.60
"Cash Flow" per sh	3.07	3.28	3.48	3.59	3.97	3.41	3.53	4.09	3.70	3.58	3.60	3.65	4.15
Earnings per sh	2.01	2.04	2.15	2.03	2.45	2.11	2.38	2.91	2.20	2.31	2.35	2.40	2.80

14

Cal-endar	QUARTERLY REVENUES ($ mill.)				Full
	Mar. 31	June 30	Sept. 30	Dec. 31	Year
1977	167.6	153.7	176.8	161.2	659.3
1978	191.1	163.9	186.5	175.6	717.1
1979	201.6	197.1	225.2	200.4	824.3
1980	217.4	198.8	260	223.8	900
1981	245	240	250	265	1000

Cal-endar	EARNINGS PER SHARE				(A)Full
	Mar. 31	June 30	Sept. 30	Dec. 31	Year
1977	.90	.65	.75	.61	2.91
1978	.53	.42	.68	.57	2.20
1979	.50	.45	.93	.43	(E)2.31
1980	.45	.45	.95	.50	.2.35
1981	.45	.45	1.00	.50	2.40

Cal-endar	QUARTERLY DIVIDENDS PAID				(B)Full
	Mar. 31	June 30	Sept. 30	Dec. 31	Year
1976	.427	.427	.427	.427	1.71
1977	.44	.44	.44	.44	1.76
1978	.46	.46	.46	.46	1.84
1979	.48	.48	.48	.48	1.92
1980	.50	.50	.50	.50	

(A) Egs. rep't due late Oct. Est'd constant-dollar egs./sh.: '79, 15¢. (B) Next tax-free in '79. ■ Div'd reinvest. plan av'. div'd meet'g about Sept. 23. Goes ex ble. about Oct. 14. Div'd paym't dates: Feb. — 15, May 15, Aug. 15, Nov. 15. Est'd 44% all'd on com. eq. in '80: 14.4%. Earn. avg.' com. eq. '79: 11.5%. Reg. Climate: Avg. (C) Excl. def. chgs. in '79: $1.86/sh. (E) Excl. cum. effect of change in deprec. Rate base: deprec. orig. cost. Rate acct'g: 11¢/sh.

Item													Est.
(D)Div'ds Decl'd per sh ■	1.44	1.49	1.52	1.55	1.60	1.65	1.71	1.76	1.84	1.92	2.00	2.08(D)	2.40
Cap'l Spending per sh	5.21	6.04	6.58	7.18	8.38	7.46	9.72	8.85	8.36	9.35	8.20	6.75	5.40
(C)Tangible Book Value sh	13.84	14.42	14.97	15.54	15.32	16.19	17.31	18.91	19.12	18.02	18.10	18.40	19.50
Avg Ann'l P/E Ratio	20.31	20.40	20.50	20.61	20.75	24.35	28.35	32.39	36.00	41.27	45.80	50.00	58.00
Avg Ann'l Div'd Yield	6.5%	6.2%	6.6%	7.1%	9.2%	9.4%	8.7%	7.9%	9.3%	10.8%	7.7	9.9%	
Revenues ($mill)	245.4	270.7	293.3	328.8	463.9	523.2	543.2	659.3	717.1	824.3	900	1000	1475
Net Profit ($mill)	40.7	41.7	49.1	49.4	60.7	64.8	81.7	111.7	99.0	113.5	133	145	195
Income Tax Rate	31.1%	26.1%	22.2%	18.3%	20.6%	14.5%	16.5%	25.5%	16.8%	20.3%	27.5%	24.0%	17.0%
Net Profit Margin	16.6%	15.4%	16.7%	15.0%	13.1%	12.4%	15.0%	17.0%	13.8%	13.8%	14.7%	14.5%	13.0%
Long-Term Debt Ratio	57.8%	52.9%	54.5%	52.9%	48.6%	53.3%	50.2%	49.2%	47.1%	45.9%	45.5%	45.5%	48.0%
Common Equity Ratio	42.3%	40.4%	34.9%	34.4%	35.3%	33.3%	34.4%	35.2%	36.2%	38.7%	39.5%	40.0%	40.0%
Total Capital ($mill)	679.2	741.3	900.9	949.8	983.0	1263.1	1488.8	1799.7	1956.9	2121.5	2315	2490	3000
Net Plant ($mill)	712.9	809.4	915.7	1035.4	1178.3	1329.7	1572.2	1816.7	2062.1	2340.6	2715	2975	3700
% Earned Total Cap'l	7.3%	7.3%	7.0%	7.0%	8.1%	7.3%	7.3%	8.0%	6.9%	7.2%	8.0%	8.0%	8.5%
% Earned Net Worth	14.2%	11.9%	12.0%	11.1%	12.0%	11.0%	11.0%	12.2%	9.6%	9.9%	10.5%	10.5%	12.5%
% Earned Comm Equity	14.2%	13.9%	14.0%	12.9%	14.6%	11.9%	12.5%	14.1%	10.8%	10.7%	11.5%	11.5%	13.5%
% Retained to Comm Eq	4.0%	3.7%	4.1%	3.1%	5.1%	2.7%	3.8%	5.7%	1.9%	2.0%	1.5%	1.5%	2.0%
% All Div'ds to Net Prof	72%	73%	73%	79%	71%	82%	76%	68%	86%	86%	88%	89%	88%

Bold figures are VL estimates

Company's Financial Strength	A+
Stock's Price Stability	95
Price Growth Persistence	35
Earnings Predictability	70

Fig. 1-2. Much of the relevant information regarding a corporation and its stock can be gathered from a concise statistical summary such as those published by Value Line (courtesy of Arnold Bernhard & Co., Inc.).

☐ Work as hard making your money earn more money as you did to earn it in the first place. Successful investing involves effort and knowledge on your part.

☐ Hindsight is always 20/20. Results of an investment decision made in the present won't become evident until the future, at which time it will be too late to do anymore about it. Like the captain who steers his ship by watching only the stern, you will run aground without a forward course to follow.

☐ Investment success should be measured in terms of positive gains. It is not necessary to "make a killing" to be successful, but your program should be making enough gains to offset inflation, taxes, expenses and still provide a reasonable profit.

☐ The best investment approach is one that suits **you**. Developing such an approach is an interesting challenge and insures priority consideration of your personal biases.

☐ Computer objectivity can be helpful in many investment programs, but is no substitute for common sense. Properly programmed, your computer can analyze and manipulate data to aid in your decision making process.

☐ "Churning" is not necessarily investing, although your broker will love the fees generated with each trade. In fact, there are times when you should not even be in the market! Look before you leap, and again before you change.

☐ Disasters are valuable learning experiences. As a matter of fact, those lessons we all learn the hard way seem to be etched indelibly in our minds. Losing a few dollars as the result of a poor decision virtually insures that same decision will not be made again, losing a bundle guarantees it!

DAMN THE TORPEDOES, FULL SPEED AHEAD!

Now that's off my chest, lets get to work developing *your* investment program. In the next few chapters we will discuss computers, investment goals and approaches, and timing. By Chapter 6, we should be ready to start the process of integrating *your* computer into *your* investment program.

Throughout the pages that follow, you will see frequent references to information contained in the Appendices. Do take a few minutes to look over those pages and pursue the topics which interest you. One of the goals of an introductory book on any subject is to provide sources of information for further study. This book is billed, and written, as a general overview of many topics that require more detailed presentation for full understanding.

Chapter 2

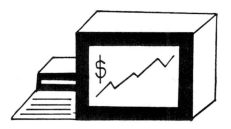

Personal Computers For Investors

Personal computers for investors vary widely depending on the scale of both pocketbook and expectations. To some of the more affluent among us, a HP3000 or IBM370 could be considered a personal computer. More realistic, however, are the low to medium priced systems such as the Apple or TRS-80. An operational definition of a personal computer should take into account the wide range of variability noted above. Perhaps the most logical definition is—"a personal computer is one dedicated to personal use".

Of course, personal use need not be a full time vacation for any computer. The small businessman who purchases a computer for the office can certainly use the same unit for personal applications after business hours. Even computer access purchased on a time-share system can be classed personal computing if that time is used for personal applications. In fact, some data processing firms solicit personal applications to keep their computers busy during the off times.

As we discuss personal computers in this chapter, time-share and large mainframe units will be somewhat neglected. Keep in mind that most applications discussed for personal units can be handled just as well in a time-share system. Often the larger system will offer advantages of more data storage and faster execution times, offset by the disadvantages of limited access and lack of data security.

All computers, from the smallest personal unit to the largest mainframe, share certain common components:

☐ **Central Processing Unit (CPU).** This is the heart of the computer where most of the actual manipulation of data occurs.

Deceptively simple instructions tell the CPU to fetch data from certain memory locations, perform an operation on the data and store the result in another memory location. As sophistication of the CPU increases, so do the number and speed of operations performed. The term *the CPU* implies only one chip, which is not necessarily the case—often there are several chips necessary to make up the CPU. Most personal computers on the market today use one of four popular CPU chips—8080, Z80, 6800 or 6502. Numerous new microprocessor chips are in the design and testing stages, so those mentioned may fall victim to advances in technology.

☐ **Memory.** As the name implies, memory is the place where data is stored. Storage capacity is usually stated in multiples of 1024 bytes, i.e., 1K. There are many types of memory available, commonly divided into *Random Access Memory* (RAM) and *Read Only Memory* (ROM). Within these major categories, numerous variations are offered. Random Access Memory is easily accessed by both the processor and user in most applications. Reading and writing to at least a significant portion of this type of memory takes place constantly during the execution of a program. Most RAM is volatile, meaning that data is lost once power is removed from the system. Read Only Memory, as the name implies, cannot be written over from a program or user instruction. This type of memory is typically programmed with languages, operating systems and frequently used routines that remain intact whether or not power is applied to the system. Programming and erasing ROM devices requires special procedures and equipment, consequently this is not done by very many personal computer users.

☐ **Input/Output (I/O) Devices.** These devices interface the computer's memory to the outside world for both input and output of data. Probably the most common input device for personal computers is the keyboard, followed closely by the cassette tape recorder or floppy disk drive. Output may be directed to a video display, printer or mass storage device.

☐ **Peripherals.** This is a generic term used to define a host of devices that can send information to or receive information from a computer. Modems, television monitors and printers are only a few of the commonly used peripherals. Devices such as graphic plotters, light pens, graphic input tablets, home security sensors, remote control systems and countless others are presently being marketed for use with personal computer systems.

In this book, we will be looking at several computer systems from a users point of view, stressing capabilities and features of interest for investment applications. We will not be delving into the actual mechanics of computer design and operation, a subject that could take several volumes the size of this one. If you are interested in more detail, several excellent publications are available as listed in the Appendices.

EXAMPLES OF SYSTEMS

The next several pages provide basic information on some of the personal computer systems presently available. This is by no means a complete directory, but is intended primarily to show the wide variation in configurations and capabilities currently offered. Prices for these systems range from just over $600 to well over $13,000, but lower and higher priced systems are readily available.

In virtually all cases, I have selected only one or two models from a more extensive selection offered by each manufacturer. My selection of both models and manufacturers is purely arbitrary, and not intended to imply the systems illustrated are the only ones you should consider for purchase.

Information contained in these pages have been provided by the manufacturers involved and is current as of this writing. The speed with which the personal computing field is moving today makes it difficult, if not impossible, to insure currency of this information for more than a limited time. More detailed and current literature may be obtained by contacting the manufacturer or your local computer retailer.

Apple Computer, Inc.

Models: Apple II, See Fig. 2-1. Apple II Plus, see Fig. 2-2.
Standard Features:

> 6502 microprocessor.
> 16K RAM, expandable to 48K.
> Color graphics, low and high resolution.
> Cassette interface.
> Game I/O connector, 2 controls included.
> ASCII keyboard.
> Display—24 × 40, upper case only.
> Assembler, disassembler and monitor in ROM.
> Integer BASIC (6K ROM)—Apple II.
> Applesoft BASIC (10K ROM)—Apple II Plus.
> High efficiency switching power supply.

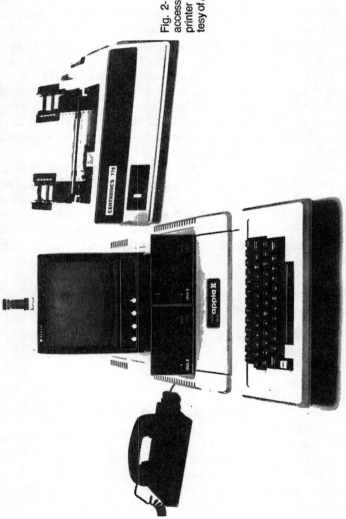

Fig. 2-1. The Apple II shown with accessory Disk II, television monitor, printer and acoustic modem (courtesy of Apple Computer, Inc.).

Fig. 2-2. The Apple II Plus (courtesy of Apple Computer, Inc.).

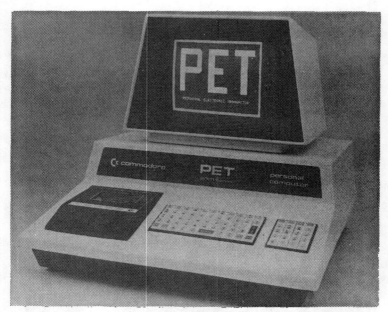

Fig. 2-3. PET 2001 (courtesy of Commodore Business Machines, Inc.).

Languages Available:

Applesoft ROM for Apple II.

Integer BASIC for Apple II Plus.

PASCAL language system.

Peripherals Needed For Operation:

Video monitor or standard television set with RF modulator.

Cassette tape recorder.

Peripherals Offered By Manufacturer:

Disk II floppy disk subsystem.

Video monitor.

Interface cards—communications, serial and parallel (several variations).

Graphics input tablet.

Clock/calendar card.

Various printers.

Numerous others.

Software Offered By Manufacturer? Yes

Expansion Compatibility:

Apple bus.

Manufacturer:
Apple Computer, Inc.
10260 Bandley Drive
Cupertino, CA 95014

Commodore Business Machines

Models: PET 2001, see Fig. 2-3. CBM 2001, see Fig. 2-4.
Standard Features:
6502 microprocessor.
16 or 32K RAM.
64 graphics characters.
2 cassette ports.
Keyboard—73 key typewriter style upper and lower case or upper case plus 64 graphics characters.
Display—built in CRT 25 x 50 and graphics.
14K ROM BASIC, machine language monitor, tape and disk file handling software.
IEEE parallel port.
Internal calendar/clock.
Languages Available:
BASIC (version 3.0) included.
Peripherals Needed For Operation:
Cassette tape recorder for standard keyboard models.

Fig. 2-4. CBM 2001 (courtesy of Commodore Business Machines, Inc.).

Fig. 2-5. Heathkit H89 (courtesy of Heath Company).

Peripherals Offered By Manufacturer:
    CMB Dual Drive Floppy Disk.
    Tractor Feed Printer.
    Cassette tape unit.
Software Offered By Manufacturer? Yes
Expansion Compatibility:
    IEEE-488 bus.
Manufacturer:
    Commodore Business Machines, Inc.
    950 Rittenhouse Road
    Norristown, PA 19401

Heath Company

Model: H89, see Fig. 2-5.
Standard Features:
    2 Z80 microprocessors.
    16K RAM, expandable to 48K.
    Floppy disk subsystem built in.
    Keyboard—typewriter format, 80 keys with numeric keypad.
    Display—built in CRT, 25 × 80 upper and lower case.
    Graphics—33 symbols included.
    Audio cassette interface included.
Languages Available:
    Floppy Disk Systems Software—included extended Benton

Harbor BASIC, assembler, text editor and disk utilities.

Cassette Systems Software—similar to above, use with cassette files.

MICROSOFT (tm) BASIC.

MICROSOFT (tm) FORTRAN.

Peripherals Needed For Operation:

Systems Software (purchased separately).

Peripherals Offered By Manufacturer:

Systems Software.

Serial and parallel interfaces.

Additional disk drives.

Printers.

Modems, cassette units, etc.

Software Offered By Manufacturer? Yes

Manufacturer:

Heath Company

Benton Harbor, MI 49022

Hewlett Packard

Model: HP-85, see Fig. 2-6.

Standard Features:

16K RAM, expandable to 32K.

Magnetic tape cartridge unit built in.

Fig. 2-6. The HP-85 (courtesy of Hewlett Packard).

Graphics—256 × 192 dot plotting area.

Keyboard—typewriter style with separate numeric keypad and special function keys.

Display—built in CRT (5″ diagonal) 16 × 32.

Printer—built in bidirectional thermal prints two 32 character lines per second, dot-for-dot reproduction of graphics display.

HP Extended BASIC and graphic system built in.

System clock and timer.

Four I/O ports.

Languages Available:
HP Extended BASIC (included).

Peripherals Needed For Operation:
None.

Peripherals Offered By Manufacturer:
Interface Modules.

Enhancement ROMs for matrix math general input/output and printer/plotter.

Numerous printers and plotters.

Flexible disk drives and operating systems.

16K memory expansion module.

Software Offered By Manufacturer? Yes.

Manufacturer:
Hewlett Packard
1000 N.E. Circle Boulevard
Corvallis, OR 97330

Intertec Data Systems

Model: SUPERBRAIN, see Fig. 2-7.

Standard Features:
2 Z80A microprocessors.

32K RAM, expandable to 64K.

2 double density minifloppy disk drives built in.

Graphics—11 line drawing characters.

Keyboard—typewriter style with separate numeric keypad.

Display—built in CRT, 25 × 80 upper and lower case.

Serial (RS232) and parallel interfaces.

CP/M disk operating system.

8080 disk assembler, debugger, text editor and file handling utilities included.

Languages Available:
MICROSOFT (tm) BASIC.

MICROSOFT (tm) FORTRAN.

All CP/M compatible languages.

Fig. 2-7. SUPERBRAIN (courtesy of Intertec Data Systems, Inc.).

Peripherals Needed For Operation:
> None.

Peripherals Offered By Manufacturer:
> S-100 bus adaptor.
> 32K RAM expansion package.

Software Offered By Manufacturer? No.

Expansion Compatibility:
> S-100 bus.

Manufacturer:
> Intertec Data Systems
> 2300 Broad River Road
> Columbia, SC 29210

Midwest Scientific Instruments, Inc.

Model: MSI-6800, see Fig. 2-8.

Standard Features:
> 6800 microprocessor.
> 8K RAM, expandable.
> 16 position motherboard.
> Disk bootstrap EPROM.
> Serial interface.
> Interface adaptor.
> Power supply.
> Chassis with card rack assembly.

Languages Available:
    BASIC (several versions).
    Compiler, text editor, assembler.
Peripherals Needed For Operation:
    Terminal (CRT or printer).
    Cassette tape recorder and interface.
Peripherals Offered By Manufacturer:
    The MSI-6800 is a mainframe unit and the basis for many
    systems offered by MSI. Multiple peripherals and accessories
    are offered.
Software Offered By Manufacturer? Yes.
Expansion Compatibility:
    SS-50 bus.
Manufacturer:
    Midwest Scientific Instruments, Inc.
    220 West Cedar
    Olathe, KS 66061

NEC Information Systems

Model: Astra Model 205 System, see Fig. 2-9.
Standard Features:
    16 bit microprocessor.
    128K RAM, expandable to 256K.
    2 dual sided/dual density diskette drives built in.
    Keyboard—typewriter style with separate numeric keypad
    and special function keys.
    Display—CRT included.
    120 character-per-second matrix printer included.
    Supports COBOL, BASIC and a macro assembler language.
    Communications protocols for network applications.
Languages Available:
    See above.
Peripherals Needed For Operation:
    None.
Peripherals Offered By Manufacturer:
    Printers.
    Disk drives.
    Others necessary for network operation.
Software Offered By Manufacturer? Yes.
Expansion Compatibility:
    Through built in communications protocols and ports.

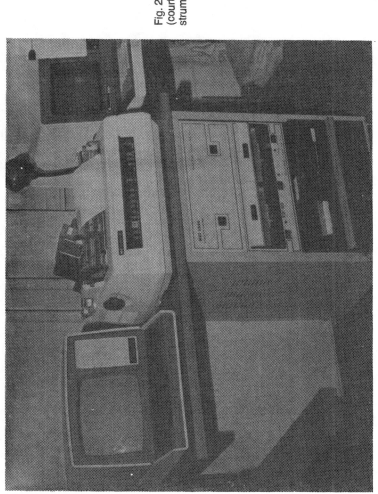

Fig. 2-8. MSI-6800, with peripherals (courtesy of Midwest Scientific Instruments, Inc.).

Fig. 2-9. Astra Model 205 (courtesy of NEC Information System, Inc.).

Manufacturer:
NEC Information Systems, Inc.
5 Militia Drive
Lexington, MA 02173

Ohio Scientific

Models: C4P, C4P MF, see Fig. 2-10.
Standard Features:
6502 microprocessor.
8K RAM expandable to 32K.
Graphics—16 colors, 256 × 512 point resolution.
Keyboard—typewriter style, 53 key.
Display—32 × 64, upper and lower case.
2 keypad and joystick interfaces.
Audio cassette interface.
AC remote control interface.
BASIC in ROM (8K).
Programmable 200-20kHz tone generator.
Model C4P MF includes all features above plus:
Real time clock and countdown timer.
Modem and printer interface.
24K RAM.
Single mini floppy disk drive.

Fig. 2-10. Challenger C4P-F, color monitor optional (courtesy of Ohio Scientific).

16 parallel lines for additional control interfaces.
Accessory bus for external 48 line I/O board.
Home security interface.
Foreground/Background processing capability.
PROM "blaster".

Languages Available:
Disk BASIC.
Assembler/Editor.
Extended Monitor.

Peripherals Needed For Operation:
Video monitor or television set with RF modulator.
Cassette tape recorder (C4P).

Peripherals Offered By Manufacturer:
GT option—includes 6502C microprocessor and fast access memory.
Printers, modems, accessory boards, etc.

Software Offered By Manufacturer? Yes.

Expansion Compatibility:
OSI bus.

Manufacturer:
Ohio Scientific
1333 South Chillicothe Road
Aurora, OH 44202

Radio Shack

Model: TRS-80, Model I, Level II, see Fig. 2-11.

Standard Features:
Z80 microprocessor.
4K or 16K RAM, expandable to 48K.
Graphics—128 × 48 point resolution.
Keyboard—typewriter style with separate numeric keypad (16K models).
Display—CRT furnished, 16 × 64 upper case only.
Cassette tape recorder and interface.
BASIC (16K) in ROM.

Languages Available:
"T" Bug monitor program.
Editor/Assembler.
FORTRAN (disk only).

Peripherals Needed For Operation:
None.

Fig. 2-11. TRS-80 Model I, Level II 16K (courtesy of Radio Shack, a division of Tandy Corp.).

33

Peripherals Offered By Manufacturer:
Expansion interface.
Mini disk system.
Voice synthesizer.
VOXBOX.
Serial interface board.
Telephone interface and modem.
Various printers and accessories.
Software Offered By Manufacturer? Yes.
Expansion Compatibility:
Through expansion interface.
Manufacturer:
Radio Shack Division
Tandy Corporation
1300 One Tandy Center
Fort Worth, TX 76102

Model: TRS-80 Model II, see Fig. 2-12.
Standard Features:
2 Z80A microprocessors.
32K or 64K RAM.
8 inch disk drive built in.
Keyboard—typewriter style with separate numeric keypad.
Display—built in 12" CRT, 24 × 80, upper and lower case.
1 parallel, 2 serial expansion connectors.
Level III BASIC furnished on disk.
Languages Available:
Level III BASIC furnished.
Peripherals Needed For Operation:
None.
Peripherals Offered By Manufacturer:
Disk expansion unit.
Additional memory.
Printers, accessories, etc.
Software Offered By Manufacturer: Yes.
Expansion Compatibility:
Through built in ports.

Manufacturer:
Radio Shack Division
Tandy Corporation
1300 One Tandy Center
Fort Worth, TX 76102

Fig. 2-12. TRS-80 Model II (courtesy of Radio Shack, a division of Tandy Corp.).

Smoke Signal Broadcasting

Model: Chieftain I, see Fig. 2-13.
Standard Features:
> 6800 microprocessor.
> 32K RAM.
> 2 mini floppy disk drives.
> 2K EPROM monitor.
> 2 serial I/O ports.
> Heavy duty power supply.
> 9 slot motherboard.
> DOS 68 Disk Operating System.
> DSB 68 Disk File BASIC.

Languages Available:
> Editor/Assembler.
> FORTRAN.
> PASCAL.

Peripherals Needed For Operation:
> Terminal (CRT or printer).

Peripherals Offered By Manufacturer:
> Disk systems.
> CRT terminals.

Printers.

Various expansion and interface boards.

Software Offered By Manufacturer? No.
(languages and utilities only).

Expansion Compatibility:
SS 50 bus.

Manufacturer:
Smoke Signal Broadcasting
31336 Via Colinas
Westlake Village, CA 91361

Texas Instruments

Model: TI-99/4, see Fig. 2-14.

Standard Features:
9900 family microprocessor.
16K RAM.
26K ROM contains operating system, BASIC, floating point, sound and color graphics.
Graphics—16 color, 192×256 point resolution.
Music and sound effects.
Equation calculator.
Display—13" color monitor furnished, 24×32.
Plug in software modules, up to 30K ROM.
Dual cassette I/O port.
Built in I/O ports.

Languages Available:
BASIC (furnished).

Peripherals Needed For Operation:
None.

Peripherals Offered By Manufacturer:
Remote controls.
RS232 peripheral adapter.
Floppy disk subsystem.
Speech synthesizer.
Telephone coupler modem.
Printers.

Software Offered By Manufacturer? Yes (Solid State Software Comand Modules).

Expansion Compatibility:
Through built in ports.

Manufacturer:

Texas Instruments, Inc.	P. O. Box 53 (ATTN: TI-99/4)
Consumer Relations Dept.	Lubbock, TX 79408

Fig. 2-13. The Chieftain I (courtesy of Smoke Signal Broadcasting).

37

Fig. 2-14. TI-99/4 (courtesy of Texas Instruments, Inc.).

As you probably noticed in looking over the last several pages, personal computers come in all shapes and sizes. Just as this is being written, one manufacturer has introduced a fully capable computer the size of a pocket calculator! With the tremendous market projected for small computers in the very near future, one would certainly expect competition to produce even more capability and price variations.

Very few systems presently on the market are totally self-contained. More commonly the basic unit requires at least one or two additional items to operate and offers many options for later expansion of capability (does this remind you of the Barbie doll and her wardrobe, accessories, etc., etc.?). A little later in this chapter we will discuss how to most efficiently personalize the capability of your system to handle the job of investment analysis.

GENERAL CAPABILITIES

Most of the personal computers considered in the preceeding pages have some capabilities in common:

—One or more high level languages are supported, increasing the ease of programming.

—Commercial and user-generated software is readily available.

—Relatively large blocks of memory can be addressed. Many have operating systems and languages in ROM, freeing more of the RAM for programming use.

—Some graphics capability. Rudimentary graphics can be generated by almost all of the systems, a few have rather extensive graphics included.

—Provision for mass storage, either on cassette tape or floppy diskette. Several support multiple tape or disk drives for more extensive data access.

—Expandability to accommodate multiple peripherals.

—High speed manipulation of data investors are likely to be dealing with most often.

GENERAL LIMITATIONS

The nature of personal computers does impose some limitations on both the type and amount of data processing that can be accomplished easily:

—Some knowledge of operating procedures on your particular computer are needed to successfully execute programs.

—Software (programs) must usually be written specifically for the type of computer involved. Despite the fact that high level languages are fairly standard, differences among systems preclude universal software development.

—Most personal systems are capable of executing only one program at a time, limiting the possibilities for time sharing and intercomputer communications.

PERSONALIZING CAPABILITIES

The capability of your personal computer system can easily be tailored to your particular requirements. In most cases, additional hardware is available to accommodate any increase in your application sophistication.

Memory

Memory, for instance, can be added to the Apple II and other systems by simply plugging the proper integrated circuit chips into sockets already supplied. Some systems use memory boards which are readily available from many suppliers. With the cost of memory chips constantly decreasing, there is little justification for operating a computer with less than its full complement of memory.

Storage

Some sort of mass storage device is a necessity unless you plan on entering your data from the keyboard each time a program is run. Most commonly, cassette tape is used as the standard storage device. Mini floppy (5 ¼″) diskettes are the next most common mass storage devices. Closely resembling a very thin phonograph record enclosed in an envelope, disks are available in two common sizes—5 ¼″ (mini floppies) and 8″ (floppies). Drives for these disks may be capable of single, dual or quad density operation on one or both sides of each disk. "Hard" disks, until recently the province of large computer systems, are becoming increasingly available for personal applications. Disks of any type offer speed and flexibility advantages over cassette tape, although the cost of disk drives is at least several times that of a good quality cassette recorder. You may want to consider both mediums in your system if your finances permit.

Displays

For those computers not equipped with a built-in video display, you will need to add one. Low cost RF converters allow the video output of a computer to be displayed on any standard television receiver, or you may select a monitor that accepts computer video output directly. If you plan to do a great deal of graphics work, a monitor will probably be more satisfactory. Color capable systems are especially sensitive to the video display quality. High quality portable color television receivers have proven quite adequate for color graphics. Recently, a moderately priced 13 inch color monitor was introduced by one of the major television manufacturers (Zenith) and more are sure to follow suit.

Languages

Most personal computers offer at least two languages—machine and BASIC. Machine language varies with the type of CPU chip used, although many commands are fairly universal. Programming in machine language is a tedious task at best. Learning to program in machine language is rewarded, however, by being able to create programs that run several times faster than those written in higher level languages. Assembly language is a low level language similar to machine code, but is somewhat easier to use and offered in many systems.

BASIC, in one of its many versions, is available for every microcomputer currently on the market. BASIC (Beginners All-purpose Symbolic Instruction Code) was developed at Dartmouth College in 1963 and has since become the defacto standard language of the personal computing world. Many variations of BASIC have appeared, some severely limited and others extended to allow special system operations such as graphics. The over-whelming majority of commercial software presently available is written in BASIC.

As suggested by the acronym, BASIC is a relatively easy language to learn and use. In *Standard* or *Extended* form, BASIC is a very capable and versatile programming language. Some of the limited versions are incapable of manipulating floating point arithmetic, string data and arrays. If you have a choice, be sure your BASIC includes all three.

Other languages are slowly finding their way into personal computers. FORTH, FORTRAN, COBOL, APL and PASCAL are currently on the market for various computer systems. Numerous language availability has done little, as yet, to diminish the popularity of BASIC.

In Chapter 6 we will further consider the role of languages in actually developing programs. Several excellent sources of information about various languages are listed in the bibliography.

SHOPPING

If you are not already a personal computer owner, many decisions need to be made before purchasing one. Articles and books to help in these decisions may be found in the bibliography, so we won't devote a lot of space to this topic. For investment analysis purposes, you may be well advised to consider purchasing as much memory capacity as you can afford. Efficient mass storage, either tape or disk, is also a priority consideration.

Within the limitations of your budget, consider also the other applications you have in mind and purchase a unit with provision for future expansion. Graphics, for instance, was not of my priority considerations when I purchased my own computer. Although some of my recent programs use graphics, they don't begin to compete with my kids who seize the computer at every opportunity to play a few of their favorite graphics games.

Local service and support can be important factors, especially if you will need someone to get you started at a very basic level (and what new computer owner doesn't?). Many of the companies selling computers by mail order provide toll-free telephone numbers and rapid service for the same purpose.

Any of the personal computers shown in the earlier illustrations, along with many more not shown, would adequately suit most investment purposes. A look through several of the personal computing magazines will give you a better idea of what is currently on the market. Good luck and good shopping!

YOUR DATA BASE

In the world of large mainframe computers, a data base is a large body of information that can be retrieved, updated, manipulated and stored by multiple users. Often the users are at some location remote to the central computer. Data file structure can be hierarchal, relational or network oriented. Data base management is a favorite buzz word that seems to fascinate both suppliers and end users of large computer systems.

While a full-blown data base management system may be of some advantage to the average investor, limitations imposed by personal computer hardware and software prevent such grandiose schemes. In the final analysis, however, the data bases we will be describing should be more than adequate for our purposes.

What Is A Data Base?

In order to more fully understand the concept of a data base, let's create an imaginary 5000 item hierarchal file structured data base. Suppose we have a file cabinet containing 100 files, arranged alphabetically. In each of these files there are 10 information sheets, numbered in ascending order. On each of the information sheets there are 5 numbers arranged in descending order. We now have a total of 5000 pieces of information arranged in a specific sequence.

For purposes of this example, lets assume the 5 numbers on each information sheet represent the closing prices for one week of trading in a specific stock. We then have 10 weeks of information on each of 100 stocks in our imaginary data base.

Data Base Management

Once this data base has been created, the information contained will become outdated rapidly. Some method of handling this data will be needed if we are to do anything but simply store it.

Suppose we now trained four employees to handle our data. The first would be responsible for adding new data, the second for deleting old data, the third for manipulating the data and the fourth for compiling data into reports. Each employee knows exactly where to find or place each specific piece of data and has only one specific function to perform with that data. We have in effect created a human data base management operation.

Data base management provides the means to do whatever manipulations are necessary to use the data stored for a specific purpose. Whether this is done in a file cabinet, as in our example, or in a computer's memory is immaterial. The computer does offer the advantage, however, of being able to more rapidly handle large amounts of data and intricate calculations.

Selecting Data For Your Data Base

Usually, information organized into a data base is accessed by several programs and multiple users. For this reason mainframe computer data base designers tend to shy away from the kinds of information that need to be updated frequently. With a microcomputer typically being dedicated to only one user and capable of running only one program at a time, this limitation is not necessarily realistic.

Data selected for inclusion in your data base may include virtually any that you can justify dedicating both file space and program overhead to managing. The 10 week stock price data included in our example, for instance, is a perfectly legitimate and manageable data base for the personal computer. Most microcomputers are capable of handling much more than 5000 items with relative ease.

Care must be exercised in selecting data base structure in order to minimize difficulty of accessing the data with multiple programs. Each item of data must be located in a specified position and remain in that position if it is to be found by every program involved.

Later, in Chapters 6 and 7, we will discuss specific examples of data base organization and programs to accomplish the necessary manipulations of your data.

Data Storage

Data may be stored in your computer's memory or on a mass storage medium such as tape cassette or diskettes. Since the capacity of mass storage is several times that of the memory contained in your computer, some means of efficiently moving data in and out of memory must be provided.

Programs direct the movement of data from memory to mass storage and back to memory. In order to accomplish this task, data must be organized in such a fashion that a program can quickly locate and move blocks of information. These blocks of data are called text or data files to differentiate them from programs, which are also contained in files on mass storage devices.

The specific form of data stored in files is largely dependent on the requirements of your computers system of operation. Data may be stored in strings, arrays, decimal notations, exponential form, etc., etc. By examples later in this book, we will illustrate several types of data storage forms.

One of the biggest challenges facing the programmer is selecting a suitable method of storing data. You may want to be sure whatever mass storage medium selected for your personal computer has the capability of storing both the amount and types of data that interest you most.

Data In And Out

As mentioned in the previous discussion, much of the data used in your programs will be contributed by mass storage devices. Some method of adding current data is needed, however, and should be considered. Typical microcomputer systems use a keyboard as the primary data input mode. For some applications, data may be inputted through a modem or other device. Stock market data, for instance, is available for input to your system through other computers. Several programs to accept this direct input through a modem are discussed in the Appendices.

Data output typically goes to either a video display or hard copy device connected to your computer. Depending on the capability of your system, output can range from printed columns of numbers to several color graphic plots. Modems may also be used to transmit data output to another computer or terminal.

Another of the challenges facing the programmer interested in designing a data base management system is the formatting of both input and output capabilities. Maximum utility and flexibility must be maintained without sacrificing system performance. The personal computer user has a distinct advantage in this area, since the program designer and user are often the same person. This allows use considerations to be made by the programmer in all areas of program development, often enabling him to simplify procedures by taking into account his level of computer sophistication.

Why Your Own Data Base?

Large brokerage firms have computers filled with all sorts of data regarding the stock market. Many advisory services maintain extensive data bases to analyze factors they consider important in reaching decisions for their subscribers. Stock market data is contained in many data bases for various purposes. The majority of computers containing this data are far more capable than anything most of us could afford to own. So why create a personal data base for investment purposes?

Your data base has one major advantage over the gigabyte jobs mentioned earlier—it contains only information relevant to you. By eliminating the unnecessary excess caused by trying to be all things to all people, you have focused the attention of your data management system to suit a highly personal investment approach.

Further, your data is readily accessible at all times. Many of my best investment decisions were made late at night when the high priced data was simply not available. By examining data at your leisure, personal data base management can truly reflect your own investment philosophy and approach.

Once a data storage and retrieval format has been developed, programs to provide desired data manipulations are relatively easy to develop. To construct a useful program it is necessary to know only two things—exactly what you want to do with your data, and where to get the data. If the data is readily available, writing the program is simplified several fold. As mentioned earlier, the same group of data can serve many programs.

It goes almost without saying that data contained in your own data base is as confidential as you want to keep it. If your investment approach calls for sensitive monitoring of a few key indicators, you certainly don't want the rest of the world to share that information. The most successful investors are those who do not travel with "the herd", so keep them guessing.

There are times you will want to gather data from one of the large data bases, either directly or indirectly. The direct approach (through modem communications or prerecorded tapes/diskettes) for personal applications is its infancy at this writing. Indirect gathering of raw data is sometimes difficult and time consuming. You need to know exactly where to find the data needed and under what circumstances that data is available. Closing price, volume and historic data on stocks is widely distributed by the media. Less common data, such as the NYSE running transaction "ticker tape", may be more difficult to locate.

The key to successful use of your own data base is found in careful selection and capable manipulation of data relevant to your investment approach. By limiting the quantity of data, you are focusing attention on what you consider to be most important.

The next several chapters of this book will consider methods and rationale for selection of relevant data to include in your data base. By the time we get to the example programs in Chapter 7, you should have a pretty good idea of the types of data best suited to your personal investment management approach.

COST EFFECTIVENESS

Your personal computer can prove its cost effectiveness in many ways. Obviously by developing your own decision making process, you are eliminating the need for a lot of high priced investment advice. The money saved by using a discount broker or not using advisory services can go a long way in paying for a personal computer. With any kind of luck at all, of course, we expect profits to also contribute substantially!

Once the initial purchase price has been amortized, operating costs for typical small computers are insignificant. Electricity consumed, even at today's high energy prices, will rarely make a noticeable difference in your total bill. Printer paper, tape cassettes, disks and miscellaneous supplies will be relatively small on-going expenses. Additional peripherals may alter the cost picture considerably, of course, and must be considered in estimating long term expenditures for the use of your computer.

Even the most sophisticated personal investment management program will not keep a computer busy full time. Other applications such as financial record keeping, household management, energy control, entertainment and word processing must be considered in assessing the overall cost effectiveness of a system.

There may be tax advantages to using a personal computer for investment purposes—some or all of the cost may be deductable from your income tax. Programs purchased, data sources, reference works and supplies are all areas that could be relevant to your tax situation. There are rather specific guidelines established for determining what is and what is not tax deductable. Since I am in no way a qualified tax advisor, you may want to investigate this possibility further with your accountant or attorney.

Any analysis of cost effectiveness must certainly include the value of your own time. Ideally, the computer should prove capable of saving significant amounts of time and adequately reimbursing the time you do spend on investment analysis by providing measurable profits. The computer hobbyist developing an investment system as an exercise in programming is likely to place a far different value on his time than is the serious investor striving to make his approach more profitable.

If your computer is to be a partner in your investment program, purchase and continued use costs must be viewed from a strictly business perspective. Careful attention to controlling both hardware and software costs will result in significant savings, increasing the net profit of your total program. Hobby and other applications for your computer may necessitate additional expenditures, but these should be considered separately when assessing the cost effectiveness of your investment management system. Any tax deduction of computer related investment management costs will, of course, help to reduce your total out of pocket expenses. Careful records should be maintained for both your own information and any tax deductions you decide to claim.

As mentioned in the first paragraph of this section, I feel the personal computer can be very cost effective in investment management applications. The final test, or bottom line, remains to be determined for each individual investment approach. If we can demonstrate ways in which computer use increases total profitability, this whole effort will indeed be justified.

PROJECTIONS, SIMULATIONS AND RECORDS

Some of the more interesting applications of your data base will involve the areas of projections, simulations and records. In the following sections we will introduce, define and illustrate by brief example all three of these concepts. More details and sample programs will be found in later chapters.

Projections

Projection, in this sense, can be defined as forward extension of various trends for the purpose of evaluating, modifying or confirming decisions.

As mentioned earlier, hindsight is not usually the investors problem. Historical data is available for virtually any factor one wishes to study. The problem, of course, is to intelligently forecast future data. Most predictions are based on projection of certain trends shown by historical data combined with the predictors opinion of what will happen in the future.

Suppose, for example, one of the stocks in your portfolio has been rising in price at the rate of ten percent a year for the last several years. If you assume nothing major will happen to change that growth rate, projection of the value of your stock for several years in the future should be a relatively simple calculation. While this may seem like an overly simplistic example, you have identified a clear trend from historical data that warrants consideration as a valid projection of future price movement of the particular stock involved.

Nothing says projections must be complicated to be effective, in fact often the opposite is true. Since you are dealing with your own data, projections can be as simple or complex as the situation dictates. Evaluating the effectiveness of projections must be left to time. Keeping records of projections you make will provide an interesting account of your prowess in this area and, perhaps, make future projections more accurate.

Simulations

Flight simulators can make the learning of skills necessary to fly a plane much simpler and cheaper than using the actual plane. Similarly, investment simulators can sharpen your skills without risking whatever capital is involved. Simulators are often used to model large systems with many interacting parts, traits common to both the airplane and the stock market.

One of the most valuable learning experiences for any investor is the construction of a stock market simulator. Designing a simulator will reinforce the multiple of factors that interact to cause the seemingly random, irrational behavior of stock exchanges and investors. In Chapter 7, a simple market simulator will be discussed and illustrated.

Commercial versions of stock market simulators are available, commonly under the guise of being games. A few of the many offered are listed in the Appendices software section.

Records

One of the obvious uses for data contained in your data base is the keeping of records. While projections attempt to predict the future and simulations provide a hypothetical learning experience, records should be the factual account of what actually has happened.

Records are simply formatted reports generated from data contained in your system. In designing a data base it is important to look ahead to the kinds of records desired and make provisions to include data necessary to generate those records.

In Chapter 8 we will further discuss records of various types and provide some ideas for generating each type.

SUMMARY

This chapter has covered a lot of ground and still provided only a cursory look at the field of personal computers for investors. Many publications providing more extensive and detailed information are listed in the Appendices. I would encourage those with limited exposure to personal computers to read everything they can get their hands on!

One of the best ways to get acquainted with your computer is to sit down with it, operating manuals in hand and just experiment. Learn the procedures necessary to efficiently use your computer. Find out for yourself what happens if you push this button or forget to press that one. See what makes it crash and why. Locate those areas in the manuals where you have questions and try to get your computer to give the answer. Run a few of the sample programs provided or listed in the manuals. Find out how some of the special features work and how they can be used in programs.

It is very unlikely that you could do anything to permanently damage the computer by engaging in these kinds of activities. As a learning experience, there is just no substitute for some "hands on" time. Time devoted to this activity will pay large dividends in terms of time and frustration saved later. It would be foolhardy, at best, to suggest you undertake a major project such as writing an investment management program (or using a commercial version) without good working knowledge of your own computer.

The next three chapters will be devoted largely to discussing background necessary to construct an investment approach. We will return to the computer in Chapter 6 and begin actually developing your own investment management program.

Chapter 3

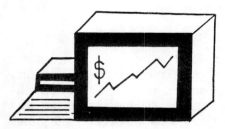

Setting Goals

Any investment program, whether or not a personal computer is involved, needs overall direction and guidance. All too often investors jump from one approach to another, depending on what is in vogue at the moment, never stopping to really think about where they are in relation to where they want to be at some time in the future.

In this chapter, we will attempt to define some goals which will provide the necessary direction for your particular program of investment management. To set realistic goals is a very time consuming process which involves decisions regarding your life style, financial status, life stage and nervous system. Each of these factors will be considered in some detail and you will be asked to construct investment goals based on your own combination of factors.

It is important that you spend the time and effort necessary to arrive at a basic set of investment goals. Most, if not all, of your later decisions will be based on whatever goals you construct at this time.

INVESTMENT OBJECTIVES

Obviously, the ultimate objective of any investment program is to make money. Contrary to the opinion expressed by some writers, I really doubt that anyone wants to punish himself by losing bundles of money in the stock market. At the very least, your primary objective should stress preservation of whatever capital has been used to establish an investment position.

Although preservation of capital and making some money sound like modest enough requirements, the average investor's track record in these two areas has been pretty dismal. To listen to cocktail party conversations, one could readily get the impression that every investor there did nothing but make a profit on every transaction. Partially true? Rarely! After all, would you be interested in a conversation that discussed in gory detail how to lose your shirt by investing badly?

The investor who has never lost money in a transaction is a rare, if not extinct, creature. Those willing to discuss losses are almost as hard to find. Preserving capital and making some money through investments involves an element of risk. As a rule of thumb, the higher potential return investment vehicles carry the most risk.

As we delve into detail in this chapter, keep in mind your ultimate investment objectives. Gains and losses must be viewed from the perspective of total results—do you have more money now than when you started? Are you making positive progress toward your goals? If the answer to these questions is yes; congratulate yourself on a job well done.

What To Invest

In considering investments, we are presupposing you have some excess capital which should be put to better use than gathering token amounts of interest in a passbook savings account. By excess capital, I mean funds that will not be needed in the immediate future for other purposes. The value of ready assets in savings must not be ignored, however, when considering just how much money you have available to invest.

Try to have sufficient savings to cover unforseen emergencies, major purchases and contingency spending. Many formulas have been offered in other publications for determining just how much ready cash is ample. Careful review of your own situation will help in identifying funds available for investment purposes. Several excellent sources of information to help you in determining what to invest are listed in the Appendices. See Fig. 3-1.

Generally, funds used for investment purposes should be those that:

—Will not be needed for another purpose soon. Nothing is more frustrating than having to liquidate an excellent position to pay for the water heater that erupted or the car transmission that got shiftless all of a sudden.

—Will not significantly affect your lifestyle if lost completely. While this is not a pleasant prospect, being prepared for the worst allows a much more casual attitude than jumping from a window because the market wiped you out.

—Are not presently providing sufficient return to offset the ravages of inflation and taxes. Stashing all your extra money in a mattress may be all well and good if you like lumpy mattresses, but the shrinking dollar is sure to rapidly take the stuffing out of this sort of investment approach.

Reasons for Investing

As mentioned earlier, the ultimate objectives for investing are twofold—preserving capital and making a profit. By examining the amount and timing of desired returns, four distinct reasons for investing can be identified.

Income. The income oriented investor is most concerned with immediate income from his investments.

Captial Gains. This investor is primarily interested in deferring income, preferring instead to depend on price increase to provide a profit at some time in the future.

Total Return. A combination of income and capital gains determine the success of this approach.

Speculation. These are the "riverboat gamblers" of the investment world, preferring to depend on long shots to provide spectacular gains.

In the real world, finding investors that suit only one of these categories is difficult. I suspect most portfolios contain some stocks that would suit each of the reasons listed above. Inside each conservative investor lives a speculator who may, from time to time, provide some interesting temptations. The conservative component of speculators is bound to surface each time a "big killing" effort results in financial disaster.

As we develop goals for our investment program later in this chapter, keep in mind your reasons for investing. Knowing the results expected makes many decisions much simpler and keeps your approach in perspective when things look unclear.

LOOK AT YOURSELF

In order to construct a set of investment goals best suited to you, some self-examination is in order. By standing back and looking into your life style, financial status, life stage and nervous system some goals will become apparent. Try your best to be objective at this stage. It's difficult to admit weaknesses, so build

Fig. 3-1. Careful review and control of your personal finances will help to identify funds available for investment. Your personal computer can help by keeping the necessary records (courtesy of Radio Shack, a division of Tandy Corp.).

on those strengths you can clearly identify in yourself. Each of the four areas that follow are important to consider in detail, listing both strengths and weakness as honestly as possible.

If you would like an interesting experience, ask someone you trust to also list your strengths and weaknesses in these areas. Compare their list to yours. Hmmmmmmmm. (Don't try this if your ego is at all fragile!)

Life Style

Is your life well organized or do details bore you? Do you have time and sufficient persistence to keep up with an investment program? Are you flexible enough to change your attitudes as the situation demands? Is there pressure to prove yourself as an astute investor? Do you enjoy new challenges?

These and many other questions should be considered in assessing your life style. Consider yourself as an individual and also as a family member. Look carefully at any pressures that may affect your investment program. Try to anticipate any changes that may occur in your life style sometime in the future.

If, for instance, you enjoy the challenge of mastering a very detailed approach to new problems, your investment goals will be very different than those of someone who abhors details. Both of you will probably be able to design successful investment goals best suited to your personality and life style characteristics. The key here is recognizing that no two investors are exactly alike, their goals should reflect the differences as well as similarities in life styles.

Once you have identified areas of strength and weakness in your life style, a basic general approach to investing should begin to surface. Build on the strength areas and attempt to minimize demands on your weaknesses. Keep in mind the investment approach that evolves from this process will need time and effort to produce results—make it one you can comfortably live with.

Financial Status

Much of the investment literature is written with rather casual references to buying a few hundred shares of this or a thousand shares of that. Nice, if you can do it. Don't panic if you can't. While the *round lot* (100 shares) buyer may be preferred by some brokers, you can buy as little as one share at a time if you like.

As mentioned earlier, funds used for investment purposes should be those not needed at the moment for some other purpose.

If you have $100 or $100,000, the basic concept still applies. Financial status considerations should revolve around not just how much money you can spare for investments, but the other demands on your cash as well. Do you have enough insurance? How about savings? Are you anticipating relatively major expenses, such as college for your children? Can you manage to set aside a certain amount for investments on a regular basis? Do you often have relatively large lump sums such as bonuses to invest? Can you afford to lose money in your investment program?

As we will see later, financial status determines many of your investment goals and serves as a significant factor in the types of stocks selected for possible purchase. Frequent examination of your net worth and financial progress will help to decide if your investment program is on target.

Help in determining your financial status is available from many sources. Some of the publications offering assistance are noted in the Appendices. Banks, brokerage houses, insurance companies and financial planners may offer services designed to help you compute and track net worth . There are commercial programs for your personal computer to aid in this process (see the software section of the Appendices).

One final thought on financial status—set goals for this area of your life. Perhaps you would like to increase your net worth by ten percent a year, or double your net worth in five years. Setting goals for both short and long term increases will aid immeasurably in determining what kind of investment goals you construct.

Life Stages

Usual practice divides life into three stages—youth, middle age and old age. For our purposes, this simplistic approach will be totally inadequate. Life stages are far more logically divided according to family situation, earning potential, income requirements, and current obligations.

The old scenario of being young and single, getting married, raising a family and settling down to retirement is no longer accurate for a large percentage of the populus. People are more in tune with "doing their own thing" which may, or may not, include parts of the traditional scenario. Marriage may involve managing the logistics of two careers rather than raising a family. Multiple marriages or no marriage at all may alter current obligations. People are living longer and better than ever before, often beginning new careers at the traditional age of retirement.

Family situation considerations revolve around planning for future obligations. Do you plan to finance college educations? Are you building an estate for someone to inherit? How soon do you expect major expense obligations? Can an investment program supplement your other plans? Have you made some provisions for your family in terms of insurance protection? What about ready cash for the inevitable little emergencies? If your spouse has a career, how does this affect your investment considerations? Are you willing to sacrifice current funds for future potential? Are there other family members you need to consider, such as, parents, grandchildren, aunts, uncles, etc., etc.?

Earning potential traditionally has been greatest through the middle age years, often peaking well before retirement. With our rapidly changing society, this is not necessarily the case today. Mid-life career changes, automation, supply and demand in your field, business conditions and hundreds of other reasons can be cited for earning potential fluctuation. Look at your own situation and others in similar positions. Do you expect to continue in your career until retirement? Are there plans in the back of your mind to open the antique store or buy that chicken ranch? Is your chosen field one that values experience? How can you increase your earning potential today? Five years from now? Will extra training or experience be of financial value to you? Would your services be more valuable to someone other than your present employer? Can your business continue to grow and prosper?

Income requirements vary widely. Although most of us find this figure only ten to twenty percent more than we currently earn, serious thought will reveal areas of mandatory spending. List these areas first, then go on to your optional expenses. Consider your total expenditures as a fine sirloin that needs the fat trimmed and attempt to define bare minimum income requirements. Both your investment program and budget will benefit from this comprehensive look at income requirements. More importantly, you will be able to set goals for income from investments should other sources of income suddenly be interrupted or reduced.

Current obligations are often, but not universally, related to family situations. The young family obviously incurs fairly substantial obligations, especially when major real estate purchases for housing are added in. The mid-life career changer may also have relatively heavy current obligations to finance the shift. Investments can also be considered current obligations, especially in a program with fairly ambitious goals. To generalize about current obligations would be rather unproductive at this time. You need to carefully analyze your situation and decide just how much of an investment obligation you are able, or willing, to assume at this time.

Your Nervous System

In any investment program, the degree of risk must be measured against the potential reward. If your investment approach is to be effective, you will often seem to be singularly swimming upstream when all the other fish in the financial pool are going down. The majority cannot win in the stock market since each transaction involves two parties, both of whom cannot be winners. For each winner there is a loser!

Consider your attitude toward risk carefully. If you get excited when the pot in your neighborhood poker game goes over a dollar, stay away from high risk investments! For those able to tolerate a reasonable degree of risk, the investment approach of choice should reflect your definition of "reasonable degree of risk".

Are you uncomfortable with uncertainty? How does not knowing exactly what your money will be worth tomorrow affect you? If your psychological make-up demands a degree of certainty, perhaps bonds would be more to your taste than common stocks. There are degrees of uncertainty, just as with risk, that should determine your investment goals. The comfort of a convertible bond or fixed return security may reduce uncertainty in at least a portion of your investment program.

Can you stand prosperity? Silly as it sounds, some investors watch and wait for their stocks to finally "break even"—and then sell before profits are realized. Knowing when to sell is every bit as important as knowing when to buy. Are you comfortable watching profits fluctuate or do you feel compelled to sell prematurely? Do you tend to hold a stock too long and end up watching your profits disappear?

Are you decisive? Can you make a decision without spending the next few weeks regretting it? Do you profit by learning from bad decisions? Once your investment program has arrived at the point of needing a decision from you, time is probably of the essence. If you seem to have problems making decisions under pressure, consider making your approach relatively decision free. For the more decisive, your computer can supply just information and leave the decisions to you.

Do you sleep well? Most problems, including investment management, seem to loom larger at night. If your investments contribute to insomnia, you may do well to follow advice attributed to the late J. P. Morgan, "If your investments keep you awake at night, sell down to the sleeping point".

Considering your nervous system really consists of nothing more than constructing an investment approach that is comfortable for you. Don't take more risk than you can handle, keep the necessary decisions manageable, and adopt a positive attitude toward your chances of success. Losing in the stock market is often nothing more than the self-fulfilling prophecy of those who insist on keeping a losing attitude.

What Did You See?

The last section encouraged a long, hard look at yourself in terms of strength and weakness areas. If you followed the suggestions, your list should be relatively complete by now. Were you surprised at the honesty and objectivity shown? Did you ask someone else to help? Were they indeed helpful?

Spend some time looking over the areas of strength you found—these will be the primary determinants in constructing a personal investment approach. Don't ignore the weaknesses, but don't dwell on them either. Think positive!

In many ways, a personal investment approach is an extension of your own personality. In order to construct this kind of system, you need to be able to communicate information about yourself. The exercise just completed gives enough of a profile to enable you to build or buy such a system. A little later in this book, we will discuss ways of translating specific traits into computer programs, so don't discard your list just yet.

WHY STOCKS AND BONDS?

Throughout this book, you will see me referring to stocks and bonds as investments. This is not to preclude other forms of investment such as real estate, precious metals, collectibles, etc. Our primary emphasis is, however, on the stock markets. Bonds will enter into the discussion because of their attractiveness to many investors during periods of stock market crises.

There are many valid reasons for the amateur investor to consider stocks and bonds as not only a legitimate investment vehicle, but an excellent source of background for activities in other areas of finance.

—Information is readily available.
—Ready liquidity and acquisition.

—Any size player can be accommodated.

—The degree of risk is relatively easily controlled.

—Approach can be structured to your level of expertise.

—Tax advantages over other forms of investment.

—Strict regulation limits the possibilities of fraud and manipulation.

Information regarding the stock market abounds. See Fig. 3-2. Brokerage houses publish numerous books and reports for their clients, as do the major exchanges. Any reasonably large public library is likely to have a surprisingly complete investment section. Bookstore shelves feature many hardcover and paperback guides to stocks and bonds. The more popular investment periodicals, such as *Barons* or *Forbes*, are loaded with advertisements for advisory services, publishers, brokerage house publications, newsletters, etc.

For the personal computer user, much historical data for both market and individual stock activities is available. In addition to hard copy information, several time-share and program firms offer data which your computer can use directly. *The Source, MicroNet, Dow Jones* and other large data bases have provision for accommodating personal computers. As noted in the Appendices, some investment oriented software comes complete with a built-in data base of market information.

Because of the amount and diversity of information available, constructing programs for stock projection and simulations is relatively easy. By preselecting certain periods and using actual data, your investment approach can be refined prior to committing actual funds. Although hindsight does not provide any guarantees of future success, glaring errors in your logic or programming can be detected early enough to avoid major problems.

Stocks and bonds are among the easiest investments to buy and sell. A phone call to your broker results in the desired transaction taking place, usually within a few minutes. The structure of stock exchanges is such that ready liquidity is maintained at all times. When you want to buy a stock, there are shares available for sale. Similarly, a sell order results in your position being readily liquidated. Certain events through the years have momentarily disrupted the stock exchanges, but recovery has been swift.

The obvious advantage liquidity provides the investor is being able to select buy and sell times with relative precision. Compare this with a real estate transaction, where a property may take

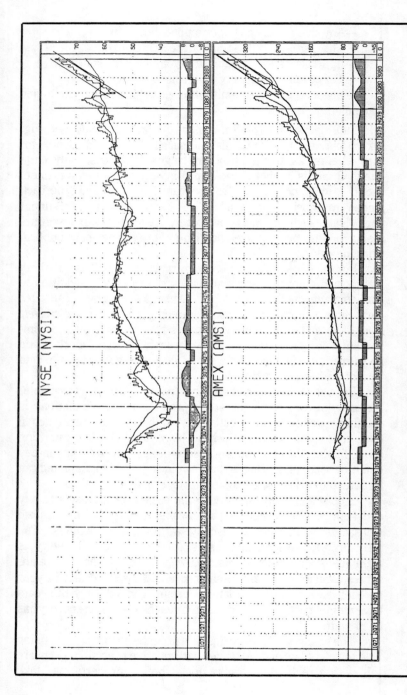

NYSE (NYSI)

AMEX (AMSI)

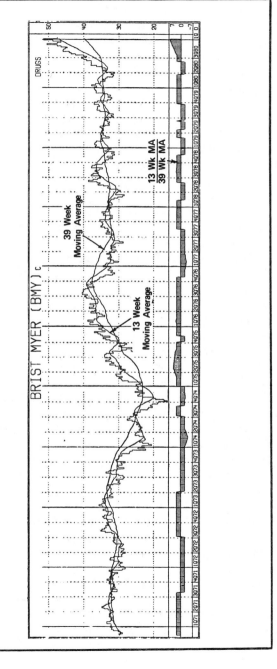

Fig.3-2. Historical data for market and individual stock activity may be obtained from charts or printed summaries in various financial publications (courtesy of Dunn & Hargitt).

61

several months to attract a buyer or seller, and the element of liquidity becomes very attractive. Small investors have another advantage, since transactions of a relatively small number of shares will not significantly affect the overall market.

Any size player can be accommodated in the stock exchanges. Prices of shares range from under a dollar to over three hundred dollars. Number of shares to buy or sell is determined totally by the investor. For the small player, special plans are offered by many brokerage houses to acquire stock in parts of shares at somewhat reduced commission rates. Larger investors can purchase as many shares of whichever stock they desire.

Many authors have attempted to suggest minimum sums you should have available to deal in stocks and bonds, primarily to justify the commission charged by brokers. While it is true that commissions can often add significantly to the purchase price of just a few shares of stock, these charges can often be reduced by using a discount broker. At this writing, several brokerage houses advertise minimum charges of $25-30. More on this in the section on choosing a broker in a later chapter.

Degree of risk incurred in an investment program is quite easily controlled in the stock exchanges. Conservative investors may select stocks with relatively little potential for dramatic moves up or down, while the more speculative types can find just as many issues to their liking. Through diversification of funds, many investors hope to reduce risk by not putting all their eggs in one basket. As mentioned earlier, degree of risk and profit potential are most always intimately related. If there is one single form of investment that is perfectly risk-free and guaranteed to produce outstanding profits, it's got to be the best kept secret in town!

Your level of expertise will certainly determine the structure of any investment program you decide to construct. Strategies in the stock market can range from simply buying and holding quality stocks to complicated combinations of longs, shorts and in-betweens. As your level of sophistication increases, changes to your investment approach can be made with some degree of confidence. Simple approaches to the stock market have often produced results equal or superior to more complex systems, so remember the *KISS* principle (Keep It Simple, Stupid).

Tax advantages available to investors in stocks and bonds are many. Among them, exclusion of certain amounts of dividends received from income tax, capability to defer income until a later time, ability to offset capital gains with losses, tax deductions for certain expenses (including investment management computer programs and advice), and others. Certain forms of securities are exempt from either state or federal taxes altogether. The subject of taxes could easily consume several volumes this size, so no detail is offered in this book. Check some of the references listed in the Appendices, your accountant or IRS publications for current and authoritative information.

Finally, the stock exchanges are among the most closely regulated businesses in this country. Numerous regulations and safeguards are imposed to lessen the chances of manipulation and fraud. Unlike some other forms of investment, you can purchase stocks or bonds with a reasonable degree of confidence that your funds will not be lost due to fraudulent activities. There are no regulations that prevent you losing money due to price fluctuations or bad decisions on your part, however. There must be some comfort in knowing that whatever losses you incur are strictly your own fault, although regulations are small consolation at the time!

SPECIFIC GOALS

The process of setting goals for your investment program requires breaking down your objectives into specific detailed units. Each goal should be measurable and capable of being reached at some point in time. Making money with your investment approach is a good overall objective, but your goals must provide the direction for when, how, where, what and why.

In this section, we shall look at several general areas requiring specific goals in any investment program. Although this will not be a complete list of areas that may be desirable to you, perhaps we will include a few you may expand on for your own situation.

Gain Knowledge And Experience

Initially, this goal may include further reading and study of various facets of market behavior. As you get further along with investing, this becomes a constant process. Be prepared to try, compare, study, refine and revise your procedures to reflect your increasing sophistication.

Increase Net Worth

Set a procedure to measure your net worth and use it regularly. Don't forget to include savings, real estate, insurance, personal property and other assets. Decide how much of a contribution your investment program should contribute to this increase and structure your goals accordingly.

Target Your Profits

Decide just how much profit you expect from each investment and sell when your profit target has been reached. You may decide, for instance, a ten percent profit per transaction is your goal. Your total annual return will be significantly greater than ten percent if several profit targets are reached in relatively short periods of time.

Timing Of Returns

This will largely be determined by your immediate needs. Postponing returns for later income is legitimate if the investment is rather safe. High yielding issues may be selected if income is an immediate need. Try to anticipate your future needs and shift your goals in plenty of time to accomplish the necessary changes in return timing.

Degree of Risk

Decide how much risk you are willing and able to accept comfortably. Often this can be expressed in a percentage of your total investment portfolio. You may decide, for instance, that a third of your portfolio will be devoted to speculative issues while the other two thirds is invested more conservatively.

Length Of Commitment

Decide which, if any, stocks in your portfolio are worthy of long term commitment. Balance those with some shorter term issues. Also look at your investment program as a whole and decide how long you think stocks and bonds will be a significant component.

Decision Making

Perhaps you want to make all your own decisions based on data supplied by your computer. On the other hand, you may wish to program logic parameters into your approach to make the decision making process as automatic as possible. The amount of flexibility you wish to retain will form the basis for several important goals.

Writing Your Own Goals

By now, you should have set several goals for your own investment approach. Check each one to be sure it is specific, attainable and measurable. Reduce each to a brief, concise statement that reflects exactly what you have in mind. Don't be concerned if there are several areas missing at this time—the next couple of chapters will provide the information necessary to fill them in.

As we discuss the areas of stock selection, methods of analysis, timing purchases and sales, and market behavior fill in the goals missing from your list. By the time we get to the actual writing or purchase of investment software, your list of goals will make the necessary decisions considerably easier.

As you construct and use your programs for investment purposes, periodically review your list of goals to insure that your program is helping to accomplish each of them. Measure your progress and revise those goals that seem unreasonably high or low on a regular basis.

A specific goal oriented approach to investments keeps your program on target. Subjective feelings must, at times, be secdary to objective facts. Regular examination of the facts helps you to eliminate those areas of weakness and poor performance that plague many less objective investment approaches.

Keep in mind your investment goals are not etched in stone. Try to anticipate changes in your own situation and revise your goals to reflect those changes. It is important, however, to avoid changing your investment goals too often. Some may take longer to reach than others, but as long as you can see progress in the right direction avoid changing goals too frequently.

Whether or not you decide to use a personal computer for your investment approach, goals constructed as a result of this and the next couple of chapters will give you a distinct advantage in the market. Keep your list handy and refer to it regularly!

Chapter 4

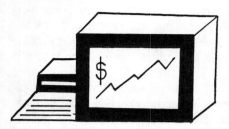

Selecting Stocks

In this chapter, we will be discussing the various methods of selecting stocks (or bonds) for your investment program. Emphasis will be placed on methods, not specific issues, that may prove useful to you. No "sample portfolio", "stocks for the aggressive investor" or "recommended master stock" lists will be found anywhere in these pages.

The total spectrum of available stocks and bonds numbers in the thousands. Unless you have an extraordinarily capable personal computer, there is no way to analyze and follow all of them. Even if it were possible to cram all that data into your computer, the desirability of trying to do so is questionable at best. Professional investors, like the exchange specialists, limit themselves to knowing intimately only a handful of stocks. Brokerage houses with research departments prefer to have analysts who are knowledgeable about industry groups and the specific stocks contained in their area of expertise.

If you were diligent in writing goals for your investment program as recommended in the preceding chapter, the information to follow should help you to select a method for picking specific stocks to help you meet those goals. Examine your goals once more before proceeding. If they seem a little vague, go back to the last chapter and rewrite any that make you uncomfortable.

Once your goals are firmly in mind, you can add the second component necessary to design an investment program—a method of selecting stocks. Whatever method of stock selection you employ, the purpose is essentially the same—to identify those issues most likely to provide maximum profit for the degree of risk you are willing to assume. While we would all like to select only those stocks that will double in price monthly, a more realistic expectation is likely to produce consistent results.

The approaches to stock selection described in the following pages are merely skimming the surface. To describe each approach in great detail would take more time and space than we have to devote. Pay particular attention to the bibliography in the appendices and study the approaches that interest you in greater detail. As you will see, selection method books are plentiful. I will leave to your own judgement the selection of information worthy of careful study. One short piece of advice—cast a jaundiced eye on claims too good to be true, they usually are!

VALUE APPROACH TO STOCK SELECTION

The value approach has often been described as the statistician's and accountant's way of selecting the right stocks for profitable investments. Much study is devoted to economic forecasts, past performance and present strength of a corporation. The result of this study is an indication of what can be anticipated in the future, provided there are no major changes affecting the corporation in question.

Financial facts are gathered from balance sheets, financial reports and news releases for the corporation under consideration. Numerous ratios are calculated, comparisons run and decisions reached according to the numbers used. See Fig. 4-1.

Value approach advocates maintain you are almost sure to pick winners when stocks are selected on the basis of the corporation's ability to make money and the basic value of its' stock. Often this promise of profit takes time to mature, leading to the inevitable conclusion that long term investments are best selected with this approach. See Fig. 4-2.

Fundamentals

The fundamentals uncovered by the value approach help to identify situations where stock of quality corporations is available at undervalued prices. Those who use this method (ersatz *Fundamentalists*) are interested in paying a dollar for two or three or more dollars of concrete assets. Rarely are they interested in buying prospects of big future earnings and/or dividends. Quite properly, fundamentalists are regarded as the skeptics of the investment community and their approach is labelled the *margin of safety* method.

Analysis of fundamentals lends itself well to the use of a personal computer. Assumming the proper information is located and used, multiple calculations and comparisons are easily accomplished.

Financial Reports

All publicly owned corporations are required to issue periodic financial reports. Often this requirement is met by combining financial data, colored pictures, inspirational messages from management and embossed covers into the *annual report*. Usually the most pertinent data is issued quarterly in a somewhat less sumptuous form.

Obtaining financial information on corporations that interest you can be accomplished in several ways. Most corporations will, on request, send their most recent reports and add you to a mailing list to receive future information. Periodicals, such as *The Wall Street Journal* and *Barrons*, publish summaries of financial reports as they are issued. Brokerage houses, advisory services, trade publications and stock summaries are all sources of financial information that may be of help to you.

The fundamentalist studies financial reports for clues regarding the operation of any corporation. Key quantities such as net tangible assets, sales costs, profits, taxes and dividends are used to derive ratios or rates for price/earnings, profit margins, net worth per share, etc. The relationship between certain ratios judged significant is used to compare the performance of the corporation against its own past performance, industry averages or other standards.

Analyzing financial reports is not a simple process for the beginner. One or more of the publications cited in the bibliography should be consulted to help gain an understanding of the process.

Price/Earnings (P/E) Ratio

One of the more popular and convenient guides to stock value is the P/E ratio, usually published along with the daily stock market reports. The P/E ratio reported is the relationship of the price of the stock to its last 12 month earnings. It is also possible to compute P/E using price vs. estimated current year profits, although the estimated profits are often pure conjecture on the part of the estimator.

Using the P/E ratio as a relative indicator of stock value is seemingly quite simple—buy stocks when P/E is low, sell when

EVANS & SUTHERLAND COMPUTER CORPORATION
Balance Sheets

Assets	1979	1978
Current Assets		
Time certificates of deposit	$3,200,000	$6,015,000
Accounts receivable:		
Trade accounts		
Current due	5,687,418	3,091,819
Amounts retained by customers in accordance		
with contract provisions	682,210	248,576
Interest..	24,426	120,634
Employees and other...	83,767	66,302
Total accounts receivable...	6,477,821	3,527,331
Inventories...	4,803,907	2,011,418
Prepaid expenses	200,520	43,563
Deferred tax charge...	203,800	88,300
Total current assets...	14,886,048	11,685,612
Property, plant and equipment, at cost...	3,264,309	1,538,768
Less accumulated depreciation and amortization	1,254,463	615,944
Net property, plant and equipment.....................................	2,009,846	922,824
Future plant site	51,000	52,500
	$16,946,894	$12,660,936
Liabilities and Stockholders' Equity		
	1979	1978
Current liabilities:		
Outstanding checks in excess of bank balances.................................	$316,815	$55,850
Accounts payable..	1,109,805	596,699
Accrued expenses...	1,560,709	671,575
Billings in excess of costs and estimated earnings on		
uncompleted contracts	818,047	554,089
Customer deposits	797,952	657,604
Income taxes..	782,117	982,913
Total current liabilities...	5,385,445	3,518,730
Stockholders equity		
Common stock of $.20 par value; authorized 2,500,000 shares:		
issued 1,093,621 shares in 1979 and 1,085,576 shares		
in 1978	218,724	217,115
Additional paid-in capital	6,336,976	6,298,360
Retained earnings..	5,005,749	2,626,206
Total stockholders' equity..	11,561,449	9,142,206
	$16,946,894	$12,660,936

ATTENTION

This New Recommendation was published on September 22, 1980 based on an analysis made at that time. It is included in this mailing as a sample of a past writeup so that investors may consider whether this type of security has a place within their investment programs. Value Line's current advice on this stock is contained only in the latest issue of the OTC Special Situations Service. In other words, this enclosure does not constitute a current recommendation for purchase and should not be constructed as such.

Fig. 4-1. Balance sheets provide much of the basic information needed for fundamental analysis of a corporation's stock. Financial information may be obtained from the company or various financial publications. If the corporations stock is deemed of interest to subscribers, services such as Value Line's OTC Special Situations Service often publish a complete balance sheet (courtesy of Arnold Bernhard & Co., Inc.).

the multiple improves. If a certain stock is selling at a multiple much lower than the rest of the market, one can assume investors have placed a low relative value on the prospects of the corporation. Conversely, stocks selling at lofty multiples have usually attracted the attention of speculators because of some particularly interesting prospect.

Sound too simple to be true? Well, it is. While P/E ratios are often valid guides, they may also indicate some problems in the corporation or industry in general. Suspiciously low or high multiples can be used as a starting point for stock analysis, but certainly need further investigation prior to making any decisions. Looking at P/E ratios of stocks in similar industries and the market in general will help to provide some perspective to those that look interesting to you.

Many studies have shown that more money can be made by purchasing stocks with low P/E ratios than buying those with high multiples. Because of the ready availability of this information and the number of investors who use it as a cornerstone of their investment decisions, you should strongly consider P/E ratio as *one* of the factors used in your stock selection approach.

Neglected Or Unpopular Stocks

The basic aim of fundamental analysis is to locate stocks that are bargain priced at the time of selection. Often these very same issues are in the Wall Street "doghouse" for some reason or another, qualifying them for consideration as neglected or unpopular at the time. The astute investor can regularly find stocks selling at a large discount by careful observation of financial facts.

Utilities, for instance, are very unpopular during periods of high interest rates. Although there is some justification for this feeling, this pendulum usually swings too far in the negative direction prior to turning positive with moderating interest rates. If, through fundamental analysis, you have identified several issues that are potential purchase candidates because of basic strength of the company this over-reaction may be just what is needed to bring the price of the stock into an attractive range.

Many examples of stocks which have been neglected or unpopular at times could be unearthed with a little digging. The herd psychology of professional money managers moves large amounts of capital into and out of industry groups at a sometimes frantic pace. If you have done your homework and can properly

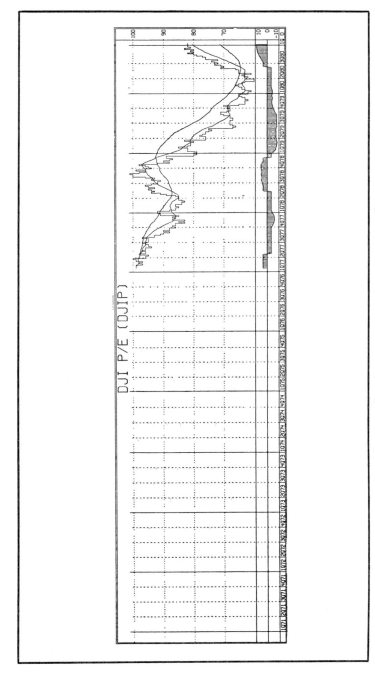

Fig. 4-2. Price/Earnings trends for stocks contained in the Dow Jones Industrial Average (courtesy of Dunn & Hargitt).

identify tomorrows "go-go stocks" from today's "no-no stocks", get ready to shift into a much higher tax bracket!

TECHNICAL ANALYSIS

Although technical analysis is generally regarded as a technique for timing market purchases and sales, there is much to be said for using some of the same principles for initial stock selection. In the next chapter, we will be discussing some of the applications of technical analysis for determining proper timing. See Fig. 4-3.

Earlier we described the value approach as one generally regarded the province of statisticians and accountants. If that is indeed the case, then technical analysts could be viewed as the alchemists of the market. Taking the lead of today mixed with the magic formula of their system, they attempt to create the gold of tomorrow. Technicians have a language all their own where phrases like "saucer bottoms", "head and shoulders", "point and figure" and "flag flying" do not relate to descriptions of human anatomy or patriotic gestures.

One of the most valuable tools of the technical analysts is the chart. The basic premise for using charts is that history tends to repeat itself. Charts are a sort of graphic ticker tape of price and volume combined with a summary of long term patterns. Primarily regarded as a timing tool, the chart can be a valuable source of information for stock selection as well. By comparing charts of individual stocks to those for the major market indices, various combinations for inclusion in a portfolio can be screened rapidly. Most charts cover a relatively long period of time, enabling the computer user to obtain much historical data from a single source. See Fig. 4-4.

Of course, there is much more to technical analysis than just using charts for selection and screening purposes. Although some of the techniques will be covered later, this may be a good time to get acquainted with some of the material cited in the bibliography on technical analysis.

OTHER SELECTION TECHNIQUES

Just when you thought we had exhausted all the methods of stock selection, along comes more! Take heart, since some of the more entertaining (and valuable) techniques are yet to be covered. Although it may seem like we are taking a tongue-in-cheek approach, many of the techniques described in this section have

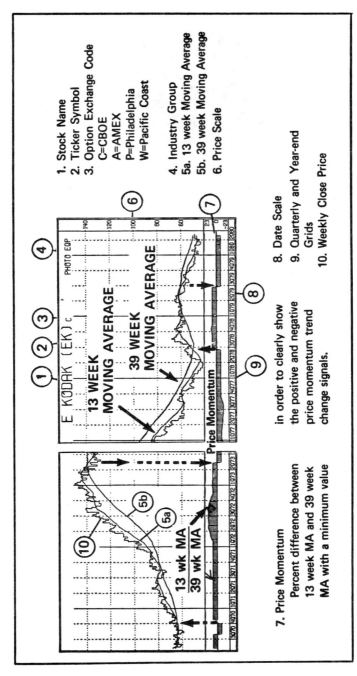

Fig. 4-3. Information contained on stock charts provides valuable clues to timing and trend analysis. This chart format is designed to be of most interest to option traders (courtesy of Dunn & Hargitt).

1. Stock Name
2. Ticker Symbol
3. Option Exchange Code
   C=CBOE
   A=AMEX
   P=Philadelphia
   W=Pacific Coast

4. Industry Group
5a. 13 week Moving Average
5b. 39 week Moving Average
6. Price Scale

7. Price Momentum
   Percent difference between
   13 week MA and 39 week
   MA with a minimum value

8. Date Scale
9. Quarterly and Year-end Grids
10. Weekly Close Price

in order to clearly show the positive and negative price momentum trend change signals.

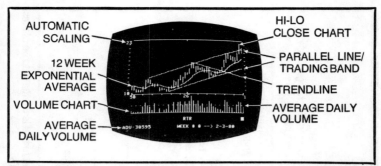

AUTOMATIC SCALING

12 WEEK EXPONENTIAL AVERAGE

VOLUME CHART

AVERAGE DAILY VOLUME

HI-LO CLOSE CHART

PARALLEL LINE/ TRADING BAND

TRENDLINE

AVERAGE DAILY VOLUME

Fig. 4-4. Some computer programs are capable of producing sophisticated stock charts. This is one of the formats available to users of *Market Charter* (tm). (courtesy of RTR Software, Inc.).

been quite successful for some investors. In fact, studies have shown that some of the more outrageous methods of selection have performed embarrassingly well, when compared over time, to some of the most sophisticated.

Advisory Services

Recently, I received in the mail a directory of advisory services—there were over 900 listed! Although not all of these concentrated on stock selection and timing, the majority did. There are services to suit virtually any method you choose to employ for selecting stocks. The more popular investment publications carry many advertisements for advisory services, often accompanied by a relatively low cost trial subscription offer.

Obviously, a group this large consists of services that range from often right to usually wrong. A common denominator seems to be price—very few, if any, could be classed as inexpensive. The cost of an advisory service could be offset by increased profits provided it's usually right, or compound your losses if it's not!

If you locate a service that uses your method of choice for stock selection and want to learn more about it, by all means do so. Request more information, try a trial subscription or check with your broker or local library to examine an issue or two. Our local library, for instance, subscribes to *Value Line*. Although quite expensive, I have found *VL* to be a convenient source of data for many of the stocks I follow. See Fig. 4-5.

Hot Tips

One of the most exciting and least dependable methods of stock selection is the good hot tip. Stock tips are usually passed with all the appropriate clandestine trappings of a state secret. Why is it that the softer the stock's name is whispered, the more exciting it becomes? Beats me! Seems to me the tipper, if he were all that convinced of the prospects, would be trying to keep the stock quiet until his last cent was so invested.

At the risk of being overly skeptical, I would certainly encourage you to further investigate any tip before selecting the stock for your portfolio. Undoubtedly there are situations where someone will steer you toward a worthwhile investment opportunity, but make him prove it! Subject any stock name received as a tip to the same scrutiny you use for others in your portfolio.

As an interesting sideline, you may want to keep a record of tips received, from whom and how the stock performed. If nothing else, this record would certainly make for lively conversation at some future cocktail party!

Gut Feelings

A somewhat colloquial description, at best, but accuracy dictates including gut feelings as a valid method of stock selection. Often, it is difficult to pinpoint the exact cause of this feeling. Maybe you've seen an exciting new product, enjoyed the fare in an emerging restaurant chain or observed a local company doing well. For whatever reason, however, you just *know* the stock is going to be a winner.

Some of the best selections I have made resulted from feelings developed at that level. The same precaution mentioned earlier for hot tips bears repeating here. Investigate and subject the stock in question to the same scrutiny used for others in your portfolio.

Dartboard Approach

Actually, this approach has been given several descriptive names and is probably the most random of all the random methods of selecting stocks. In its usual form, this consists of pinning the financial pages on a dartboard and buying those stocks under each dart you throw. You may also just close your eyes and randomly select points on the page, draw names from a hat or take only the names you can read after the dog has chewed your paper.

Despite the less than serious nature of the above descriptions, there is some evidence to suggest an entirely random approach to stock selection can produce gains similar to more orthodox methods. There are market conditions, of course, where picking a winner is not overly difficult. Conversely, there are also market

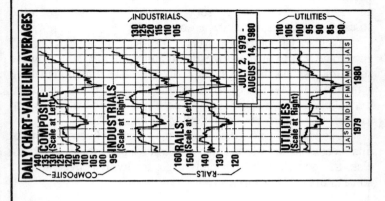

DAILY CHART–VALUE LINE AVERAGES

JULY 2, 1979 - AUGUST 14, 1980

COMPOSITE (Scale at Left)

INDUSTRIALS (Scale at Right)

RAILS (Scale at Left)

UTILITIES (Scale at Right)

RELATIVE PRICE PERFORMANCE
LAST SIX WEEKS

7 Best Performing Industries		7 Worst Performing Industries	
Aluminum	+28.2%	Bank (Southwest)	−0.7%
Toys & School Supplies	+24.9%	Bank	−1.1%
Drug Store	+23.8%	European/Diversified	−2.7%
Computer/Data Proc.	+23.8%	Savings & Loan	−4.1%
Precision Instrument	+23.5%	Electric Utility-West	−4.1%
Steel—Specialty	+23.2%	Electric Utility-Cent.	−4.2%
Electronics	+21.0%	Electric Utility-East·	−5.3%

The corresponding change in the
Value Line Composite Average is +10.4%.

THE VALUE LINE AVERAGES

	Composite (1687 stocks)	Industrials (1490 stocks)	Rails (18 stocks)	Utilities (179 stocks)
8- 8-80	137.90	145.00	160.94	98.45
8-11-80	138.70	145.95	161.21	98.50
8-12-80	137.96	145.12	160.48	98.24
8-13-80	138.06	145.24	160.70	98.18
8-14-80	139.71	147.12	163.08	98.56

The Value Line Averages, which are geometrically averaged and equally weighted, provide a superior picture of the price action of the typical stock.

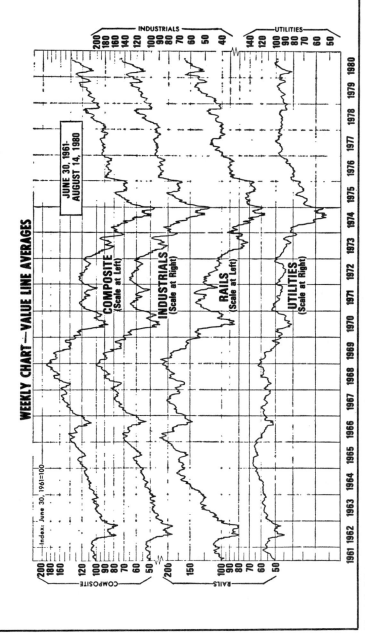

Fig. 4-5. Advisory services, such as Value Line, often include broad market information summaries with their profiles of individual stocks and recommendations (courtesy of Arnold Bernhard & Co., Inc,).

conditions where nobody seems able to pick stocks correctly. As a means of increasing your chances of consistent profits in any market condition, this approach leaves much to be desired.

Salesmen (Brokers)

Most investors recognize three things as inevitable. In addition to the two (death and taxes) commonly used, investors add a third—commissions. Every transaction, profitable or not, results in a commission for your broker. Recognizing this, it also follows that lots of advice and no transactions result in no commissions. If you were a broker, which would you prefer?

Among the many reasons brokers recommend stocks, there are a few to which heed should be paid and many which should be politely ignored. If you happen to be a good customer, the broker may be inclined to let you in on some stock that really is a good buy just to keep your account. Perhaps he has discovered some new information from the research department that may be of value to you or knows about a new issue that looks like a winner.

There are, however, some less than charitable reasons brokers recommend stocks. Special commission arrangements, company "hype" stocks, churning your account to generate commissions and taking a flyer with your bucks are not all that uncommon.

If your broker recommends a particular stock to you, ask why! Why this stock? Why now? Why me? Don't be afraid to press for answers to these whys! This is one of the times in your life when it pays to be a "whys" guy! After all your questions have been answered, give yourself a chance to do some research and form an independent opinion. Very few opportunities in the stock market are so time sensitive that a day or two here and there will make a huge difference. Check it out yourself, think about it and then make your decision.

The relationship between you and your broker can make a large difference in the amount of confidence you are able to place in recommendations made. In the next chapter, we will enlarge on the topic of selecting a stockbroker and how to insure your desired degree of dependability in recommendations.

Lists

Many publications print lists of stocks recommended for this or that type of investment portfolio. In addition to the advisory services mentioned earlier, magazine and paperback book publishers are flooding the market with lists of all kinds. Often these lists can be part of self-fulfilling prophecy. Lets say that Rip-Off magazine publishes a list of 25 stocks guaranteed to rise at least 50 percent in the next six months. Further assume this ficticious magazine has a circulation of two million, and half of those readers decide to buy every stock on the list. What happens when a million people are all buying the same stocks at the same time? The price rises! Rip-Off's prediction of a significant price rise are fulfilled, subscribers are happy and awaiting next month's list.

Obviously, the above example is a cross exaggeration of what is likely to happen with a published list of recommended stocks— or is it? Lists do, however, often provide a good starting point for your selection process. Look first at who compiled the list, check the track record of previous lists offered, and further investigate those stocks that look interesting. Locate and use lists as components of your selection process if you feel comfortable with the necessary precautions mentioned above.

The Eclectic Approach

Webster defines eclectic as "1. selecting from various systems, doctrines, or sources. 2. composed of material gathered from various sources, systems, etc.", *Webster's New World Dictionary, Concise Edition*. A sizable number of investors seem to qualify for this category of methods of stock selection. There is much to be said for using the best of the many approaches in combination when attempting to locate stocks with profit potential.

Also inherent in the eclectic approach, however, is the danger of selecting only the most convenient and insignificant parts of each method of stock selection. A large amount of bad information is certainly not as effective as a limited amount of valuable information.

Over the last several pages, we have discussed methods of stock selection in a rather pure sense. Finding the investor who adheres exclusively to only one of these methods could be difficult, if not impossible. Even the most dyed-in-the-wool technician has been known to sneak a peek at financial reports, hot tippers glimpse at charts and so it goes.

DETERMINING YOUR OWN APPROACH

We have reached the point of action in this chapter, you must determine a method of stock selection most consistent with your investment goals and projected program. Hopefully, you have taken the opportunity to do some homework in some of the references found in the bibliography. Careful study of the various "standard" methods of stock selection may have shown an approach entirely satisfactory to you—if so, use it! If, on the other hand, you have not yet made your decision, perhaps an individualized approach is needed.

Most investors commit a portion of their funds to growth stocks, some to income and a percentage to more speculative issues. The preferred method of selection for each of these types of stocks need not necessarily be the same. In fact, methods of selecting one type of stock may be entirely inappropriate for another.

Some time ago, I became interested in the use of moving averages as indicators of proper timing to buy and sell stocks. Although we will be discussing timing in the next chapter, the method used to select stocks for this approach is somewhat unorthodox and deserves mention here. Most investment guides discourage selection of stocks that vary widely in price with fluctuations in the market, the so-called *cyclicals*. Zahorchak, in his book, *The Art Of Low Risk Investing*, Van Nostrand Reinhold Co., 1977, advocates selecting stocks that vary at least one hundred percent in price over the period of a year. The basic premise to this approach is that the price volatility can be harnessed to provide good buying and selling opportunities repeatedly using the same small group of stocks.

The preferred method, according to Zahorchak, to select stocks for his approach is a chart book that shows long term trends for both stock and market indicators. Charts and other tools of technical analysis can also assist in locating stocks that are currently in market disfavor, relatively stable in price, or move in harmony (or disharmony) with market trends.

Procedures necessary to accomplish technical analysis lend themselves well to the use of a personal computer and may well be used to select at least a portion of your stock portfolio. Most computers have at least a rudimentary graphics capability, some have outstanding capacity to produce intricate charts and figures. If you have some reservations about your ability to program for graphics, there are several outstanding commercial programs available (see the software section of the Appendices).

Some of your funds may be designated for relatively long term investments with good growth possibilities. The value approach to selection may provide some good candidates in this area. As mentioned earlier, you may want to use charts to screen potential candidates—but the real reasons *why* a stock has good growth potential or is presently undervalued must be ferreted out of financial reports and detailed information. Your computer can be a great help here, too. Calculating ratios, diplaying comparisons, storing information and logical deductions are all among the primary reasons personal computers justify their existence.

In constructing your own stock selection approach, take in to account your own personal strengths and weaknesses. Remember the exercise we did in Chapter 3? If, for instance, you have a real knack for spotting significant trends before the rest of us who may want to gear your stock selection technique to choosing small companies with good prospects. Currently popular trends such as solar energy, gasohol, cable television, and personal computers have provided perceptive investors many excellent opportunities. The best of these opportunities presented themselves long before gasohol was sold at every station, computer stores were plentiful and the IRS provided tax incentives for installing solar systems. Yesterdays speculators who took a chance on flyers in these fields have proven themselves fortunate indeed. I guess everyone has a little speculation hidden away. If yours is allowed to surface, make room for it in your stock selection system.

Stock selection is a dynamic, evolving process. I really rather doubt anyone has constructed a perfect system, no matter how many tries he has made. It is a bit presumptious of us to think we can come up with one just because a computer is involved. By carefully studying the failures and flaws in our approach, we can certainly improve performance significantly.

The development of a stock selection system is a difficult, demanding process. By breaking this process into several steps, we can follow a logical progression in this development. First, we need to become acquainted with as many methods as possible. This will involve some hours of reading and study. Although none of the methods may be your eventual selection, other investors use them! Knowing why some investors react in response to this or that development in the market can put you in the position of spotting good issues at bargain prices. Every book and article you read will provide some small piece of information that may prove the cornerstone of a very effective approach.

Second, you will need to commit your selection system to paper. Draw diagrams, write descriptions, clip pertinent data from publications and fully document whatever your plan involves. Look over your system with an eye toward possible flaws, oversights, vague descriptions, logic errors and incomplete information. Revise, redraw, and fine tune your paper description until it reflects exactly what you want your system to do. This step is especially important if your computer is to be involved in the stock selection process! Those who have written computer programs before will recognize this stage as the first, and most difficult, part of writing any program.

Third, select a time somewhere in the past—five years or so would be ideal. Gather as much information about market conditions and stocks at that time as possible. Use your selection process to identify several that would have been part of your portfolio at that time, some that may have, and a few that you would have avoided. Check those same issues today and see what kind of results your procedures yield. Look for reasons for success or failure, factors that you may have neglected to consider and flaws in logic. Although this type of exercise is somewhat artificial, much learning can take place as a result.

Fourth, repeat steps two and three until you feel confident that your stock selections are compatible with your investment goals and personal preferences. At this time, market timing should be ignored—we are only interested in improving the efficiency of the selection process.

Fifth, use your selection "program" to locate some stocks that interest you today. Again, identify some that you would buy, a few to watch, and those to avoid. On paper only, "buy" a few hundred shares of each and write down the relative investments made. Like the currently popular jokes, this "investing on paper" process has good news and bad news. The good news is that you can't lose money that was never ventured. The bad news is that you can't make any either! This step, like the third, will provide some excellent opportunities to refine and revise your thinking about the whole process of stock selection.

Don't attempt to shortcut the development of a stock selection approach! The stocks you choose with this process are the only vehicle you will have to carry your investment program to ultimate success or failure. Some final thoughts on stock selection:

☐ Select only those stocks you would feel comfortable owning, should your market approach indicate a buy. If you have strong negative feelings about a particular company or industry group, don't buy those stocks.

☐ Emphasize industry groups and companies in your particular area of expertise. Draw as much as possible on your vocational background, hobby interests, geographic location and sources of information.

☐ Diversify some of your funds and interests. This may seem to contradict the previous statement. Not so! Putting all your eggs in one basket can be devastating if the basket gets crushed. Try to locate some groups that do well when the market doesn't, some that do well when your favorite groups don't, etc.

☐ Keep a few good stocks "in the bullpen" at all times. You will find, from time to time, that some of your selections are not doing as well as expected and need to be dumped. Call in the reserves from your bullpen at that time.

☐ Don't rush to change your stock selection methods at every turn in the market. Realize that some stocks do well regardless of market trends, some don't. Give yourself and your approach time to be effective, but don't hang on when there is obviously a major problem that needs correcting.

☐ Discretion can be a major asset when selecting your own stocks. It's one thing to be angry at yourself for picking a loser, quite another to have all your friends incensed because you recommended the loser to them.

If you have religiously followed the steps outlined earlier, you now know more about stock selection than the vast majority of investors in the stock market. Putting that knowledge to work will be discussed in the next chapter, where we will add the last few essential ingredients for a successful stock and bond management system.

Perhaps your stock selection process is fairly complete at this time. If so, you may want to try incorporating your ideas into an actual program for your personal computer. To give you a preview, Chapter 6 discusses programming, followed by some sample programs in Chapter 7. After you have completed a selection program, don't forget to come back to Chapter 5 for those essential ingredients we mentioned earlier!

Chapter 5

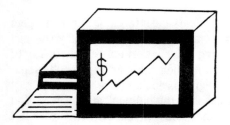

Approaches To The Market

This chapter will concern itself with the several details left before we can construct a viable system for stock market investments using a personal computer. Actually, most of the information will be just as applicable to those who do not plan to use a computer at the present time but may be considering one in the future. In previous chapters, we have considered the nature of both machine and investors. Hopefully, by this time you have made some important decisions about yourself, your investment goals, method of stock selection and sources of information. From this point forward, our thrust will be devoted mainly to methods of implementing those decisions.

TIMING THE MARKET

Your method of stock selection has probably by now yielded a group of stock that look interesting and potentially profitable to you. If you were to buy all of those stocks today, chances of realizing those potential profits could be significantly less than expected. Why? Numerous studies have demonstrated potential profits are much higher if stocks are purchased at market bottoms and sold at market peaks than if the same stocks are simply purchased and held over the same period of time. Of course, most of these studies are done in retrospect (the only sure way to identify market peaks and bottoms!). As we have repeatedly mentioned, hindsight is always 20/20 when it comes to making astute investment decisions.

If we can be permitted to extrapolate from those studies a bit, it is also logical to assume that purchases and sales made somewhere near market extremes can be nearly as profitable. The trick, or course, is to successfully identify those optimum periods for transactions. Many systems have been developed in an effort to successfully time the market. Some work, some don't. None are infallible.

A few of the more popular approaches to market timing use combinations of indicators to identify market momentum. Among the better known of these is the *Dow Theory*. Others consider volume versus price trends, such as the *On-Balance Volume* approach advanced by Granville. Some use price action in a very limited number of stocks, such as the *General Motors Bellweather Theory*.

Moving averages are a popular component of many market timing approaches, including my own. This school of thought suggests that market behavior can be indicated by the interaction of various length averages. In some cases, this is combined with numeric comparison indicators such as *Advances vs. Declines* or *New Highs vs. New Lows*.

Most of the advisory services have a preferred method of market timing which can be discerned from their promotional material. The actual process, however, is usually an almost mythical combination of indicators interpreted by elaborate computer programs or sages on their mountain tops. It may seem that I am having some fun at the expense of advisory services, and indeed I am. Many have an impressive record in correctly identifying major market moves. Most don't.

Why Buy A Particular Stock?

Stocks should be purchased because they are compatible with your investment goals. This implies the potential for profit versus risk is such that you feel confident this issue is the best possible place to establish a position. Perhaps the corporation has an idea whose time has come. New technology, exciting products and increased profitability are certainly valid enough reasons to buy a stock. Consider also those companies "turning around" poor past profits, take-over candidates and leading issues in various industry groups.

One of the major factors to be considered when deciding why to buy a stock is price. If you have done your homework in the selection process, price history will be a vital part of the data you have gathered on each stock. You should know where the price today is in relation to historical pricing. Price versus earnings (P/E) data also provides a clue. Other things being equal, stocks with lower P/E ratios have greater potential profitability than those with more lofty multiples.

Knowing the corporation's past history in areas such as stock splits and distributions, dividends, profit growth and efficiency will help you in making the necessary decisions. Why buy this stock instead of that one, when both are attractive purchase candidates, can be a difficult choice. In fact, if your stock selection process is good enough you will never have an easy choice of just one issue to buy.

When To Buy

Although it seems life for the investor is full of decisions, the real "biggies" are only two—when to buy and when to sell. In this section, we will be discussing the simpler of those two decisions—buying. Buying is the simpler decision because it only establishes a position. Money is not made or lost buying stock. That comes with the sale, making selling the hardest decision for most investors.

Throughout the ensuing discussion, we must take for granted your stock selection process has identified one or several issues that interest you. Although the strictest advocates of timing maintain that any stock can be profitable if bought and sold properly, buying the right stock at the right time will prove infinitely more profitable if sold with the same finesse.

As mentioned earlier in this chapter, timing the market in general is important. One of the more accurate adages from Wall Street is "Don't try to fight the tape". Making a large investment in stock when the market is on one of its sharp declines can be downright dangerous, as can "chasing the tape" upward to buy a particular stock. Although the specific stock you are interested in buying may not be overly market sensitive, often a sharp movement in one direction or the other spills over to almost every issue on the board.

The ideal time to buy your stock, of course, is at a market bottom. Following a decline, stock markets eventually reverse direction and begin to advance again. If your system of timing can identify those movements for both the broad market and your stocks in particular, buying is considerably simplified. In actual practice, even the best timing systems will give you an indication of the primary trend sometime *after* the reverse takes place. Trend information, even though somewhat delayed, can serve you well by pointing out relatively good times to buy. The same information can be just as valuable by pointing to times when buying is foolhardy.

Applying the same criteria to each of your potential purchase stocks can further increase chances of buying wisely. Having several stocks in mind at any one time allows the investor to select each issue at an optimum time for purchase.

The Decision To Buy

In summary, the decision to buy is reached after careful consideration of both the issue and the market where it is traded. Properly selected stocks with good potential can be considerably more profitable when purchased at the optimum time.

Some bits of "barnyard wisdom" may also provide some guidance in fine tuning the optimum time to buy. The months of June, September and November traditionally provide good buying opportunities. Often the market is stronger around the beginning and end of each month, making mid-month a good time. Monday is a much better day to buy than Friday, and the last hour of the trading day often provides whatever price decline is going to take place.

One of the poorest reasons to buy stock is having some money that is "burning a hole in your pocket". Better to park the funds in a money market or savings account than to rush out and buy stock at an inopportune time. By exercising some patience, these same funds will allow you to take advantage of good buying opportunities as they come along.

Why To Sell A Stock

Selling stock is an infinitely more difficult decision than buying. The sale culminates all the planning, sweat and patience that have gone in to the selection and purchase process. Hopes are realized (or dashed) when the order to sell is issued.

Ideally, stock should be sold to make room in your portfolio for some other stock that will better help you to reach your profit goals. This implies that your portfolio, like a garden, must be periodically weeded of the weakest performers. The natural temptation is to sell those stocks that have provided maximum profits and hope the others eventually come through. Selling the weakest stocks takes courage but pay handsome dividends in an overall investment program.

Often, a stock must be sold because it has taken off in the opposite direction of what you expected. Some nerve! Losing money with each tick of the tape is a compelling reason to sell stock. Taking the loss early enough will prevent disaster, so move with decisiveness when this unfortunate event occurs. The question of timing also enters here, and we will discuss losses again (Gulp!) in the section on when to sell.

Unless you plan to live forever, every stock you buy must eventually be sold. In the final analysis, stocks are sold for only two reasons:

☐ Your selection process was right, in which case you can take your profits and move on to bigger and better things.

☐ Your selection process was wrong, in which case you would like to limit losses as much as possible.

When To Sell

The absolutely ideal time to sell is when the stock has reached the pinnacle of its price rise by peaking at a level never to be reached again. As you may have gathered by now, identifying that exact moment is a goal set by many and reached by virtually none.

On a more realistic level, timing sales should reflect your overall investment goals and approach. If you have set a profit target for each stock in your portfolio, the sell point has been predetermined. Although further profits may be possible, there is much to be said for sticking to your target unless there is some compelling reason to do otherwise.

In the absence of specific price goals, stock should be sold whenever the original reasons for purchasing that stock no longer apply. If your selection process showed a stock was undervalued, purchased, and is no longer undervalued—sell it! By periodically reapplying your selection criteria to stock already in your portafolio, proper times to sell should be clearly indicated.

As promised earlier, here's the proper time to sell a stock that is losing money—**yesterday**! Learning to recognize those stocks in your portfolio that are potential or actual losers and selling promptly is the most valuable timing technique you will ever develop.

Always sell too soon. Hanging on for the last few points of profit in the face of significant risk of severe decline is downright dumb. Don't get greedy and you will be able to take your profits into another situation that will provide similar profits in the future.

Tax considerations may also enter in to your timing of sales. Through capital gains treatment, some tax advantages are realized by holding a profitable stock for the period required to qualify as a long term investment. On the other hand, taking a short term loss is generally more advantageous. While tax considerations are important, assuming an unreasonable degree of risk to qualify may prove disastrous. It's far better to have some profit on which to pay taxes, even short term, than to have long term losses to deduct!

The Decision To Sell

In summary, the decision to sell a stock should be based on specific criteria built in to your stock market system. By constant refinement, you can learn to cut your losses and let profits run. Whatever method of stock selection you employ can, and should, be "trained" to point out the time when a particular stock is no longer consistent with your investment goals.

Behavior of the market in general is not as important in your sell decision as the behavior of the stock in question. Some stocks do well in spite of poor market conditions and vice versa. Constant awareness of general market conditions can, however, provide valuable clues as to the degree of risk you are assuming by holding the stock.

Sometimes the decision to sell is reached for reasons not directly related to any market approach. Perhaps the money is needed for some other purpose or can be invested in something else with more profit potential. If you are able to anticipate these kinds of situations far enough in advance, sales can be timed to provide maximum returns.

If your stock market approach is effective, you will often be making decisions to both buy and sell at a time when everyone else is doing the opposite. Selling stock when all the experts are saying we are in for untold prosperity takes a certain amount of courage. So does buying stocks when these same experts are preaching doom and gloom.

In a roundabout way, I am suggesting that one of the poorest reasons for reaching a decision to sell is simply because everyone else is. Although "fighting the tape" is not recommended, following the herd may prove equally disastrous.

Keeping Things Simple

Sophisticated investors will recognize this strategy as effective only for the simple buying and selling of stocks. There are effective methods of capitalizing on major market movements in either direction, most of which are beyond the scope of this book.

Several of the references listed in Appendix C will provide detailed information on these methods.

Although buying and selling stock successfully seems simple enough, let me assure you not many investors do it consistently! When you have developed a system that allows accurate identification of issues and times for transactions, the cornerstone of a more sophisticated system has been laid. The very same information can be adapted for use in short sales, option strategies and other investment techniques that may interest you in the future.

THE MECHANICS OF MARKET TRANSACTIONS

In this section, we will be discussing not only the actual transaction process, but also several related areas. To maintain a somewhat logical progression, we will follow the entire process from choosing a broker to reinvesting your profits.

Choosing A Broker

The vast majority of transactions in the stock markets are carried out by brokerage firms. Each of these firms has at least one seat on each of the exchanges where stocks are bought or sold for their customers. There are two major types of brokerage firms—full service and discount. Within these categories, numerous differences exist, so our discussion will be rather general.

Full service borkerage firms, like Merrill Lynch or E. F. Hutton, have offices in various cities throughout the United States. In addition to providing simple transaction services, these firms provide many other extras. Research reports, for instance, are provided to clients for virtually any stock on the market. Specialized financial and account services are provided at little or no cost, as are numerous publications. The cost of all these extras is added in to the commission rate schedule.

Discount brokerage firms, like StockCross or Ovest Securities, Inc., tend to show more variation in the number of extras offered to their clients. Some are "bare-bones" transaction only, others offer limited special service. Commission rates are generally much lower than those charged by the full service firms, reflecting the savings afforded by not offering special services.

The first decision you need to make is what kind of brokerage firm interests you. If your approach calls for much information to be obtained from your broker, full service may be the way to go. If, on the other hand, you have developed your own sources of information and like to make your own decisions, a discount broker may suit your needs as well. All the firms listed in the Appendices will send information on their services, and many will include a rate schedule, on request.

Actually, the term "broker" is somewhat outdated. In all likelihood, most or all of your dealings will be with a registered representative of a brokerage firm. Registered representatives, as a group, are well trained in the art of selling services of the brokerage firm and usually receive a percentage of the commission fees they generate. Some firms, particularly discounters, have salaried representatives who receive no commission—but this is the exception rather than the rule.

Choosing a registered representative can be one of the most important decisions you will face in your investment program. If you have chosen a firm with an office in your area, visit with several reps before selecting one. Make sure that he is well aware of your financial situation, investment goals, biases, preferences and interests. Don't hesitate to ask some tough questions and expect straightforward answers.

Many investors deal with brokers they have never met except by long distance telephone contact. This is particularly true with discount brokers, since one of the primary ways of saving money is by not having an office in every corner of the country. Although your opportunities to choose an individual are somewhat limited in this situation, make sure whoever is servicing your account knows at least something about you besides your account number.

I would discourage splitting your account among several brokerage firms, unless the account is considerable in size. Getting research reports from your full service firm, then actually buying and selling the stock through a discounter is not exactly the way to win friends and influence people! Most registered representatives are more than willing to work new investors and small accounts, knowing full well that someday the small account may yield enough to justify the time spent. If you are inclined to use a discount brokerage firm, the commissions saved will reflect your involvement in your own investment program.

A few more words on brokers, then on to accounts, etc. Probably the single best understanding you can have with your broker is "Don't call me, I'll call you!". Assuming you have properly designed your investment approach, the last thing you need is a phone call relating the daily whims of the market or news of some hot new issue the company happens to be pushing that day. In return, you can promise to make your calls brief and to the point. Sound good? It is, and it works!

Opening An Account

In order to retain the services of a brokerage firm, you will have to open an account with them. Most small investors start off with a cash account, which is exactly what it says—stocks purchased must be paid in cash within five business days after purchase and proceeds from sales will be credited to this account or paid in cash shortly after the transaction has been completed. The application is relatively simple, asking only for some financial information, banking and credit references and necessary signatures. You will be notified when the application has been approved and stock trading can begin.

A margin account is often the next step for investors. This type of account allows you to buy stocks by paying only a portion of the total cost and your broker extends credit for the balance. Credit charges are added to your account for the amount borrowed. The obvious advantage of a margin account is the ability to control a larger block of stock than could be purchased by cash alone. Leverage provided by this method can significantly increase your profits, but also can compound losses. Initial equity and margin requirements are set by the New York Stock Exchange and the brokerage firm involved. Further information on margin and other types of accounts available can be readily obtained from your broker.

How To Buy Stocks

Stocks are sold in either "round lots" or "odd lots". Round lots are multiples of one hundred shares, odd lots less than one hundred. Actually, you can buy as many or as few shares of any stock as you desire. In most instances, odd lots are subject to a slightly higher brokerage fee per share than are round lots. Some firms eliminate the odd lot differential by selling you stock from their inventory, although the odd lot differential usually amounts to only pennies per share.

Once you have decided how many shares to buy, the next item on the agenda is the type of order to place. For buying stock, two types of orders may be placed—the market order or a limit order. Entering a market means you have instructed your broker to execute the order as rapidly as possible at the going market price. Unless you are dealing with a very volatile stock or a large number of shares, the market order is perfectly adequate. A limit order tells your broker to buy the stock at a specific price, subject to time and certain other conditions you can specify. You may, for instance, place an open limit order for one hundred shares of General Chaos at ten dollars per share. If and when GC reaches the ten dollar level, one hundred shares will be purchased for you. The limit order may be cancelled at any time prior to the actual purchase being made.

Since you and your broker have previously agreed how the stocks in your account will be registered and the method of payment, all that remains is placing the order. For most investors, orders are placed by phone to your registered representative in a simple and brief conversation. Once you have given your name (and account number, if requested), try something like "Buy me one hundred shares of General Chaos at the market" or, "Buy me fifty shares of General Chaos at ten, open". The transaction will be executed as specified and you will be notified when it is completed. That's all there is to it! Old hands at this business of buying and selling stocks may be in mild hysteria after reading the last few sentences. Nervous newcomers are quite another story. I remember being severely tongue-tied as I attempted to convey my first buy order to a broker! You, at least, have something to read if all else fails. Don't, however, attempt to order General Chaos (crummy stock, you know!).

The Sell Order

If your intention is to sell a certain number of shares at the time you enter a sell order, instruct your broker to sell at the market. Like the market order to buy, the sale will be made as soon as possible at the prevailing market price and the proceeds credited to your account.

Limit orders may also be entered, although more commonly stop orders are used when selling. Once called the stop loss order, a stop order becomes a market order once the stock sells at or through the specified price. A combination stop limit order may be entered which specifies both the stop price and a limit below which the order must not be executed. The stop limit may be impossible to execute in a fast moving market, eliminating much of the advantage afforded by either.

Sell orders may be entered for a variety of reasons. Protecting a profit is possible by placing a stop order several points below the market but above your cost for the stock. Using the previous example, lets say your General Chaos, purchased at ten dollars per share, is now selling at twenty five. By placing an order to sell at twenty dollars stop, good till cancelled you have assured yourself of approximately a ten dollar per share profit. If the price of the stock continues to rise, the order will never be executed. On the other hand, if good old GC drops to eight you should have been sold out at around twenty. In a nervous market, stop orders should be regularly reviewed and revised as necessary.

Obviously, sell orders can be used to limit losses in much the same fashion as above. By setting the stop price at or near your break-even point, you can effectively limit any losses that may be incurred. As in the case of buy orders, many variations of sell orders can be entered. For the beginning investor, market orders again emerge as the most commonly used.

Reporting Transactions

Once an order for a transaction has been entered, your broker will do his best to execute that order according to your wishes. The usual method of confirming market orders is first by phone, then a mail follow-up. In some instances, your broker may be able to confirm the transaction within minutes of your placing the order. Limit orders are confirmed by mail when they are entered and often by the phone and mail process when executed. Notice of expiration is also sent for orders no longer in effect.

Stock purchases, unless there are sufficient funds in your account, will result in a request for remittance from your broker. Funds must be received within a specified time to comply with NYSE requirements. Stock sale proceeds will be credited to your account or sent directly to you within the same time frame mentioned above.

Stock held in "street name" by your brokerage firm will simply be credited to your account when purchased and deleted from your account when sold. If you elect to have stock certificates sent to you for each purchase, these will be received shortly after you have paid for the stock. Certificates must be delivered to your broker to validate your order to sell and receive the proceeds. Holding stocks in "street name" is one of the most valuable services provided by many brokerage firms. In addition to providing a good measure of safety, your broker will see to it that dividends received are credited to your account and any information addressed to company stockholders is forwarded to you. Unless you have some compelling reason to obtain stock certificates and hold your own securities, I heartily recommend the "street name" approach.

Once a month, or so, you will receive an itemized statement of activity in your account. This statement will list all transactions, present holdings, any dividends received and account status. Some firms include extra information on the account statement, some don't. Any questionable items should be reviewed with your broker immediately.

The Care And Feeding Of Brokers

The preceeding sections have outlined procedures for selecting and instructing your broker. Not much has been said to this point about enhancing the relationship between brokers and investors. Aside from the "Don't call me, I'll call you" advice, I haven't helped much so far.

Any broker worth his salt is more than willing to help a beginning investor better understand the market. Few, if any, can afford to provide this education during a time when the market is jumping and all the phones are ringing. Lesson one—when asking for information that doesn't pertain to the immediate business at hand, allow your broker the option of sending it by mail or calling you back when he has more time to talk.

Although most brokers will express an opinion if pressed, decisions are yours alone. Blaming your broker for bad decisions may be convenient, but not very realistic. Don't expect a lot of sympathy, or plaudits, when you order this transaction or that. Lesson two—your broker is there to execute your instructions, not to tell you what to do!

Instructions given to brokers come in all varieties. Most credence is given, I suspect, to those clients who habitually leave no question about their intentions. Question, repeat and reword as necessary to be sure you are both on the same wavelength. Lesson three—be sure your instructions are clearly communicated to your broker and that both he and you understand exactly what is to happen as a result.

Brokerless Trading

There are some special situations where the investor can add to or sell from his portfolio with out using the services of (and paying commission to) a broker. The most common of these situations is *automatic dividend reinvestment*, offered by many corporations. This plan requires you to purchase a few shares of stock in the market and register the shares in your own name. Once these shares are registered, you may elect to participate in the

ADR program by notifying the stock transfer agent. Dividends paid on the stock you own are used to purchase additional stock, often at a slight discount to the market and without brokerage commissions. So where's the trading? Well, most plans allow periodic cash payments to be applied to stock purchase. These stocks are purchased for your account on the dividend date, usually at the market average for the day and little or no brokerage fee is incurred.

Stocks held in your ADR account by the transfer agent may be sent to you, if desired, or sold subject to certain limitations. Plans offered by various corporations differ slightly in both procedures and limitations, so check the one that interests you carefully before deciding to participate. We will be discussing ADR again shortly as part of a formula plan for investing. If you are able to live with the limitations imposed, this program is an excellent way to invest relatively small amounts of money without incurring cumbersome brokerage fees.

FORMULA PLANS FOR FUN AND PROFIT

Many investors, in an effort to minimize the effects of timing on their portfolios, turn to one of the formula plans for buying and selling stock. These plans may rely on automatic signals to buy, sell or revise holdings and/or require periodic investments of either money or time.

By its very nature, a formula plan is designed to limit losses (which most do) at the expense of also limiting profits. Plans which generate buy and sell signals tend to work well in cyclical markets by encouraging purchases in bear markets and sales in bull markets. Periodic investment plans which call for investing a fixed amount of money at fixed intervals are intended to allow you to reduce the average price per share on a long term basis.

Any formula plan requires time and patience to produce results. Often the results produced are surprisingly good, particularly when compared to the random and impulsive investing we are all guilty of at times. Properly selected stocks for this type of investment approach should include only those you feel merit a relatively long term commitment.

We will be discussing three such formula approaches. Variations of these basic plans lend themselves well to the use of a computer. As an exercise in programming or for actual use in your investment approach, formulas deserve your careful consideration.

The Constant Dollar Formula

Undoubtedly the easiest of the formula plans; this formula calls for you to decide in advance exactly how many dollars are to be invested in stocks. At regular intervals, your holdings are totaled and compared to the figure decided on earlier. If your total holdings exceed the maximum figure, stock is sold until the limit is reached. Conversely, if your holdings do not reach the predetermined limit, more stock is purchased to bring your total back up to the maximum level. Profits from sales and funds for additional purchases are assumed to be in bonds or a savings account until needed.

The constant dollar approach assumes you will be selling stock during peroids when the market is high and buying stock when the market drops. In reality, your gains are severely limited by both the timing and relatively high brokerage fees incurred in buying and selling odd lots of stock.

Ratio Plans

Unlike the constant dollar plans, a constant ratio approach calls for deciding in advance what percentage of your total investment funds will be in stocks. The remaining funds may be in bonds or savings accounts. As in the case of constant dollar plans, your holdings are periodically reviewed to determine their current market value.

The total market value of your holdings is compared to savings by calculating the percentage each constitutes in your total funds invested. For instance, you decide that your funds will be invested 50% in stocks and 50% in savings. With an initial nest egg of $20,000 you would buy $10,000 worth of stock and place the remaining $10,000 in savings. During a later review, your stocks have doubled in price and are currently worth a total of $20,000. With the $10,000 savings and stocks, your total funds invested are now $30,000. Based on your preselected ratio, $5,000 worth of stock would have to be sold and the proceeds added to savings to restore the 50-50 balance.

Under the constant ratio plan, stocks are bought and sold to maintain the set ratio regardless of the level of stock prices. Generally more effective than the constant dollar approach, constant ratio plans work best over complete market cycles that include relatively wide price swings.

It is also possible to construct variable ratio plans which automatically change the percentages for stock and savings as stock prices fluctuate. If we were to use the same $20,000 nest egg mentioned earlier for this type of plan, perhaps only 25% would be in stocks at market peaks and 75% at bear market bottoms. Variable ratio plans can be valuable if they direct you to buy more stocks at low prices and sell more when prices are high. It must be presumed that you have successfully determined a central average, above which stock prices are high and below which prices are low.

Determining a central average can be a hit or miss process. It is possible to link this determination to some market indicator which the investor believes adequately reflects or anticipates the level of stock prices. Using your computer to project levels based on historical data may be of great help in this process.

Dollar Cost Averaging

If, like many of us, you don't happen to have a sizable nest egg available for investment, this approach will help you to accumulate funds. Dollar cost averaging assumes you have selected a quality stock and invest a set amount of money in shares at regular intervals. In periods of relatively low prices, your dollars will purchase more shares than when prices are higher. Averaged over a relatively long period, your cost per share will be less than if the stock was purchased all at one time. The ideal stocks for this type of approach are relatively volatile issues with good long term growth possibilities.

There is an inherent "fly in the ointment" if you are dealing with relatively small amounts of money at a time—brokerage fees. As mentioned earlier, fees are proportionately higher for small puchases. Dividends paid on your stocks may help to offset commissions or you can seek some method of reducing commissions. Some brokerage firms offer discounts for cash in advance, fixed dollar purchases under titles such as "share builder accounts". Dividend reinvestment plans which allow periodic cash stock purchases at little or no brokerage fees are ideally suited to dollar cost averaging approaches.

Time, not timing, is your major ally when using dollar cost averaging as an investment technique. For accumulating funds, it is one of the few approaches which will *always* result in a profit *if* your stock selection was on the mark and you give it enough time to work for you.

Your computer, of course, is ideally suited for the record keeping and calculations necessary to closely monitor a program of dollar cost averaging. One such program is included in Chapter 7, or you may design your own as a good exercise in acquiring programming skills.

Formulas In Perspective

Formula plans are, by their very nature, relatively mechanical and decision free processes. For many investors the prospect of not having to make decisions under the pressure of uncertain market activity is attractive. Those who enjoy the freedom of making decisions and can resist the trap of emotional overreaction will probably not stick with a formula plan long enough to obtain the desired results. Looking back over the list of personality traits you constructed in Chapter 3 may help to decide whether or not a formula plan should be part of your investment program.

Investors new to the market would do well to consider some stocks as candidates for dollar cost averaging, whether or not any other formula plan is selected. While investment capital is being accumulated, dollar cost averaging provides the possibility of greater returns than savings accounts for small amounts of capital.

Formula investing does take a relatively long time to produce results. Most systems work best when carried through a complete market cycle, a period of four to six years. Be sure you have the courage to face the possibility of losing ground for some of those years before positive results are obtained.

Constructing a formula based investment approach can be a tedious process, especially if portions of the formula are particularly market sensitive. Extensive use of historical data will help to point out areas of weakness in your formula. Because of the long term nature of formula plans, it is especially important to be sure the plan has had at least a theoretical trial before actually commiting funds through its use.

SUMMARY

In this chapter, we have covered many details of buying and selling stocks. There are countless others that have not even been mentioned. Since this book is intended for the novice investor who is interested in computers, we have emphasized the basics (no pun intended!). If you have pretty much followed along to this point, simple stock market transactions should no longer be a mystery.

Don't underestimate the power of these so-called simple transactions. Many investors have reaped handsome rewards by applying their knowledge of a few simple principles. Numerous others have over complicated and emotionalized their approaches with disastrous results. By starting slowly and proceeding deliberately, you can avoid many of the pitfalls along the road to successful investing.

Chapter 6

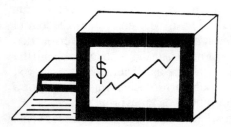

Where Does The Computer Come In?

Using a computer for investment purposes involves many decisions, some rather clear cut and others quite vague. The first five chapters have been devoted to the study of investment basics, with a little exposure in Chapter 2 to the personal computer. Hopefully, as a result of those studies, you have already made many decisions crucial to your investment program. If you have followed the suggestions made in those chapters, your investment program should be organized into a logical progression of measurable steps. From this point forward, we will assume decisions relating to investment goals, stock selection, market approach and timing have been duly considered and made. If such is not the case, perhaps some time completing this part of the process would be well advised.

In this chapter we will be considering the role of a personal computer in your investment program. We will be switching attention to some of the finer points of computing and relating these points to your background in investments. As we have repeatedly noted, further information may be obtained from sources noted in the Appendices. Take time to study any concepts that are unclear to you, and try some of the ideas suggested if you already own a computer.

Throughout the chapters to follow, "computer" will be used as a generic term not referring to any one machine in particular. You will often note references to the Apple II, primarily because this is the computer with which I am most familiar. Programs presented will be written in either Applesoft or Apple Integer Basic, with accompanying suggestions for adapting them to other versions of BASIC.

NECESSARY DECISIONS

As mentioned in the introduction to this chapter, we will be focusing our attention here on the processor. Hardware and software considerations are needed to implement your selected approach to the stock and bond markets. Placing this section near the end of the text has hopefully resulted in a clear definition of a process that may or may not be suitable for use with a personal computer.

Before proceeding any further, two questions need to be answered objectively:

☐ Just how useful will a personal computer be for my investment purposes?

☐ What is my desired level of involvement in the process of marrying an investment program with a computer program?

The first question becomes even more pressing if you do not presently own a computer and are considering purchasing one. If

Fig. 6-1. The same personal computer that entertains your family can be a helpful investment management tool if properly programmed (courtesy of Texas Instruments, Inc.).

your investment program consists mainly of sending in a quarterly check to add shares to your dividend reinvestment plan or purchase mutual fund shares, perhaps a computer is not needed at all. An ambitious regime of tedious calculations and comparisions, on the other hand, clearly justifies involving a computer in the process. Look carefully at the investment program you have developed so far and weigh the potential benefits of a computer against the additional profits necessary to help pay for even the simplest unit. If the facts say not to buy a computer, don't do it! Just following that gem of advice may save you many hours of frustration and several kilobucks.

Even the proud owner of a personal computer should spend some time pondering these questions. Despite the fact your computer can play a mean game of chess, balance the checkbook, entertain the kids and keep you off the streets—it may not be a suitable partner for your investment program. Additional hardware, software and time expenditures may simply not be justified if potential benefits are not obvious. There is little that's more frustrating than trying to develop a program or system that you don't feel will prove worthwhile. See Fig. 6-1.

If you can honestly demonstrate some potential benefits in using a personal computer for your investment purposes, proceed to the next questions. How much time and money are you willing to spend on developing an investment system? Should you program it yourself or buy commercial software? What additional hardware will be needed? No need to answer these additional questions now, we will be discussing them in some detail for the next few pages.

Approaching The Market

Your investment approach will determine the nature and extent of your computer use. Stock selection, for example, is an area ripe for fresh programming ideas. Let's say, for instance, that your selection process depends heavily on manipulation of data found in financial reports. Since this selection process is rather rigidly defined, it is an excellent candidate for computer assistance.

Computers are lousy cocktail party conversationalists and rarely, if ever, share a round of golf with your favorite source of hot tips. If your method of stock selection relies on either of these methods, programming computer assistance becomes a difficult, if not impossible, task. If you hear of a "great stock buy" at a party and buy without investigating further, you don't need a computer to help you lose money!

Approaches that emphasize timing are good candidates for integration into a computer program. Data manipulation, the forte of any computer, can be effectively used to reinforce or disprove timing considerations. The objectivity demonstrated by an efficient timing program can offset any tendency you have toward second guessing your selected market indicators.

Portfolio management and keeping of necessary records are natural applications for your computer. Properly designed and utilized programs can be of invaluable assistance in determining profits and losses, tax liabilities and market approach effectiveness. Since relatively simple mathematics and logic are needed for record keeping applications, many personal computer owners concentrate their initial programming efforts in this area.

Hardware Capability

Once you have decided to involve a computer in your investment program, the amount of hardware necessary to handle your application must be acquired. As we saw in Chapter 2, personal computers come in all shapes and sizes. To briefly review, a minimal system for investment applications will consist of the following four elements.

☐ A Central Processing Unit (CPU), memory and associated components necessary to integrate the two. In most systems, these are mounted on one or more printed circuit cards contained in a master cabinet.

☐ Some method of getting data into and out of the processor. The keyboard usually provides for data input and a video tube displays data output. Often the keyboard and video display are integrated into one unit (a terminal) or are combined with CPU, memory and power supply to form a self contained computer.

☐ Mass storage device, either cassette tape or diskette. Some computers have one or the other built in, others rely on external units.

☐ A high level language suitable for your abilities and interests. BASIC, PASCAL, or some other language may be contained in Read Only Memory (ROM) or fed into your computer from a mass storage device.

From the discussion earlier, you may have gathered that the above requirements are quite easily met by most personal computers. Quite often computer manufacturers or retailers will offer a basic package containing all the necessary items at an attractive price. Check your local computer store or the ads in personal computing magazines for systems offered for sale by mail order. See Fig. 6-2.

Don't underestimate the starting level units offered by many companies! As an example (and not a commercial), my initial system consisted of an Apple II with 16K memory to which I added a cassette tape recorder, an RF modulator (to provide video display signals to an old TV set) and Applesoft (floating point BASIC) on ROM. Actually, Applesoft was furnished on tape with the computer, so the ROM card was a luxury. Excluding the language card, my total accessory expenditures amounted to less than one hundred dollars.

Using the system described in the preceding paragraph, I was able to construct and use an investment program for over one hundred stocks. As described in the November, 1979 issue of *Microcomputing*, this system computed moving averages, market and stock recommendations, provided for splits and updated the files on each run. While my approach may or may not suit your investment goals, it is important to note again its use of a minimal system. Many other worthwhile programs can be written and run successfully on similar basic systems.

The decision you must make is whether to buy an entry level system and add capability as necessary or to buy all the capability available and hope you need it. Although I certainly cannot make this decision for you, my biases run toward starting off with the entry level system. Why? The minimal system lets you learn the capabilities and limitations of the computer itself without the additional complication of multiple peripheral devices.

Programming skills developed using an entry level system will center on your computer, providing a good background for later work with more capability. In my case, for instance, early programming efforts were done on a time-share system with virtually unlimited memory and disk storage. A 16K microcomputer looked more like a toy than the very capable machine it turned out to be. I spent considerable time re-learning skills and solving problems that could have been avoided if my own advice had been followed. As it turned out, the microcomputer was far more capable at executing programs than I was at writing them!

Once you have gone through this learing phase, hardware additions to your system become a matter of providing capability in areas of real need. Adapting or writing programs to take advantage of expanded system capacity is easier because of your understanding of the basic unit. Again considering my own

Fig. 6-2. An entry level system—the TRS-80, Model I, Level I from Radio Shack (courtesy of Radio Shack, a division of Tandy Corp.).

experience, which may be fairly typical of the new computer owner, hardware additions were made as particular needs arose. First, memory was expanded to 48K to allow more elaborate programs to be written. Next a printer was added to ease the task of program listing and troubleshooting. A disk drive came shortly after I discovered loading multiple data files from tape was a lengthy and cumbersome process. Lower case capability through a hardware adapter proved necessary when a word processing program was added to my collection. See Fig. 6-3.

What's next for my system? Well, a second disk drive will be needed soon to provide disk copies and data access for a new program in the works. Perhaps a color monitor, modem, graphics tablet or other device will be needed later. It seems new devices are being introduced almost daily, so future system expansions will depend on what is available and whether or not my particular applications are appropriate to the device.

Despite the fact that your situation and mine may be vastly different, there is a point here to consider. One of the very real dangers in personal computing is over-buying. Devices with limited application potential are often purchased on impulse and left to gather dust once those limited applications are no longer of interest. It seems infinitely more logical to expand hardware capability in response to a demonstrated need. In this fashion, your system sophistication can roughly reflect your own abilities and applications.

Since the whole field of personal computing is moving so rapidly, applications unheard of today will be commonplace in a few years. It would be sad, indeed, to find yourself burdened with unused, outmoded hardware. The price of added devices can easily equal several times the initial cost of your computer, so consider carefully any additions to your system. By all means buy what you need, but be sure what you have is what you use.

Since we are considering only investment applications in this book, few of the more exotic additions available for most systems will be discussed. We will be making use of the two I consider most important—large blocks of memory and floppy disk mass storage. Since both are relatively inexpensive, you may want to consider them as candidates for initial expansion of your hardware capability. Additional memory is readily available for most systems at an attractive price, either from the manufacturer of your system or many alternate suppliers. Disk drives are several times more expensive than cassette tape units, but the additional flexibility

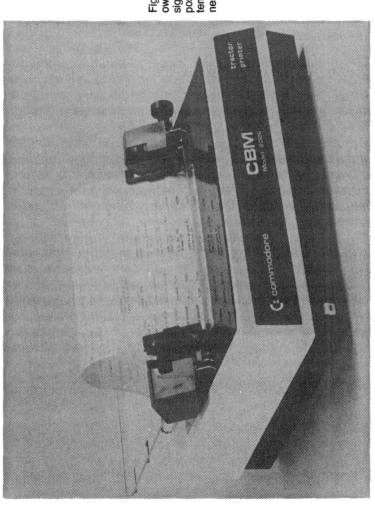

Fig. 6-3. Many personal computer owners find the addition of a printer significantly increases the number of possible applications for their system (courtesy of Commodore Business Machines, Inc.).

107

offered is well worth the price. One disk drive will suffice for nearly all investment purposes, although many computers have the capacity to utilize two or more if necessary.

Software

Programs, often referred to as software, are the fuel that makes your computer run. Even the most sophisticated computer can operate only as efficiently as it has been instructed by the programmer. There are many sources of programs for most computers. Among the most common sources are computer manufacturers, software houses, magazines and books, other computer owners, software exchanges and yourself. Most commercial programs are supplied on disk or tape ready to be read directly into your system. Listings, published in books and magazines, may be entered via the keyboard and saved on mass storage. Some special purpose programs are supplied in ROM and must be hardwired into the system. Your own programs, of course, must be typed in on the keyboard.

In this section, we will be considering the relative merits of commercial versus your own programs. Later, we will discuss some methods of programming and ways to evaluate commercial programs you may be interested in purchasing. In the Appendices, you will find a section describing some of the programs available commercially.

The question of whether to buy or write your own software often has no easy answer. The temptation to buy a program rather than write your own is usually strongest in the early stages of computer ownership. With some programming experience, you may find writing programs easy for some applications and difficult for others. I find, for instance, that games and complex machine language programs are the types I buy commercially. On the other hand, I prefer to write my own investment and specific application programs where BASIC can be used effectively.

Commercial Programs. New commercial programs are being introduced at an astounding rate for most computer systems. Some are offered by major software houses and publishers of other materials, particularly magazines. There also exists a sizable "cottage industry" of computer owners and hobbyists who are marketing a limited number of their own programs. Any computer oriented magazine carries numerous advertisements describing programs available from both these sources. See Fig. 6-4.

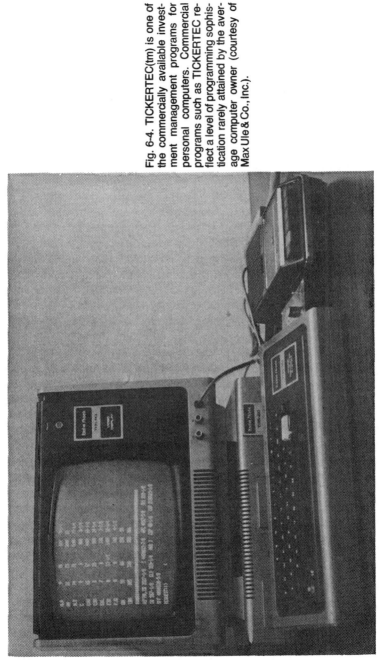

Fig. 6-4. TICKERTEC(tm) is one of the commercially available investment management programs for personal computers. Commercial programs such as TICKERTEC reflect a level of programming sophistication rarely attained by the average computer owner (courtesy of Max Ule & Co., Inc.).

Advantages to buying commercial software include documentation, support and sophistication. Most commercial programs are well documented in that users manuals contain sufficient instructions to get the program up and running in your system. Often additional material describing modifications and expanded applications is also found in the documentation. Some suppliers offer documentation separately so you could purchase just that and decide whether or not to buy the program after some study.

Support for the program often comes from at least two sources—the supplier and other users. If the program was purchased from a reputable supplier, some sort of guarantee was obtained. Terms of guarantees vary widely, but most provide for replacement of defective disks or tapes and some method of obtaining updates as they become available. Other owners of the same type of computer system and program may be able to help if your copy of a program doesn't perform as expected and answer questions as they arise. User groups can put you in touch with any other owners of a particular program and offer support in many areas.

Program sophistication is the third advantage to commercial software. Some programs have been written by experts in both programming and the particular area of interest. Chess programs written by proficient players of the game should be considerably more sophisticated than those written for someone who doesn't know a knight from a rook. A little searching will reveal many such experts who have programs for sale. Similarly, other applications for your computer can be handled best by programs with a fair degree of sophistication. If you don't possess the expertise to write a program for such particular application, perhaps buying a commercial program would be preferable. My own library, for instance, contains a few very sophisticated commercial game programs that provide an interesting diversion at times. You may also want to buy commercial programs that you need for an immediate application. Again referring to my own situation, I purchased a word processing program because of an immediate need to use such a system. As a matter of fact, this whole book was composed, written and the manuscript printed using my computer and word processing program.

Commercial software is not without disadvantages. Complication, adaptability and reliability are three areas that loom dark over the software display in your local store. Many commercial programs are unduly complicated for the relatively simple duties they perform. Data base management and business systems seem to be the worst offenders, although there are many others. Complex data display options, unusual input systems, long drawn-out loading procedures and lack of proper prompting for the user make some programs an absolute nightmare to use.

With some notable exceptions, most commercially available software requires the user to adapt to the program. A few top notch offerings build in flexibility for the user and a simple method of modifying the program to accommodate differing applications. To further complicate matters, program listings and variable identification data are rarely furnished to allow user modification. Program locks, made necessary by unauthorized copying and distribution, often preclude the user generating a listing or easily modifying the program.

Reliability, or lack of same, is noteworthy in two areas. First, does the program work at all? A few years ago several of the personal computing magazines carried ads for an astoundingly capable and low priced terminal unit. The picture in the ad certainly looked legitimate enough. The whole thing sounded too good to be true. It was! The terminal shown in the pictures was a mock-up containing no working components at all. Similarly, the company behind the ads was a mock-up, never intending to actually deliver terminals that had been ordered and paid for! While similar cases involving software are not quite so dramatic, beware of the ad that promises the moon. Secondly, will the program reliably do what the supplier said it would? Are there some "bugs" that have not been worked out? Was the program honestly represented as to its capabilities and limitations for your particular application? Do you have any recourse if the program is not what you expected? In many cases, you must actually purchase the program to answer these questions. If the answer to any one of them is no, you may be left holding the bag.

Reliable software companies are doing their best to provide top rate software that does indeed work and work well. One of the better ways to check both a company and a specific program is the check with someone else who purchased it. If your circle of acquaintances can't help, ask the company to give you the names of some other people in your area who have purchased similar programs. Look through the popular computing magazines to see whether someone may have reviewed the program, or at least some program from that company. If all else fails, check with the magazine publishers to see if any of their readers have reported problems with either the company or the program that interests you.

"Home Grown" Programs. Writing your own software offers distinct advantages in many situations. Since you have a certain level of computer sophistication, the program will obviously reflect it. The best way to insure a program will do exactly what you would like is to write it that way! By knowing what kinds of input and output are desired, you can eliminate the wide range of options that are often necessary in commercial programs. If the program is for your own use, error trapping and handling can be greatly simplified. Knowing how and why the program works make modifications much simpler to do. Programs you write can easily be tailored to suit the configuration of your own computer and peripheral devices. See Fig. 6-5.

Writing your own programs does not mean that every line must be original and unique to that program. Many program articles and listings are published in computer oriented books, magazines and newsletters. These programs may be used as written, or often provide useful ideas to incorporate in your own work. From your own writing and other sources, one can rapidly build up a library of subroutines that can be used in many programs. As we will see in the discussion on learning to program, such a library will make your programming efforts considerably easier.

There are, of course, disadvantages to writing your own programs. Effective programming is a time consuming process requiring patience and persistence to achieve the desired results. Often much time is spent "re-inventing the wheel" by trying to devise routines that are readily available from other sources. User generated programs are often abandoned before completion because of frustrations associated with solving the inevitable problems that crop up along the way.

As mentioned earlier, the decision of whether to buy commercial or write your own software is not always easy. There are tremendous satisfactions achieved by writing a program that successfully fulfills an application need. These satisfactions must be balanced against the ease of simply purchasing a program to do whatever it is you have in mind. At the risk of injecting personal philosophy, let me suggest an approach. Buy those commercial programs that are beyond your programming abilities or not of sufficient interest to devote the time necessary to write your own. Write programs for those applications that reflect your own individual requirements and write some simply to gain programming experience.

Fig. 6-5. Successfully writing your own programs provides a great deal of satisfaction. Each program you write helps to build your programming skills (courtesy of Texas Instruments, Inc.).

Time Demands

As your computer is called on to do more and more chores, demands on your time will increase proportionately. Both system operation and programming are relatively time consuming activities. In order to earn its keep, your computer must demonstrate that it is able to help you use time more effectively or provide an interesting deversion for time you would have wasted otherwise.

As an example, let's consider two applications that illustrate time effectiveness. K. Byte spent many hours developing a program to help him keep track of his many social activities and appointments. This program displayed month by month schedules and printed lengthy agendas on request. For each run, this program required K. to load it in, type new information or revisions and wait for prints to be made. The exact same functions could have been provided by an inexpensive pocket calendar book from the local

113

office supply store. Effective use of a computer? Hardly! I. N. Vestor, on the other hand, developed a computer program to handle multiple calculations necessary in his investment approach. Once the program was up and running, time for doing the calculations was reduced three fold. In addition, Vestor devised a system of printing the results so as to eliminate the necessity for hand writing them on record sheets. More like it? Definitely!

While the preceeding examples may sound like fiction, I have been in the positions of both K. Byte and I. N. Vestor. It is indeed a shattering experience to find that a program you have nurtured from concept to completion is not worth the time spent. Hours spent inputting large amounts of data to a commercial program which proves largely useless can create the same feelings of frustration. A few such experiences force you to consider time a valuable commodity not to be wasted on "busy work" applications. Negative experiences do have some value in that they help you to appreciate the satisfaction achieved by devising or purchasing a program that is indeed a time and effort saver.

Many applications, particularly in the investment area, require consistent amounts of time at regular intervals for success. Consider not only the time you have to spend now, but try to look a few weeks or months in the future before starting any new commitment.

BUILDING A SOFTWARE LIBRARY

There are many ways to build a collection of programs for your computer. As mentioned earlier, you can buy commercial offerings, type in programs from articles and listings in publications, or write your own. Each of these methods has its place in acquiring software. Most personal computer owners use all three at some time or other in their quest to provide fuel for more applications. Since we have already discussed the relative advantages and disadvantages of these approaches, this section will concentrate on the actual processes involved in their use.

Buying Commercial Programs

In order to purchase programs, you must first know what is available and from whom. Sources of information are rather numerous in the personal computing field, if you know where to look. The obvious place to start is wherever you purchased your computer. Whether you bought from the neighborhood computer store or some mail order firm halfway across the country, programs are probably available from the same source. If you are lucky enough to have a computer store nearby, often demonstration programs are available for examination prior to purchase. Computing magazines and newsletters are a valuable source of information about commercial offerings. Advertisements, new product announcements, articles and software reviews help to keep you abreast of new developments.

Most software suppliers offer an easy method of obtaining more information about their products. Some have toll-free telephone numbers or clip out coupons in their advertisements. Others participate in the "bingo card" reader information service offered by several magazines. Mailing lists are maintained by the major software houses for the purpose of sending new product information, etc. Any reputable supplier will send more detailed information in response to a direct request made by any of the above methods or a letter directly to their marketing department.

In the case of an elaborate (and often expensive) offering, documentation is sometimes available separately. Usually credit toward the purchase of the program package is allowed buyers of documentation. Such an offer implies integrity on the part of the seller, since the inner workings of the program are discussed in some detail. The potential buyer, of course, assumes an obligation to carefully study the material since documentation prices are usually kept low enough to be a break-even proposition for the supplier. Ideally, this approach offers distinct advantages for both parties involved—the seller provides detailed information which he hopes will lead to the sale of a program, and the buyer can decide whether or not the cost of the total package is justified for his situation. Buying a documentation packet to accompany a "bootleg copy" of the program obtained somehow is the basic reason many software companies are reluctant to offer more "documentation only" prices. It's unfortunate that the few who resort to this method of building a software library spoil it for those of us who would like to see more information prior to purchasing a program.

Some program suppliers are now offering guarantees for their products that go further than just stating they will indeed work. Provisions for replacement of defective or damaged media, low or no cost updates, customer assistance for individualizing or solving application problems and unconditional refunds are getting more common. As competition increases, look for better guarantees to be forthcoming.

The actual process of buying a program couldn't be simpler.

Local stores sell programs in much the same way as any other retail item. Mail order suppliers usually offer a variety of ways to pay and toll-free order numbers for those who pay by credit card or c.o.d. Sending a cashier's check or money order instead of a personal check will often speed up handling of your order, since most firms will not ship before personal checks clear for payment—a process that can take up to two weeks. If you are unsure of the reputation of a software supplier, consider using a credit card to purchase your programs. Often the credit card company can help in settling disputes resulting from deceptive advertising or shoddy business practices.

Software Soapbox

The process of designing, writing, producing and marketing programs involves the same risks and rewards as any other type of investment. The writer has devoted many hours and all of his skills to developing a program he feels has commercial appeal. Testing, revising, updating and finally selling the program have created a considerable investment of time, talent and funds for which he has a legitimate right to be compensated. The software producer, distributor and retailer also have an investment in the finished product that deserves some compensation in the form of profits. If the product is successful and sufficient profits are generated, more and better programs are sure to follow. The same free enterprise system that created the stock markets is alive and well in the computer software business.

Once a program is loaded into a computer's memory, there is little to prevent unlimited copies from being made. Sure, some protection is afforded by copyright laws but they are, except for the most blatant violations, nearly impossible to enforce. Elaborate program locks and security codes have helped to stem the tide, but the basic responsibility lies with each of us. By distributing or accepting a "bootleg" program copy, you are discouraging the active development of more commercial programs. Be fair! If you want a particular commercial program, buy it! By all means, look at your friends copy running on his system if you like but resist the temptation to run off a copy for your own use.

In return, the software companies should return to the practice of supplying listings for those of us who would like to modify the program. It would also be very nice if those who have purchased a program could make a back-up copy for our own use without having to wade through several security devices. Maybe the personal computing field is ripe for non-disclosure agreements similar to those used for large computer software!

It would be naive to assume that all commercial software suppliers are shining examples of integrity and sound business practice. Despite all the precautions we can employ, the prospect of "being taken" does exist. If you honestly feel that you are the victim of an unscrupulous operator, carefully document your efforts to obtain satisfaction. Write first to the company in a calm, rational tone and explain the problem. Be specific in requesting some sort of solution to the problem. Often a copy of this letter sent to your local Better Business Bureau, postal authorities or consumer protection agencies will work wonders in speeding a response. Copies of follow-up letters, if needed, can be directed to magazine editors, software reviewers and appropriate agencies. Stay cool and calm—usually you will collect. If not, chalk it up to experience or pursue the matter further depending on your inclination at the moment.

Learn To Program

To many new computer owners, writing programs looks like an enormously complicated undertaking. As more understanding of the computer is gained, the process of programming becomes simply that of translating your instructions into a language the computer can understand. In our brief discussion of languages in Chapter 2, several requirements for a language suitable for investment programming were offered. These requirements included the ability to handle floating point arithmetic operations (decimals), string data (alphabetic as well as numeric), and arrays. Many versions of BASIC easily fulfill these requirements, as do PASCAL, FORTH, FORTRAN, COBOL and APL. Since BASIC has become the defacto standard of the personal computing world and is easily obtained for all systems described earlier, our discussion will be confined to BASIC. The information included with your computer and version of BASIC provides a good starting point for your study of programming. Excellent references for further information on all the languages mentioned may be found in the Appendices.

As a result of reading whatever information was furnished with your system, you are probably acquainted with at least the more elementary operative statements contained in BASIC. These statements include LET, INPUT, PRINT and REM. Although not usually thought of as commands, the arithmetic operators (+, −,

×, /) have a specific order of execution that differs slightly in various versions of BASIC. Perhaps you have tried a few programs using various combinations of these and other commands. If not, try them out and get well acquainted—they are used heavily in everyday computer operations.

Any program you construct must have some sort of purpose. By carefully constructing the preliminary design, actual program writing is simplified several fold. While it may be all well and good to just jot a few notes for a simple program design, intricate programs require comprehensive preplanning to function effectively. Flow charts describing all the contingencies likely to be encountered are preferred by some programmers. Others like to write a sequential plan and work from that.

One of the best ways to develop a usable program has been described in the last few chapters. If your investment approach has been properly constructed, writing programs for that use should be relatively easy. You already know exactly what has to be done, all that remains is getting your computer to do it! Look carefully at your investment approach and take one of the rigidly defined processes as an area to start your programming efforts. Nobody says an investment approach must be all one computer program, in fact most are comprised of several. Your system most likely has the capability to renumber, revise, save, delete and combine multiple programs—so start with the easiest part and work your way up.

Although this book is not intended as an authoritative treatise on the art of programming, I would like to share with you the development of a program for one specific investment application. For purposes of illustration, several versions of the same program will be constructed to utilize progressively more of the computer's capacity and programmers skills. Each version of the program will accomplish the same basic purpose and may actually be used in your system. Keep in mind, however, that the concepts used are offered only as programming examples. Do not attempt to use the program as a stock selection device unless you are willing to study the references cited for more detailed information on how to do so. Operational differences and sample runs will be described as we go along.

DEVELOPING THE FUNDAMENTAL ANALYST

The name of our sample program gives away the purpose for which it is intended. If you recall our earlier discussion of methods of stock selection, fundamental analysis was described as a way to identify those stocks that are presently undervalued. Much use is made of information found in financial reports and comparisons generated from that information.

Specifically, our program will generate seven figures that have been described by Hardy (*Dun & Bradstreet's Guide to $Your Investments$*) as the *Seven Keys To Value*. In addition, Graham's (*Security Analysis*) corporate cash position approach will be used to determine whether or not a stock is undervalued.

The following pieces of information will be required from a financial report in order to generate the desired figures:

- —Operating profit.
- —Total sales.
- —Current assets.
- —Current liabilities.
- —Total of cash and its equivalent.
- —Long term debt.
- —Par value of all preferred stock.
- —Capital surplus.
- —Retained earnings.
- —Value of plant, equipment and land before depreciation and amortization.
- —Year end inventories.
- —Net income.
- —Number of common shares outstanding.
- —Market value of preferred stock.
- —12 month high—common stock.
- —12 month low—common stock.
- —Total assets of the company.

Using the preceeding figures, we can calculate the following ratios and percentages to aid our stock selection process:

☐ **Operating Profit Margin.** Defined as the ratio of profit to sales, this figure should increase with volume of sales.

☐ **Current Ratio.** The ratio of current assets to current liabilities, this figure should center around two to one for most corporations. Very low or high ratios may indicate problems in liquid asset management.

☐ **Liquidity Ratio.** Defined as the ratio of cash and its equivalent to current total liabilities, this ratio may be used as in indicator of a corporations ability to meet current obligations.

☐ **Capitalization Ratios.** These ratios show the relative percentages of each type of investment as part of the total investment in a corporation. Often capitalization ratios are used as indicators of relative leverage and risk for each of the types of securities offered.

☐ **Sales To Fixed Assets.** Computed by dividing the annual sales by the value of plant, equipment and land, this ratio helps to determine effectiveness of funds spent to enlarge production facilities.

☐ **Sales To Inventories.** Dividing annual sales by year-end inventories shows the rate of inventory turnover. High ratios, especially important to retailers, indicate marketing effectiveness.

☐ **Net Income To Net Worth.** Defined as the result of dividing net income by the total of preferred stock, common stock and surplus accounts, this figure indicates the percentage of profits the company is earning on the stockholders' investment. More profitable companies are indicated by similarly higher ratios.

☐ **Asset Value Per Share.** Using Graham's approach, the current liabilities, long term debt and total market value of preferred stock are subtracted from the current assets. This result is divided by the number of common shares outstanding, producing an asset value per share figure. If this figure exceeds the current price per share, the stock is considered undervalued.

☐ **Price Variation.** Shows the relative price volatility of the common stock over the 12 month period.

Version 1.0

With no more information than we now possess, it is possible to construct a relatively simple program to handle this application. All that remains is to determine how to display the results obtained. For now, lets just print the figures on our video display. In order to write such a program, we need to be acquainted with only a handful of commands and a few ground rules. The first version of our program will use REM, PRINT, INPUT, LET, INT and END statements along with the four basic arithmetic operators (+, −, *, /) and parentheses for directing numeric operations. Check your software manual if you are unsure how to use these commands in your version of BASIC.

Since we have defined our problem, outlined the procedures to solve it and not added any extravagances, Version 1.0 of Fundamental Analyst meets our needs. Notice in Listing and Sample Run 6-1 a relatively straightforward sequence of events.

The REM statements in the first few lines explain the purpose of the program and allow for some self-documentation. PRINT merely displays the information in quotes on the video display each time the program is run. The next several lines use INPUT to obtain the desired information for use in later calculations. INPUT, as used in this program, also prints a prompt (enclosed in quotes) for the desired information. Letters following the semicolon in INPUT tell the computer which variable it is accepting. Many versions of BASIC allow for elegant variable names, but single or two letter combinations work just as well.

Once all the information has been received, a series of LET statements handle the actual calculations. LET is used to define the variable on the left side of the equals sign as the value of the operation specified on the right. In many versions of BASIC, LET is implied in statements containing a variable on the left and an operation, value, or other variable to the right of the equals sign. Therefore, the statement:

$$X = 2 + 5 + 9$$

is, for all practical purposes, exactly the same as:

$$LET X = 2 + 5 + 9$$

Both statements will cause the computer to add all three numbers and designate the sum as the variable X.

INT merely cuts off decimal values and returns the largest whole number contained in the statement. By using slightly more complicated arithmetic operations, we can calculate the desired results and round the results to any number of decimal places. In this instance, percents are returned as whole numbers and ratios limited to two decimal places. Without these additional steps, your BASIC will carry results to the maximum number of decimal places it is capable of manipulating.

Calculations now completed, the program looks for some way to display the results. PRINT, a rather versatile command, is used to provide the necessary format. Most BASICS will print literally the information enclosed by quotes and the value or string represented by a variable without quotes. Although conventions vary slightly, Applesoft requires a semicolon to separate the two. By using a second string enclosed in quotes, we can provide the proper symbol for the result displayed. END, required in some BASICS and not in others, simply identifies the conclusion of a program.

If you have followed the program to this point, try typing it in to your computer and running it. As you will see, it does indeed work for the intended application. To avoid having to type it in again for the next use, SAVE it to tape or disk if you like. If you have a similar application, try writing a program using only the commands discussed thus far. You will not only learn just how simple programming can be, but may also develop a very useful part of your investment approach program(s).

Developing Version 2.0

If you had a chance to use version 1.0 of our program, several areas of improvement may have occurred to you. Since the data generated is often used for comparative purposes, it would be helpful to be able to compare two different companies or the same company over two different time periods. New data must be supplied for each run of 1.0, since no provision for data storage was included. Prompts for mass storage handling should be included to cue proper operation of the tape unit. A little "tidying up" of both input and output displays would certainly enhance readability.

Without unduly complicating the original program, we can resolve several of the problems noted and make our program much easier to use. The absence of many "bells and whistles" found in some commercial programs may be a little confusing, but keep in mind we are bent on designing the simplest way to accomplish the desired results. Several new commands are used in this version, but no tricks peculiar to Applesoft have been employed. Little rewriting is necessary to use version 2.0 in your own computer. Most of the actual program commands should work as is. Methods of storing and loading data vary slightly, so check your manual for more details. The syntax of INPUT and PRINT may also be somewhat different in your BASIC version.

This version of our program, along with version 1.0, will run on a bare minimum system. A 16K Apple II, TRS-80, PET or similar unit will do very nicely. The only additional requirement for version 2.0 is some sort of mass storage device, which you probably have added if none was furnished with your computer. For the sake of simplicity, we will assume your mass storage media is cassette tape. A later version of this same program will use floppy disks as the storage media.

Version 2.0 Details

As may be seen in Listing and Sample Run 6-2, the program has grown in both length and complexity. The same straightforward sequence of events noted earlier is still there, but may not be quite as clear. Several new commands have been used in this version and we have added a few subroutines to handle the input, calculation and storage functions. In order to better understand the new commands used here, let's go through the program listing and describe the function of each in the line where it first occurs.

CALL -936 (line 40) clears the video display screen and returns the cursor to the upper left position. HOME serves the same function in Applesoft. Your BASIC should have an equivalent command, although the term may be slightly different.

INPUT A$ (line 110) allows a combination of letters and numbers to be designated as the string variable A$. The "$" is a standard designation for strings, making A and A$ distinctly different variables. In this case, we are asking for the name of Stock #1.

IF-THEN (line 160) is the first logical operator most programmers learn to use, and one of the most powerful. Used with $<$ or $>$ in this instance, the statement actually makes two comparisons and acts accordingly. If X is less than ($<$) 1 or greater than ($>$) 2, the program returns to line 120. Since we have asked for either a 1 or 2 response in the previous statement, this line is a form of error trapping in that program execution will not continue until the condition is satisfied. Once the proper response is obtained, the IF conditions are no longer true so THEN is ignored and the program continues on to the next line. Although this line uses GOTO another line number following THEN, other commands may be used as we will see later.

GOSUB (line 170) directs program execution to the subroutine starting at line 1500. Operations will continue sequentially from line 1500 until a RETURN statement is encountered, causing program execution to return to the statement immediately following the GOSUB command. Line 710 uses an IF-THEN statement to invoke the GOSUB command if Z=1. If Z is not equal to 1, program execution continues in the next numbered line. GOSUB and RETURN may be used without any logical operator to direct program operation to any subroutine you have included.

There are five subroutines used in this program, primarily to direct input of data and calculations. Lines 1000-1250 constitute an entry routine for inputting data from the keyboard. This same routine can be used for both sets of data. Lines 1300-1410 perform the calculations necessary to generate the results for stock #1. Similarly, lines 1700-1810 generate results for stock #2 data. The other two subroutines, located from lines 1500-1560 and 1600-

1660, read data directly from cassette tape files. Note that each subroutine MUST end with a RETURN to prevent the computer from executing only that portion of the program following the subroutine currently in use.

STORE and RECALL are the Apple commands to store and retreive data in an array from tape. STORE A, for instance, will save to tape all data contained in either a single or multi-dimensioned array A(x) or A(x,y). RECALL will read array data back in to memory. Arrays must be properly dimensioned by the program, since no file identification data is contained on the tape.

GET accepts single character input from the keyboard. Line 480, for instance, prompts either a Y or N response for saving data to tape. GET, in line 490, accepts the response character and assigns it to the variable C$. No return is necessary after typing the character requested by a GET command, in fact the return character will be accepted as a response in itself! Used judiciously, this command can lend a very professional air to your programs.

So, there you have version 2.0. We have fulfilled our goal of keeping the program as simple as possible to do the required task. If you fully understand the role of all the commands used so far, you may want to type the program in to your system and modify it to better suit your own specific requirements.

In the next chapter, you will find version 3.0 of The Fundamental Analyst. You will recognize much of the program from what we have covered in the last few pages. Rather extensive error trapping, disk files, display options and increased ease of use are the major changes made in version 3.0. Each of these areas will be discussed more fully in the section describing the program.

CONTINUING YOUR EDUCATION IN PROGRAMMING

As mentioned earlier, programming is simply the art of telling your computer what you would like it to do in language it understands. Although it may sound trite, the single best way to learn programming is to program! Your first efforts may be something less than fully successful, but each one will provide valuable experience you can get no other way.

Many excellent references are available to help you along in your programming efforts. Some are listed in the Appendices. Check the shelves at your local computer store and watch advertisements for new material. Subscribing to one or all of the periodicals oriented toward personal computers will provide another source of programs and information.

Studying other people's programs can be an interesting learning experience. Often you will find a solution to one of your problems or an interesting routine in a program seemingly unrelated to your specific applications. I, for one, am not shy about "stealing" a routine or idea from someone elses program to make my programming life easier!

I really doubt that your programming education will ever be finished. Just about the time you think you have a pretty good grasp of your system, along comes another language or disk operating system or peripheral or capability, etc., etc. With the personal computing field moving as rapidly as it is today, just keeping abreast of new developments can be a very time consuming chore.

EVALUATING SOFTWARE

Once you have purchased or written a program, thorough evaluation will help to point out areas of strength, weakness and possible modification. Although you may have considerable ego involvement in your own programs, it is important to subject them to the same scrutiny you would give a commercial product. Any program, yours or someone elses, needs to be carefully tested prior to devoting a lot of time to its use.

In this section, we will discuss some ways to evaluate programs. Hopefully, you will come up with some other ways not mentioned here. Try to put yourself in the position of a writer charged with reviewing the particular program for a magazine and look carefully at all the areas usually covered. Reading a few reviews may give you some ideas about questions to ask yourself. As a matter of fact, you may decide to actually try writing a review of some program and submit it to one of the popular magazines—who knows, you may be able to recoup the cost of the program!

Back to the matter at hand—evaluating software. The next several paragraphs may suggest some ways to conduct your own evaluation. In addition to the areas mentioned, try to add any others pertinent to your own situation.

Documentation

Commercial programs should be supplied with at least enough information to let you intelligently use the product. Some software suppliers provide very extensive documentation, including program listings. Unfortunately, these operations are all too rare. More often the documentation consists of a sheet or two of brief use instructions. Unless you are considering a very simple program, quality of documentation is often closely correlated to the quality of the program itself.

Programs you generate yourself should be documented closely. It's amazing how much you can forget about the inner workings of a program over a period of time. If the program does not require almost all of the memory you have available, generous use of REM statements in the program itself will be extremely helpful for later modification or debuggings. Another advantage of REM statements in the program itself—listing the program will provide another copy of the documentation when you misplace the originals.

Applicability

Does the program actually do what it is supposedly intended to do? Evaluating this area for a simple program is relatively easy, but can become a major chore when considering a complex task. A checkbook balancing program, for instance, can be compared to your paper records to see how accurate it is. Checking the operation of a program like The Fundamental Analyst we developed earlier involves hand doing the same calculations, rounding the results and comparing them to those generated by the program. For even more complex programs, much time can be consumed in this necessary chore. Your own programs can be checked for applicability a little easier by developing the program in stages and carefully trying each step along the way. Trusting valuable data to a program you have not checked is indeed a foolhardy move that may cause considerable problems sooner than you think!

Ease Of Operation

Commercial programs often excel in this area, since the user was not privy to the development of the program. Look for logical prompting, good error trapping and availability of options. Prompts should tell you what type of information is requested, how to input the data and what actions are necessary to terminate the sequence. For example, the statements:

PRESS RETURN TO CONTINUE

CONTINUE? (Y/N)

are infinitely easier to use than the often used:

CONTINUE?

which gives absolutely no clue as to what response is expected.

Simplicity is the real key to effective prompting—look for it in commercial programs and use liberally in your own.

Error Trapping

Error trapping refers to the ability of a program to inform the user what error was made and, hopefully, how to correct the error. Poorly designed programs include little, if any, error trapping, depending on the computer itself to generate error messages. Most often what happens in that instance is program termination in an error state, causing loss of any data contained in variables. Incorporating error trapping in a program is a relatively simple process and should be done for your own as well as commercial programs. Using the example of CONTINUE? (Y/N) again, error trapping is accomplished by testing for the desired character input with an IF-THEN statement something like: IF A$ <> "Y" OR A$<> "N" THEN PRINT "TYPE Y OR N". Of course, there is nothing to prevent error trapping being combined with another statement directing further program activity. Using the same example, we can combine desired activities into two IF-THEN statements: IF A$ = "N" THEN STOP and IF A$ <> "Y" THEN PRINT "TYPE Y OR N". Each error message line should then direct the program to return to the original prompt, allowing the user a "second chance" to get it right. In your evaluation of a commercial program, test the error trapping by deliberately making mistakes. If the program bombs or depends on a computer generated error message, avoid the program if at all possible. Do the same for your own programs and provide more error trapping than you think necessary—it will save a lot of frustration later.

Program Options

This is an area that can inhibit, as well as enhance, ease of program operation. Many data base management programs currently available are examples of option overkill. The user is forced to spend a great deal of time designing input and output formats with each use of the program, definitely causing at least me to think twice before even bothering! Thoughtful use of options like providing for the use of a printer or changing the base parameters of the program can be a definite plus. Look carefully at the options provided in commercial programs to see whether or not they are applicable to your intended uses. In your own programs, providing options can be as simple as leaving a large enough gap in line numbers to fill in new steps later or as complicated as you care to make them.

Other things, of course, contribute to the ease with which any program is used. One or two step loading rather than a complicated series of commands certainly helps. Messages displayed during long sorts or operations help assure the user all is well. Distinctive markings on the tape or disk aid in locating the program on cluttered shelves (doesn't every computer user have them?). In designing your own programs, think about the easiest to use programs in your library and try to model further efforts after those.

Efficiency

Finally, look at the efficiency offered by the program. Is it memory efficient or does it gobble up all the bytes you have? Speed of operation is a good clue to efficiency, as long as accuracy is not sacrificed. Does use of the program save you time and effort or could the same chore be done easier in some other way? It makes little sense to load an extensive telephone directory program, for instance, if you could locate a desired number more quickly in a $2.98 phone index.

If you write or buy a program that fulfills your application, operates easily and efficiently, provides enough documentation to answer your questions and won't let you get too far astray—pat yourself on the back for a job well done! Make a back-up copy, sit back and let your computer demonstrate just how wise you were.

SUMMARY

We have covered a lot of ground in this chapter and perhaps raised more questions in your mind than were answered. Obviously an area as complex as integrating a computer into your investment program requires careful consideration of all the available alternatives. Take some time to look over some of the material listed in the Appendices to clear up any questions you may have in specific areas.

By the time you leave this chapter, I hope you have reached some of the many decisions necessary regarding the areas discussed. In deciding to use a personal computer as an investment tool, you are committing yourself to a relatively large expenditure of both dollars and time. Efficient utilization of this new tool is vital if your investment program is to benefit significantly.

Only through careful construction of your total investment approach and strict attention to the details of your computers role will provide the necessary efficiency. No one can sell you either a computer or program capable of making foolproof investment decisions. As a tool, the personal computer is unique in its capability to aid you in reaching intelligent decisions. Control of your investment program must not, however, be delegated to your own or any other computer.

I hope we have been able to at least whet your appetite for doing some of your own programming as a way to learn more about your own computer. The programs described in the next chapter may give you a good place to start accumulating a software library, or at least provide a few ideas to use in your own programs.

Program Listing 6-1

```
10   REM   Fundamental   Analyst  V1.
     0
20   REM   by L. Schmeltz
25   PRINT
30   PRINT "ENTER THE FOLLOWING IN
     FORMATION"
40   PRINT "FROM THE FINANCIAL REP
     ORT"
50   PRINT
60   PRINT "BE SURE ALL NUMBERS AR
     E IN THE SAME"
70   PRINT "QUANTITIES, I.E., 000,
     000 OMITTED"
80   PRINT
90   INPUT "OPERATING PROFIT?";A
100  INPUT "TOTAL SALES?";B
110  INPUT "CURRENT ASSETS?";C
120  INPUT "CURRENT LIABILITIES?"
     ;D
130  INPUT "CASH AND ITS EQUIVALE
     NT?";E
140  INPUT "LONG TERM DEBT?";F
150  INPUT "PAR VALUE OF ALL PREF
     ERRED STOCK?";G
160  INPUT "PAR VALUE OF ALL COMM
     ON STOCK?";H
170  INPUT "CAPITAL SURPLUS?";I
```

```
180   INPUT "RETAINED EARNINGS?";J
190   INPUT "VALUE OF PLANT, EQUIP
      . & LAND?";K
200   INPUT "YEAR END INVENTORIES?
      ";L
210   INPUT "NET INCOME?";M
220   INPUT "COMMON SHARES OUTSTAN
      DING?";N
230   INPUT "MARKET VALUE OF PREFE
      RRED STOCK?";O
240   INPUT "12 MO. HIGH--COMMON S
      TOCK?";P
250   INPUT "12 MO. LOW--COMMON ST
      OCK?";Q
260   INPUT "TOTAL ASSETS?";R
270   HOME
280   LET S =  INT ((A / B) * 100)
290   LET T =  INT ((C / D) * 100 +
      .5) / 100
300   LET U =  INT ((E / D) * 100)

310   LET V =  INT ((F / (G + H +
      I + J + F)) * 100)
320   LET W =  INT ((G / (G + H +
      I + J + F)) * 100)
330   LET X =  INT (((H + I + J) /
      (G + H + I + J + F)) * 100)
340   LET Y =  INT ((B / K) * 100 +
      .5) / 100
350   LET Z =  INT ((B / L) * 100 +
      .5) / 100
360   LET AA =  INT ((M / (G + H +
      I + J)) * 100)
370   LET AB =  INT (((R - (D + F +
      O)) / N) * 100 + .5) / 100
380   LET AC =  INT ((P / Q) * 100
      ) - 100
385   PRINT : PRINT
390   PRINT "OPERATING PROFIT MARG
      IN  ";S;"%"
400   PRINT "CURRENT RATIO   ";T
```

130

```
410   PRINT "LIQUIDITY RATIO  ";U;
      "%"
420   PRINT "CAPITALIZATION RATIOS
      ;"
430   PRINT  TAB( 5);"LONG TERM DE
      BT  ";U;"%"
440   PRINT  TAB( 5);"PREFERRED ST
      OCK  ";W;"%"
450   PRINT  TAB( 5);"COMMON STOCK
      & SURPLUS  ";X;"%"
460   PRINT "SALES TO FIXED ASSETS
      ";Y
470   PRINT "SALES TO INVENTORIES
      ";Z
480   PRINT "NET INCOME TO NET WOR
      TH  ";AA;"%"
490   PRINT "ASSET VALUE PER SHARE
      ";AB
500   PRINT "PRICE VARIATION  ";AC
      ;"%"
510   END
```

Sample Run 6-1

```
ENTER THE FOLLOWING INFORMATION
FROM THE FINANCIAL REPORT

BE SURE ALL NUMBERS ARE IN THE SAME
QUANTITIES, I.E., 000,000 OMITTED

OPERATING PROFIT?267.9
TOTAL SALES?3283
CURRENT ASSETS?1280.8
CURRENT LIABILITIES?1087.5
CASH AND ITS EQUIVALENT?18.1
LONG TERM DEBT?4928.2
PAR VALUE OF ALL PREFERRED STOCK?786
PAR VALUE OF ALL COMMON STOCK?760
CAPITAL SURPLUS?1147.1
RETAINED EARNINGS?629
```

```
VALUE OF PLANT, EQUIP. & LAND?12011.12
YEAR END INVENTORIES?667
NET INCOME?591.3
COMMON SHARES OUTSTANDING?152.2
MARKET VALUE OF PREFERRED STOCK?790
12 MO. HIGH--COMMON STOCK?31.75
12 MO. LOW--COMMON STOCK?24.25
TOTAL ASSETS?13377.1


OPERATING PROFIT MARGIN  8%
CURRENT RATIO  1.18
LIQUIDITY RATIO  1%
CAPITALIZATION RATIOS:
    LONG TERM DEBT  59%
    PREFERRED STOCK  9%
    COMMON STOCK & SURPLUS  30%
SALES TO FIXED ASSETS  .27
SALES TO INVENTORIES  4.92
NET INCOME TO NET WORTH  17%
ASSET VALUE PER SHARE  43.18
PRICE VARIATION  30%
```

Program Listing 6-2

```
10   REM   FUNDAMENTAL ANALYST 2.0
20   REM   BY L. SCHMELTZ
30   DIM A(10): DIM B(10)
40   CALL  - 936
50   PRINT "THIS PROGRAM ALLOWS YO
     U TO ANALYZE"
60   PRINT "TWO DIFFERENT STOCKS O
     R THE SAME STOCK"
70   PRINT "FOR TWO DIFFERENT TIME
      PERIODS."
80   PRINT
90   PRINT "DATA MAY BE LOADED FRO
     M TAPE OR KEYBOARD": PRINT
100  PRINT "ENTER NAME OF STOCK #
     1"
```

```
110    INPUT A$
120    PRINT "DATA FROM:"
130    PRINT  TAB( 5);"1.   TAPE"
140    PRINT  TAB( 5);"2.   KEYBOARD
       "
150    INPUT "WHICH?";Z
160    IF Z < 1 OR Z > 2 THEN  GOTO
       120
170    IF Z = 1 THEN  GOSUB 1500
180    IF Z = 2 THEN  GOSUB 1000: GOSUB
       1300
190    PRINT "ENTER NAME OF STOCK #
       2"
200    INPUT B$
210    PRINT "DATA FROM:"
220    PRINT  TAB( 5);"1.   TAPE"
230    PRINT  TAB( 5);"2.   KEYBOARD
       "
240    INPUT "WHICH?";Z
250    IF Z < 1 OR Z > 2 THEN  GOTO
       210
260    IF Z = 1 THEN  GOSUB 1600
270    IF Z = 2 THEN  GOSUB 1000: GOSUB
       1700
280    CALL  - 936
290    PRINT "STOCK #1: ";A$
300    PRINT "STOCK #2: ";B$
310    PRINT
320    PRINT  TAB( 26);"#1"; TAB( 3
       3);"#2"
330    PRINT
340    PRINT "OPER. PROFIT MARGIN";
        TAB( 26);A(0);"%"; TAB( 34)
       ;B(0);"%"
350    PRINT "CURRENT RATIO"; TAB(
       26);A(1); TAB( 34);B(1)
360    PRINT "LIQUIDITY RATIO"; TAB(
       26);A(2); TAB( 34);B(2)
370    PRINT "CAPITALIZATION RATIOS
       :"
380    PRINT  TAB( 5);"LONG TERM DE
       BT"; TAB( 26);A(3);"%"; TAB(
```

```
          34); B(3); "%"
390   PRINT   TAB( 5); "PREFERRED ST
          OCK"; TAB( 26); A(4); "%"; TAB(
          34); B(4); "%"
400   PRINT   TAB( 5); "COMM. STOCK+
          SURPLUS"; TAB( 26); A(5); "%";
          TAB( 34); B(5); "%"
410   PRINT "SALES TO FIXED ASSETS
          "; TAB( 26); A(6); TAB( 34); B
          (6)
420   PRINT "SALES TO INVENTORIES"
          ; TAB( 26); A(7); TAB( 34); B(
          7)
430   PRINT "NET INCOME/NET WORTH"
          ; TAB( 26); A(8); TAB( 34); B(
          8)
440   PRINT "ASSET VAL. PER SHARE"
          ; TAB( 26); A(9); TAB( 34); B(
          9)
450   PRINT "PRICE VARIATION"; TAB(
          26); A(10); "%"; TAB( 34); B(10
          ); "%"
460   PRINT
470   PRINT
480   PRINT "SAVE DATA TO TAPE? (Y
          /N)"
490   GET C$
500   IF C$ = "N" THEN  GOTO 620
510   PRINT "SAVE WHICH DATA?"
520   PRINT   TAB( 5); "1.   "; A$
530   PRINT   TAB( 5); "2.   "; B$
540   PRINT   TAB( 5); "3.   BOTH"
550   INPUT Z
560   PRINT "READY TO RECORD DATA?
          (Y/N)"
570   GET C$
580   IF C$ = "N" THEN  GOTO 560
590   IF Z = 1 THEN  STORE A: PRINT
          A$; " DATA STORED"
600   IF Z = 2 THEN  STORE B: PRINT
          B$; " DATA STORED"
610   IF Z = 3 THEN  STORE A: STORE
```

```
          B: PRINT "ALL DATA NOW SAVED
          "
620   END
1000   CALL  - 936
1010   PRINT "ENTER THE FOLLOWING
       INFORMATION"
1020   PRINT "FROM THE FINANCIAL R
       EPORT."
1030   PRINT
1040   PRINT "BE SURE ALL NUMBERS
       ARE IN THE SAME"
1050   PRINT "QUANTITIES, I.E., OO
       O,OOO OMITTED"
1060   PRINT
1070   INPUT "OPERATING PROFIT?";A

1080   INPUT "TOTAL SALES?";B
1090   INPUT "CURRENT ASSETS?";C
1100   INPUT "CURRENT LIABILITIES?
       ";D
1110   INPUT "CASH AND ITS EQUIVAL
       ENT?";E
1120   INPUT "LONG TERM DEBT?";F
1130   INPUT "PAR VALUE OF ALL PRE
       FERRED STOCK?";G
1140   INPUT "PAR VALUE OF COMMON
       STOCK?";H
1150   INPUT "CAPITAL SURPLUS?";I
1160   INPUT "RETAINED EARNINGS?";
       J
1170   INPUT "VALUE OF PLANT, EQUI
       P. & LAND?";K
1180   INPUT "YEAR END INVENTORIES
       ?";L
1190   INPUT "NET INCOME?";M

1200   INPUT "COMMON SHARES OUTSTA
       NDING?";N
1210   INPUT "MARKET VALUE OF PREF
       ERRED STOCK?";O
1220   INPUT "12 MO. HIGH--COMMON
       STOCK?";P
```

```
1230  INPUT "12 MO. LOW--COMMON S
      TOCK?";Q
1240  INPUT "TOTAL ASSETS?";R
1250  RETURN
1300 A(0) =  INT ((A / B) * 100)
1310 A(1) =  INT ((C / D) * 100 +
      .5) / 100
1320 A(2) =  INT ((E / D) * 100)
1330 A(3) =  INT ((F / (G + H + I
      + J + F)) * 100)
1340 A(4) =  INT ((G / (G + H + I
      + J + F)) * 100)
1350 A(5) =  INT (((H + I + J) /
      (G + H + I + J + F)) * 100)
1360 A(6) =  INT ((B / K) * 100 +
      .5) / 100
1370 A(7) =  INT ((B / L) * 100 +
      .5) / 100
1380 A(8) =  INT ((M / (G + H + I
      + J)) * 100)
1390 A(9) =  INT (((R - (D + F +
      O)) / N) * 100 + .5) / 100
1400 A(10) =  INT ((P / Q) * 100)
      - 100
1410  RETURN
1500  PRINT "LOCATE THE ";A$;" FI
      LE"
1510  PRINT "ON THE TAPE AND LOAD
      IT"
1520  PRINT "AT THIS TIME"
1530  RECALL A
1540  PRINT
1550  PRINT  TAB( 15);"DATA LOADE
      D"
1560  RETURN
1600  PRINT "LOCATE THE ";B$;" FI
      LE"
1610  PRINT "ON THE TAPE AND LOAD
      IT"
1620  PRINT "AT THIS TIME"
1630  RECALL B
1640  PRINT
```

```
1650  PRINT  TAB( 15);"DATA LOADE
      D"
1660  RETURN
1700 B(0) =  INT ((A / B) * 100)
1710 B(1) =  INT ((C / D) * 100 +
     .5) / 100
1720 B(2) =  INT ((E / D) * 100)
1730 B(3) =  INT ((F / (G + H + I
     + J + F)) * 100)
1740 B(4) =  INT ((G / (G + H + I
     + J + F)) * 100)
1750 B(5) =  INT (((H + I + J) /
     (G + H + I + J + F)) * 100)
1760 B(6) =  INT ((B / K) * 100 +
     .5) / 100
1770 B(7) =  INT ((B / L) * 100 +
     .5) / 100
1780 B(8) =  INT ((M / (G + H + I
     + J)) * 100)
1790 B(9) =  INT (((R - (D + F +
     O)) / N) * 100 + .5) / 100
1800 B(10) =  INT ((P / Q) * 100)
      - 100
1810  RETURN
```

Sample Run 6-2

THIS PROGRAM ALLOWS YOU TO ANALYZE
TWO DIFFERENT STOCKS OR THE SAME STOCK
FOR TWO DIFFERENT TIME PERIODS.

DATA MAY BE LOADED FROM TAPE OR KEYBOARD

ENTER NAME OF STOCK #1
?SAMPLE UTITLLITY CO.
DATA FROM:
    1.   TAPE
    2.   KEYBOARD
WHICH?2
ENTER THE FOLLOWING INFORMATION
FROM THE FINANCIAL REPORT.

```
BE SURE ALL NUMBERS ARE IN THE SAME
QUANTITIES, I.E., 000,000 OMITTED

OPERATING PROFIT?267.9
TOTAL SALES?3283
CURRENT ASSETS?1280.8
CURRENT LIABILITIES?1087.5
CASH AND ITS EQUIVALENT?18.1
LONG TERM DEBT?4928.2
PAR VALUE OF ALL PREFERRED STOCK?786
PAR VALUE OF COMMON STOCK?760
CAPITAL SURPLUS?1147.1
RETAINED EARNINGS?629
VALUE OF PLANT, EQUIP. & LAND?12011.2
YEAR END INVENTORIES?667
NET INCOME?591.3
COMMON SHARES OUTSTANDING?152.2
MARKET VALUE OF PREFERRED STOCK?790
12 MO. HIGH--COMMON STOCK?31.75
12 MO. LOW--COMMON STOCK?24.25
TOTAL ASSETS?13377.1
ENTER NAME OF STOCK #2
?SAME COMPANY FROM TAPE
DATA FROM:
     1.   TAPE
     2.   KEYBOARD
WHICH?1
LOCATE THE SAME COMPANY FROM TAPE FILE
ON THE TAPE AND LOAD IT
AT THIS TIME


              DATA LOADED


STOCK #1: SAMPLE UTILITY CO.
STOCK #2: SAME COMPANY FROM TAPE

                         #1        #2

OPER. PROFIT MARGIN      8%        8%
CURRENT RATIO            1.18      1.18
LIQUIDITY RATIO          1         1
```

```
CAPITALIZATION RATIOS:
     LONG TERM DEBT          59%        59%
     PREFERRED STOCK         9%         9%
     COMM. STOCK+SURPLUS     30%        30%
SALES TO FIXED ASSETS        .27        .27
SALES TO INVENTORIES         4.92       4.92
NET INCOME/NET WORTH         17         17
ASSET VAL. PER SHARE         43.18      43.18
PRICE VARIATION              30%        30%


SAVE DATA TO TAPE? (Y/N)
SAVE WHICH DATA?
     1.   SAMPLE UTILITY CO.
     2.   SAME COMPANY FROM TAPE
     3.   BOTH
?3
READY TO RECORD DATA? (Y/N)
ALL DATA NOW SAVED


]
```

Chapter 7

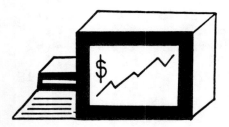

Sample Programs

In this chapter, we will present and examine in detail some sample programs that could be used for investment purposes. Perhaps as importantly, these programs may give you a few ideas or subroutines to use in developing your own programs. Rather than try to cover all the possible programming techniques, each program discussed will use somewhat different approaches to solve the problem presented. All are written in Applesoft (floating point BASIC), but may be readily adapted to other versions of BASIC by following the suggestions given at the end of each program discussion.

Although each of the programs has been tested and "debugged" on my own computer, there is certainly room for any refinements you care to add. If you are at all interested in learning to write your own programs, take the time to study each subroutine. Learn how and why it operates, look for areas of possible improvement and try to rewrite it to better suit your purposes. For instance, some of the lines have been left short and slightly awkward for purposes of clarity. By combining statements and using shortcuts, memory efficiency can be improved several fold.

Should you decide to use any one of the programs presented here in your investment management system, be sure it does exactly what you think it should. Using the Fundamental Analyst to select stocks, for example, will not guarantee success for you unless that approach agrees completely with your investment goals and objectives. Slight modifications to change the factors considered, methods of calculation or data presentation may make the program more suitable for your own use.

For those of you unwilling or unable to spend the time necessary to rewrite and type in the following programs, similar versions are available through LeSoftware. See the software section of the Appendices for further details.

BECOMING A DISK JOCKEY

Before getting in to the actual programs presented, a little more information on mass storage is needed. In the preceeding chapter you had occasion to use cassette tape storage files for both programs and data. No doubt you have also had the opportunity to load and save other software using the cassette capabilities of your system.

There is much to be said for the use of cassette tapes as media for data storage. Relatively low cost of both transports and tapes, ready availability, good dependability, and the capacity to store large amounts of data are plusses easily recognized. On the negative side are limitations on the types of data stored easily, slow access and loading, and difficulties in locating the specific data needed at any one time. It has been my experience that tape storage works best for programs and files needing infrequent access and modification.

Disk based storage, in most cases, is considerably faster and more convenient for applications requiring any type of files that must be frequently changed. The programs presented in this chapter will use the Apple II Disk as a primary mass storage medium. Specific operating details may differ from system to system, but most disk based storage has capabilities remarkably similar to those offered by Apple. See Fig. 7-1.

Several types of files are used in disk applications. Our initial excursion into the world of the disk will use three of these:

□ **Program Files.** As the name implies, programs are stored using named program files. Using the commands SAVE, DELETE, LOAD, RUN, LOCK and UNLOCK followed by the name assigned to a particular program allow rapid program access. Although there are other commands that can be used, those listed accomplish the basic functions of program storage and operation. Program listings do not usually include these commands, unless one program is called from within another.

□ **Sequential Access Text Files.** Limited to data storage, sequential access files are very similar to those used in cassette based systems. Data is stored in a serial fashion, one item directly following another. Usual operating procedures for this type of file structure call for reading and writing the file in a specific order. Specific pieces of data are relatively difficult to locate for the average programmer. Sequential files may be quite long, since they are limited only by the amount of memory available for reading and writing them. APPEND allows data to be added following the last item currently in the file.

☐ **Random Access Text Files** are most easily visualized as a group of fixed length sequential access files. The maximum length of each record must be specified each time the file is opened. Once the file has been accessed, individual records may be read or written by specifying their record number. Locating a specific record in the file is considerably simplified, at the expense of more complexity in program design.

Disk commands for the Apple may be either immediate or deferred execution types. Immediate execution commands are merely typed in on the keyboard and the desired disk operation is done when return is pressed. Deferred execution commands are contained in a program and must be preceeded by CTRL-D in order to operate. Usual programming practice calls for defining a printing character to equal CTRL-D, in the sample programs the string variable D$ is so defined.

In the program descriptions that follow, disk operations will be pointed out as they occur. If your operating system requires different syntax for disk commands, knowing the desired result of each operation will aid in translating the line to work properly for you.

THE FUNDAMENTAL ANALYST 3.0

If you followed the discussion on learning to program in the last chapter, the name of this program should sound very familiar. As you may recall, the first two versions of Fundamental Analyst were developed to show two different ways of attacking the same programming problem. From the relatively simple direct data input and display of version 1.0, provisions for mass storage and subroutines were added to form version 2.0. Despite the fact that both earlier versions were quite different in construction and operation, the end results were the same.

Listing 7-1 shows version 3.0 of Fundamental Analyst. Grown a bit, hasn't it? As promised earlier, this version incorporates many of the "bells and whistles" missing from the two earlier programs. The seeming complexity of the program may lead you to the false conclusion that operation is also more difficult. Not so! Most of the

Fig. 7-1. Floppy disk mass storage systems offer significant advantages in versatility, speed and capacity. Drives are available for virtually every personal computer. Dual drives, as seen here, provide a convenient means of using both program and data disks simultaneously, creating back-up files and disk-to-disk copying (courtesy of Commodore Business Machines, Inc.).

refinements added have been designed to increase ease and convenience of operation.

The Problem

To quickly review the problem we are attempting to solve with this program, look back at the section titled Developing The Fundamental Analyst in Chapter 6. As noted there, 17 pieces of information readily available from corporate financial reports are used to calculate ratios and percentages often in stock selection. Since the raw data requested and calculated results have already been discussed, we will not bore you with repetition here.

An additional set of problems are posed to make the program more useful to the serious investor:

☐ Often it is helpful to be able to compare data for one, two or three stocks simultaneously.

☐ Both raw data and computed figures should be readily available for each stock under consideration.

☐ The program should be self-prompting and error trapped in such a way that the user can easily recover from an error.

☐ Adding new data and deleting unwanted information should be a relatively simple process.

☐ As much as possible, capabilities and limitations peculiar to the Apple II should be avoided.

☐ Disk files of various types are used to show the relative capabilities of each.

The Program (Listing 7-1)

Keeping in mind the constraints imposed by the problem, version 3.0 does offer some interesting alternatives to techniques demonstrated earlier. Version 2.0 used a limited menu to select input from keyboard or tape. Additional selection options have been added here, resulting in a program entirely driven by the menu displayed in the first few lines. In order to maintain some semblance of logic in discussing this program, subroutines will be discussed as they are called rather than following a line number sequence.

Line 30 sets the string variable D$ equal to CTRL-D, as required for disk operations later in the program. The DIM statements in Line 40 set up arrays to handle data and directory listings. A$ and E$ are arbitrarily dimensioned for 100 strings, the maximum number that will be accepted by the directory file. You may want to set the limit higher or lower to accommodate memory capacity in your system.

Line 50 calls subroutine 5000, which prints some background information on the screen and allows the user to create both the disk files needed for program operation. DATA-L205 is a random access text file which will contain the raw and computed data. Maximum length of each record in this file is 205 bits, hence the strange name to help remember to use the length figure in the proper places. DIRECTORY, as the name implies, will contain a directory of the stocks and dates contained in the system. Since DIRECTORY is a sequential access file, no length parameter is needed to create or use it. Notice each deferred execution disk command is preceeded by PRINT D$, as discussed earlier. Lines 5000 and 5220 contain a FOR-NEXT loop used to delay program execution long enough for the message on the screen to be read.

The eleven lines, 60 to 160, direct all further action of the program according to the option selected when the menu is displayed. Following completion of each subroutine, line 60 is specified as the return point so the menu is repeatedly displayed. Z and Z$ are variables reserved for responses to input prompts, used repeatedly throughout the entire program. Error trapping for the menu, Line 150, limits the range of acceptable responses and chides the user with an error message for unacceptable responses.

Selecting option 1 on the menu causes the program to branch to Line 4000 and accept data for a new stock. The first few lines of the Data Input For New Stock Subroutine set up a screen format for ease of inputting data. Once the format is in place, the input statements actually accept the data. Rather than using extensive error trapping in this subroutine, the user is given the opportunity to change data following the last input statement. Since the stock name and date variables are strings, either numeric or alpha characters will be accepted. All the rest of the prompts require numeric characters to avoid the RE-ENTER message generated by Applesoft.

Line 4280, in response to RETURN, initiates several processes. First, the name and date of the new data are added to the DIRECTORY file. Next, the raw data is manipulated to compute the percentages and ratios desired. Finally, all the data is printed to the DATA-L205 file for random access later. As in the other subroutines, GOTO 60 returns the program menu to the screen.

Option 2 calls the Directory Display Subroutine which begins with Line 3000. After reading the DIRECTORY file in its entirety, this subroutine titles the top of the screen and displays record number, stock name and date information for all the records currently in the file. To keep this display from scrolling off the screen, records are displayed one screenfull at a time. Lines 3200-3230 determine the number of records remaining and print the appropriate prompt at the bottom of the screen. Once all the records have been displayed, RETURN again displays the main program menu.

The Delete Data Subroutine, selection 3, begins at Line 3300. First the user is reminded of the procedures to be used and given an opportunity to obtain a record number from the directory routine. If a negative response is received, a record number is requested. To double check, the name and date for that record are displayed and again a Y or N response is requested. Since this routine will remove access to the particular data in question, the extra caution may save a lot of typing to recover data lost through error.

If all the proper responses have been received, this routine then proceeds to delete the directory listing for that particular data. Since access to data is gained with the record number, deleting the record number allows overwriting of that record in the random access file. In a flash, the data's gone and the main program menu reappears.

The two display options, 4 and 5, on the menu are closely related and share some common subroutines. Selecting either option indirectly calls the Select Data For Display Subroutine at Line 2000. By following the prompts given, the user may select display of up to three stocks simultaneously. Record numbers, obtained from the directory routine, are used to identify each stock. Stocks selected are then read from the DATA-L205 file, the display is captioned and program execution returns to either the raw or computed data subroutines.

Another shared subroutine occurs at Line 1500, where tab settings to justify the data display are calculated. Depending on the number of stocks for display, up to three tab settings are calculated before RETURN is encountered.

Selecting menu option 4 activates the Raw Data Display Subroutine starting at Line 1000. Once the K$ array elements have been defined, actual display is handled in the FOR-NEXT loop starting at Line 1210. Line 1290 provides for two options—returning to the program menu or viewing computed data for the same group of stocks. Pressing ESC results in a rapid display change to computed data, and the same option for display of raw data. Although this may seem a bit frivolous, I find myself skipping back and forth quite often when examining actual data.

Option 5, the Computed Data Display Subroutine, begins at line 500 and is virtually identical in operation to the display routine just discussed. Pressing 6 when the menu is displayed results in a very unceremonious end to the program—the Applesoft prompt bracket character tells you the deed has been done.

Operation

Actual use of this program is a very simple process. Once the RUN command is executed in your system, everything else is selected from the menu. There are, of course, some areas where common sense must prevail. As noted in both earlier versions of Fundamental Analyst, all figures used (except for stock prices) must be in the same units, i.e., 000,000 omitted. If the files contain no data and you request a directory or data display, error messages will chide you vigorously.

Obviously, it is impossible to recreate interactive video displays on the printed page. Rather than try to artificially create them, I have chosen to leave the sample runs for a pleasant surprise once you have gone through the trouble to enter the program into your system. Although the 40 character display width offered by the Apple causes some squeezing to fit all the data on the screen, readability is quite good. The ability to see data in a side-by-side comparison compensates, at least for me, the minor inconvenience of any squeezing noted.

Adapting To Other Versions Of BASIC

If you followed the advice given earlier and obtained a version of BASIC that handles arrays, strings and floating point calculations adapting this program will not be an overly complicated process. For this first sample program, we will point out areas possibly requiring adaptation on their first occurence.

Line 30. D\$ = CTRL-D sets up the disk access character as the string variable D\$.

Line 40. The DIM statements dimension arrays. It is not necessary in Applesoft to dimension the length of string variables. Some versions of BASIC require at least two dimension arrays, in which case you could use DIM A\$ (10, 10 or DIM A\$ (1,100).

Line 60. CALL -936 clears the display and returns the cursor to the upper left (home) position. Similar commands are HOME or CLS.

Lines 130 & 140. GET and VAL are used to input a single character and convert it to a numeric variable. If your BASIC does not allow for either operation, an INPUT statement will do the job.

Line 150. IF-THEN statements in Applesoft execute the next numbered line if the conditions are not met. Any statements on the same line are executed only if the argument is true.

Line 520. INVERSE and NORMAL switch the video display background and print color. Primary use in this program is for contrast outlining expected responses. Can be eliminated altogether or replaced by underlining, expanded letters, etc.

Line 800. CALL -958 clears the display inside the text window from the current cursor position to the bottom margin of the screen.

Line 2210. Disk access commands must be preceeded by CTRL-D (defined earlier as D$) when used within a program. In this line, the random access text file DATA-L205 is opened. The ,L025 parameter following the name indicates each record has a maximum length of 205 bytes.

Line 2220-2270. This series of lines retrieves data from records F, G and H of file DATA-L205. Once a READ command is used, subsequent INPUTs accept data from the disk file. By closing the file in Line 2270, the read operation is terminated.

Line 3130. POKE 34,4 sets the text window at the fourth line from the top of the display. The purpose, in this case, is to preserve the directory display heading. Various POKESs may be used to define all four boundaries of the text window. TEXT, found in Line 3260, returns the next window to the full 24 × 40 default size.

Multiple statements per line are permitted, using the colon (:) as a separator. VTAB amd HTAB, used in several lines, move the cursor to the vertical and horizontal positions specified. In FOR-NEXT loops, the variable name may be omitted in the NEXT statement.

If your BASIC offers PRINT USING, IF-THEN-ELSE, or other extended functions, parts of this program can be rewritten with a considerable savings in memory usage and programming effort. More limited versions of BASIC may not offer all the features used here, but the program can be adapted with a little ingenuity. For those systems limited to cassette storage, the DIRECTORY file may be used as is. The random access DATA-L205 file could be simulated by creating a series of sequential access files on tape, one for each record.

Displays capable of more than 40 characters per line permit

neater data displays without the squeezing evidenced here. Changing the tab settings for print spacing, or setting PRINT USING values appropriately, will enhance readability of the displays several fold. Some adjustment of vertical display values will be necessary if your system permits less than 24 lines on the screen.

Program Modifications Possible

Although this program was designed to analyze the factors noted, it is entirely possible and relatively easy to modify its operation. All data display labels are contained in the 29 elements of array K$. Input prompts for data are found in the PRINT statements, Lines 4020-4210. All numeric data, both raw and computed, is contained in the 29 elements of array A. Lines 4450-4550 calculate the various ratios and percentages, assigning each result to one of the array elements.

By changing the statements noted in the preceding paragraph, this program could be set up to analyze virtually any combination of factors you desire. If you have very limited memory available, each subroutine could be set up as a separate program called by the main menu program. Resourceful programmers could probably add a great many features, such as hard copy capability, light pen input, voice or sound routines, etc.

STOCK TREND ANALYST

Michael G. Zahorchak, in his book, *The Art Of Low Risk Investing*, presented an interesting approach to investment management using moving averages to determine both market trends and individual stock positions. By selecting volatile stocks, Zahorchak demonstrates how capitalizing on market cycles can provide relatively good gains.

To use this approach, one needs to calculate 5, 15 and 40 week moving averages for each stock followed and at least one broad market index. In addition, a 15 week advance-decline line is calculated. Deciding which stock to buy and when is determined by various combinations of moving average interaction. Both broad market and individual stock trends are considered for purchases. Selling a stock is determined primarily by its own moving average activity.

Weekly data for each of the indexes and stocks is used to update the program. At least 40 weeks of data must be available to calculate all the moving averages.

As I mentioned in Chapter 1, this approach lends itself well to development of a computer program because of its well defined parameters. Actually, one of the first programs I wrote was based on Zahorchak's principles. This program (Listing 7-2) is one of many versions that have been developed since that first one.

If you are tempted to use this approach in your own investment program, I would strongly recommend reading, *The Art Of Low Risk Investing*, from cover to cover! Much of the information contained in the book does not enter into the computer program and yet could be equally important in helping you to make intelligent investment decisions.

The Problem

Moving average techniques are based on the storage and manipulation of long term price and index data. In this instance, 40 week data must be available for each stock and market index you select. Some means of updating the files by including only the latest 40 weeks must be designed.

Logical analysis of 5, 15 and 40 week moving averages results in general market trends being indentified and individual stock recommendations made. Multiple comparisions are necessary for the various combinations of factors to be adequately considered.

Additional factors have been considered in the construction of this program to permit the user to easily accommodate his own group of stocks and particular computer system:

☐ Data file dimensions should be easily adjusted to fit any number of stocks, within user system memory limitations.

☐ Sequential access files are used to permit users of cassette storage systems to readily adapt the program to their needs.

☐ Relatively standard input and output routines should be used to allow for the easy addition of more stocks.

☐ Demonstrate a different programming approach while providing a tested, usable product.

The Program (Listing 7-2)

As structured here, this program provides for handling a 15 week advance-decline line, 2 broad market indexes (the Dow Jones Industrial Average and New York Composite Index) and only 7 stocks. Later in this discussion, the procedure for adding additional stocks will be demonstrated. A basic 16K Apple II will handle this program and data for at least 30 stocks on a tape file. Since most disk based systems have more than 16K memory available, proportionately larger numbers of stocks may be added.

We will again discuss the subroutines as they are called rather than follow line number sequence. In this program, as in The Fundamental Analyst, most of the actual work is done by subroutines. Notice, however, that the data strings are incorporated in the program rather than in a text file as we did earlier. The primary reason for using this approach is the limitation on string data storage imposed by the Apple cassette system, for those who decide to use tape rather than disk storage.

The stock names and trading symbols used here are fictional examples. To paraphrase the old movie disclaimer, any resemblance to companies living or dead is purely coincidental. When using the program, names and trading symbols for your own stocks should be substituted for the examples.

Line 20 dimensions array A to receive the numeric data. This dimension should consist of 40 elements for each market index, 15 elements for the advance-decline figures and 40 elements for each stock you want to include. The 374 figure here reflects 7 stocks and 2 market indexes at 40 each (360) plus 15 for the advance-decline figures. 360 plus 15 equals 375, from which 1 must be subtracted since Applesoft does use the O array element for data.

Lines 30-60 are included to determine whether or not a data file exists. On an "N" response, program execution branches to the data entry routine.

The Data Entry Routine, lines 8500-8700, provides for the initial entry or replacement of all price data necessary for program operation. Since this routine completely replaces any data contained in the file, the user is given another chance to change his mind before any data is lost. Closing price data, rounded to two decimal places, is inputted starting with the most recent weekly closing and proceding backward in chronological order. Once the data has been entered, DATA FILE is created to store the information for later use. Since the data for this program is in memory at the conclusion of the entry routine, line 8700 causes the main program menu to appear on the screen.

If the program has been used before, a data file is assumed to exist, A "Y" response to the prompt allows the program to proceed without invoking the entry routine. Lines 70-100 retrieve data from the file.

Lines 110-150 comprise the rest of the menu program and direct traffic to the subroutines. Menu option 1 causes the program to produce a video directory of the file by calling the File Directory Subroutine at line 8020. Stock name, trading symbol and array locations for the data are included in the display. This routine works well for less than 20 or so stocks, any more than that will cause the top of the display to scroll off the screen.

Menu option 2 provides for a printed version of the file directory produced by selecting option 1. Although more elegant ways to produce a printed page are available, the method used here is adequate for most purposes. Selecting 2 causes the File Directory Subroutine to start at line 8010 and proceed as described in the previous paragraph. Assuming you have a printer card in slot #1 of your Apple, directory information is sent to the printer as well as the video display. The PR#0 in line 8150 disengages the printer card if it was selected, and has no effect if only the video display was used.

Option 3, the Data Entry Routine, was described earlier. The primary reason for including this option in the menu was to allow the user to replace all his data, should a different group of stocks be selected or a different time period desired.

To verify or correct data in the file, option 4 is selected. Lines 8200-8450 comprise the Verify Or Correct Data Routine. First, this routine presents an abbreviated directory type menu and asks for identification of the data to be examined. Number 11 allows the user to gracefully exit the routine. Data is displayed one item at a time, with a CORRECT? prompt. Pressing any key but "N" allows the FOR-NEXT loop to go on to the next item. An "N" response branches to the mini subroutine in lines 8440 and 8450, allowing the user to input the correct data for that item. In my own use of a similar program, this routine was one of the most valuable. Inevitably a decimal point would be missed, a wrong number typed or some such disaster would occur that required corrections to be made. After the last data item has been displayed and corrected or verified, the main program menu reappears on the screen.

Stock Analysis (option 5) gets to the primary purpose of the program and involves four subroutines, one to calculate the advance decline figures, one for moving average calculations and two logic routines. In addition to those already mentioned, there is a user called routine to adjust the data in any stock file for splits. If no information is available for a particular stock, entering SKIP causes the program to advance to the next issue.

Notice the advance-decline information is a single figure in the file. This figure is computed by the following process:

☐ Collect the last 15 weekly totals of prices that have advanced and declined on the particular exchange that interests you.

☐ For the *least* recent week, subtract the declines from the advances and add an arbitrary figure to the total to keep long term results positive (20,000, for instance).

☐ For the next least recent week, subtract the declines from the advances and add the result to the figure obtained at the end of the previous step.

☐ Continue as above for each succeeding week, each time adding the figure obtained to the total from the previous week. (Obviously, if the resulting figure is negative, it should be subtracted from the previous week's total). The last calculation made should be for the current week.

☐ When entering this data into the file, enter the current weeks first, then last weeks, etc. until all 15 weeks have been entered.

☐ Once the initial data has been calculated and entered, the program automatically follows the same process during the Stock Analysis Routine.

Advance-decline line calculations and logic are contained in the subroutine starting at line 5800. After doing the actual calculations, this routine displays the derived figures and a statement of movement direction. For purposes of this approach, it is necessary to know only if the primary advance-decline line trend is up or down, the figure display could be eliminated if you so desire. Line 5840 updates the array by dropping the last item and incorporating the current data for a total of 15.

Moving averages for the market indexes and stocks contained in the file are calculated and displayed by the subroutine starting at line 5000. There are some elegant mathematical methods for calculating moving averages, none of which are used here. This subroutine simply totals the price information for the appropriate number of weeks and divides by that number, rounding the result to two decimal places. Actually, two sets of moving averages are calculated—one for the past week and the other for the current week. The two figures are used in determining the primary direction of movement of the averages. Following computation of the moving averages, this routine updates the file by dropping the last item and incorporating the current figure as part of the data array.

After the moving average figures have been calculated, one of the two logic subroutines is invoked. If the moving averages are for market indexes, the Market Comment Subroutine starting at line 6000 is called. For individual stocks, the logic routine starts at line 7000. In order to better understand the operation of these two subroutines, some background information is needed. The following few paragraphs will provide a very brief overview of the logic involved. Again I would recommend, however, that you carefully read the Zahorchak book before attempting to actually use the program yourself.

The general market comment is derived from the moving averages for a broad index and the advance-decline line. If both the 5 and 15 week are below the 40, and the advance-decline line is down, a bear market is assumed to exist. When the 5 week figure makes an upward move, a probable bear market rally is indicated. If the 5 week penetrates the 40 or the advance-decline line turns positive, this could be interpreted as the first sign of a new bull market and provides a preliminary buy indication. When the 5 week figure has penetrated the 40 and the advance-decline line is advancing, the second sign of a bull market is flashed. If both the 5 and 15 week figures are above the 40, the advance-decline line advancing and the 40 week moving average advancing from week to week, a bull market is in progress. If the 5 week then drops below the 40 or the advance-decline line starts dropping, the market becomes uncertain. If the 15 week line drops below the 40, a bear market is indicated.

For individual stocks, the moving average figures generate generalized recommendations. If the 5 and 15 are above the 40 week, the stock is to be held regardless of market trend. If the 5 week drops below the 15 or 40 week figures, the stock should be held in a bull market and sold in a bear. A stock should be purchased in the early stages of bull markets if both the 5 and 15 week averages have been below the 40 and the 5 rises sufficiently to penetrate the 40. As long as the 5 and 15 week averages remain below the 40, the stock should be avoided regardless of the general market trend.

The logic subroutines at 6000 and 7000 are generally modelled after the logic just explained. Once the market comment has been displayed, the program goes on to individual stock analysis without regard for the market conditions indicated. An interesting variation could be added to the program so market conditions would become part of the analysis logic for each stock. Keeping in mind that this is a sample program, however, will point out the reasons this was not done there.

The necessary weekly closing price for each stock is prompted and handled in a four line sequence. Lines 360-390 are the first of these. Line 360 accepts the price input, sets the display variable T$ and sets the array locations X and Y. Line 370 looks for SPLIT instead of a price input and calls subroutine 9000 if it is found. Line 380 looks for SKIP and, if present, causes the program to skip to the next input statement (400, in this case). If neither SKIP nor SPLIT is found in the price input, the variable is then assumed to be numeric and converted to a numeric variable by the VAL statement in line 390. Subroutines 5000 (moving average calculation) and 7000 (stock analysis) are called in succession from the same line.

Stock splits cause the data array to be adjusted by the subroutine at line 9000. Once this routine has been called, the user is asked to enter the split divisor. A divisor of 2 is used to adjust 2 for 1 splits, 3 is used for 3 for 1, etc. Stock dividends or distributions may also be adjusted with the proper divisor (1.05 for a 5% stock dividend, for instance). Each element in the array is divided and the result rounded to two decimal places. The CURRENT PRICE? prompt should then receive the post split current price for the stock. Both the current and past moving average figures displayed for the split stock will then reflect the adjustment.

There are more elegant ways of prompting input and handling the operations assigned to the four line input series just described. Since this program calls for the user to enter his own stocks (and most investors follow more than seven), the sequential approach used here provides for easy completion of the program.

Once the stock analysis sequence has been completed, the program updates the file and returns to the menu line 110.

Operation

Using this program is a relatively time consuming process if a significant number of stocks are involved. All the data necessary should be at hand when the program is run. Quite likely you will want to jot down some notes or copy some figures from the screen. You will find the program most effective during times of definite market movement one way or the other, least effective during prolonged periods of little change.

Moving averages, by design, react slowly to changes in market conditions. This means that buy and sell conditions are likely to occur long before they are recognized by the program. In following a similar approach over a period of two years or so, I have noticed the sell signals particularly slow to occur.

Program execution is a relatively straight forward process. Only one data file is used, so even a tape version is not excessively cumbersome to handle. Some accuracy in entering price data is required, since there is no error trapping included in that operation. If you get some strange changes in your figures, use the verify and correct routine to see whether or not some input error occured.

Adapting To Other Versions Of BASIC

There are few significant problems involved in a conversion of this program. An earlier version I wrote in HP BASIC is virtually identical, except for the file handling commands. Lines 320 and 330 first use a sequence repeated often throughout the program— PRESS SPACE BAR TO CONTINUE prompt, and the POKE, WAIT, WAIT values and commands. Actually, line 330 works with any character whose ASCII code is even. Using something like "Press any key to continue" and a GET command would work as well. Be especially wary of the PR#1 command used in line 8010. If you are using an Apple with a printer card in some slot other than 1, change the number or your system will perform some interesting operations on whatever peripheral you have in the slot. Your version of BASIC may require a completely different statement, such as LPRINT.

The detailed conversion information presented following the description of The Fundamental Analyst should also be of help to you for this program.

Program Modifications Possible

As listed, this program will not perform any useful function for the investor. By design, each user must at least insert the name and trading symbol for each of his stocks in place of the fictional ones printed here. By expanding the file dimensions and adding additional four line input sequences, considerably more stock may be analyzed. Cassette users can use this program by changing the disk commands to the appropriate tape versions, along with a few printed prompts to start and stop the recorder.

Digging further in to the logic subroutines could certainly identify areas needing some improvements. Changing parameters and printed statements may make the program more compatible with your own investment goals.

Some investors have suggested different time periods be used for computing the moving averages. No problem! A few changes in divisors, display labels and file parameters will let you use any time periods desired.

Feel free to modify wherever you see the need to do so. This program is billed as a sample to demonstrate a particular approach to the problem defined in the initial description. As such, personalization is the responsibility of the user. It is important to keep in mind, however, the same caveat applies to this program with or without modification—Study both the program and the book on which it is loosely based *carefully* before actually attempting any investment application!

DOLLAR COST AVERAGING ANALYST

As mentioned in Chapter 5, dollar cost averaging is a widely accepted technique to accumulate investment funds. Under this plan, a quality stock is selected and a set amount of money is invested at regular intervals. In times of relatively low stock prices, your dollars will buy more shares of stock than when prices are higher. By averaging the results over a long period of time, it becomes apparent your cost per share is less than if the stock were all purchased at once. Relatively volatile stocks with good long term growth possibilities are excellent candidates for dollar cost averaging.

Commissions paid to your broker can be rather significant if you are investing small amounts at a time. Some methods of reducing the brokerage fees were suggested in Chapter 5. Let me again reinforce the idea of using dividend reinvestment plans for dollar cost averaging stocks. Under these plans, dividends are used to purchase additional shares of stock for your reinvestment account. In addition, many plans allow periodic cash payments to purchase additional stock with little or no brokerage fees involved. While dividends paid by growth stocks are often minimal, the opportunity to purchase additional stock is a definite advantage to participants in dividend reinvestment programs that accept cash payments. Specific information on dividend reinvestment plans can be obtained from corporations which offer them.

Periodic monitoring of the progress of your dollar cost averaging plan will help to insure that your goals are being met. The usual method of doing this is to divide the total number of shares held by the dollars invested to obtain a cost per share figure. Obtaining a current quote and comparing that to your cost per share will point out the general direction of your progress. If you are involved in dollar cost averaging for only one or two stocks, this method may suffice. Several stocks with some shares purchased by dividends, others by cash payments and numerous fractional share figures can be quite a challenge to monitor.

The Problem

Dollar cost averaging plans are characterized by relatively infrequent transactions, usually no more than four or five per year. Following the progress of dollar cost averaging for several stocks involves rummaging through confirmation slips, computing running cost per share and comparing that figure to a current quote per share. For total portfolio performance monitoring of dollar cost averaging, total cost and total current value figures for all the shares involved can be used. From the figures mentioned, percentages can be calculated to provide additional information.

Obviously, the record keeping and calculations involved in dollar cost averaging are ideally suited to computer use. In addition to the factors already mentioned, several additional problems have been posed in constructing this program:

☐ Demonstrate the use of multiple serial access disk files, using each for separate and merged operations.

☐ Allow the user to create additional files in routine operation of the program.

☐ Provide detailed transaction information for each individual stock and a summarized display of total portfolio results.

☐ Illustrate different methods of generating and justifying data for display.

☐ Provide subroutines that may be used in other investment management applications.

☐ Demonstrate yet another type of approach to solving a specific programming problem while providing a usable program in its present form.

The Program (Listing 7-3)

As configured here, the Dollar Cost Averaging Analyst will handle 17 stocks, allowing 17 transactions for each stock. By limiting the program in this fashion, we have eliminated the need to reuse the screen length counting routine for data display shown in The Fundamental Analyst 3.0. Systems with limited memory should be able to run this program with little difficulty, since the disk files serve to keep minimum amounts of data in RAM at any one time.

As in our other sample programs, most of the actual operation takes place in the subroutines. We will again discuss each subroutine as it is called rather than following a strict line number sequence.

Variables, in most versions of BASIC, may be identified in several different ways. Applesoft, for instance, allows variable names to be up to two letters or one letter followed by a number. The different types of variables are identified by the presence or absence of additional characters. In this program, several different variables with very similar labels are used. S$ is used for the stock symbol input, while S$(X) denotes the same symbols in an array. NS, a variable denoting number of shares is used in several ways; NS single number of shares, NS(X) number of shares contained in array and NS$ the numeric variable converted to its string equivalent for length determination. Converting from numeric to string variables and back again is done using the VAL and STR$ functions.

Line 30 dimensions all the array variables used:

DT$ for dates.

T$ transaction types.

NS number of shares.

C cost.

S$ stock symbol.

CQ current quote.

VL value.

If you would like to change the capacity of the program, it is necessary to re-dimension these arrays. Since Applesoft uses the 0 element, each array is presently dimensioned for 17 elements.

Following the timed display of program name found in line 60, the user is asked if this is the first use of this program in line 70. If a "Y" response is received, the routine starting at line 1500 creates and writes an initial value of -1 to the DIRECTORY file which contains both the number and symbols for all stocks used in the program.

Once the file has been opened, or an "N" response received, the main program menu routine at line 100 is executed. As in our other programs, the menu routine merely directs operations to the appropriate subroutines and provides for exiting the program.

Option 1 provides an additional menu to allow the user to select from display of all stocks in the portfolio or individual stocks starting at line 3000. If the individual stock option is selected, a directory of stocks in the file is displayed. Proper operation of this routine is obtained only if there are stock files present and the current quote routine (described later) has been executed at least once for each stock in the files. Although none is included here, adding a line to display the need for stock files and current quotes could easily be added.

Once the display has been selected in line 3010, the DIRECTORY and CURRENT QUOTE files are read. Since these files are used in both display modes, a common input routine saves unnecessary duplication of program lines. If the portfolio display option has been selected, program execution continues by titling the display in lines 3150-3180. Headings for stock symbol, shares, cost, value and gain/loss figures are printed. This routine then reads every transaction in each stock file to obtain the necessary data. Each transaction is evaluated for BUY or SELL, causing the routine to add or subtract the share and cost figures to calculate present holdings. CURRENT QUOTE data is used to compute the value of shares held as of the last update. Cost and value totals are then used to derive gain/loss amount and percentage.

Data for each stock in the portfolio is displayed prior to the next stock file being read. Figures in the display have been reduced to the greatest integer by the INT function, eliminating decimal points from this display in order to conserve screen space. A slightly different method of justifying the numbers on the display has been used here in lines 3310-3360. Each variable has been converted to a string, the length of which is then subtracted from predetermined screen positions to coincide with the headings used. The variables T1-T5 are used for TAB values in the actual printing process.

After the last stock file has been displayed, totals for number of shares, cost, and value are displayed. Total portfolio gain/loss figure and percentage is also calculated and displayed at this time. Pressing RETURN when this display is complete causes the GOTO 100 statement to return the main menu to the screen.

Individual stock display, starting at line 3510, is somewhat different than the total portfolio routine described above. Once a particular stock has been selected from the directory display, headings for date, transaction type, shares, shares held, total cost and cost per share are printed. Each transaction date, type and number of shares is read and displayed. Total shares held and total cost are displayed as running totals.

Cost per share is recalculated following each transaction. This routine has no provision for totals at the bottom of the screen, since the last transaction displayed reflects the totals for shares held and cost along with the latest cost per share figure. Computing cost per share in this fashion provides a vivid indication of the effect each transaction can have on overall effectiveness of the dollar cost averaging approach. Changing the method of determining cost per share to display the figure for each individual transaction is simply a matter of dividing C(X) by NS(X) rather than the running total CT and ST variables used in line 3670. Again, pressing RETURN at the completion of the display returns the main menu to the screen.

Menu option 2, updating the current quote, branches program execution to line 2000. This routine rewrites or creates the CURRENT QUOTE file each time it is run. After a brief explanation and CONTINUE? option, the DIRECTORY file is opened and read. Input prompts request the date and current price quotes for each stock in the system. Once input has been completed, the new CURRENT QUOTE file is written. Data in the file is of two types, the string DT$ date, and numeric elements CQ(X) for individual quotes.

As mentioned earlier, the display routines use the date and quotes from the CURRENT QUOTE file to calculate total portfolio value and gain/loss figures. If no such file is located, the program terminates in a nondestructive error state with an END OF DATA or FILE NOT FOUND statement displayed.

Transactions are entered by selecting menu option 3. The Enter Transaction Subroutine, located beginning at line 1000, sets up a self-prompting screen display in lines 1020-1070. Lines 1080-1120 place the cursor at the proper position for each successive INPUT statement. Line 1130 is used to determine whether or not a file already exists for this stock. If a "Y" response is received, the DIRECTORY file is modified and a new file for the stock is created by lines 1410-1590. Prior to any action being taken by this routine, the user is asked to press RETURN if all data is correct or ESC to change. Since reasonably concise data is requested, the "second chance" provision of this line is an acceptable substitute for elaborate error trapping procedures in the program. Using ESC resets the screen and all data must be entered again.

If the data input was correct, the file for that stock is read into memory. The transaction counter variable T is incremented and all data is printed to the file. Following each transaction, program execution returns to line 100 for display of the main program menu.

Menu option 4 provides for necessary file adjustments due to stock splits or dividends paid in shares. Starting at line 300, this routine first asks for the stock symbol and then whether adjustment for a split or dividend is required. In either case, the individual stock file is read into memory. An "S" response invokes line 390, which prompts the split divisor and adjusts the total number of shares accordingly. A "D" response, beginning in line 410, results in a request to enter the dividend percentage. The number of shares is adjusted by adding the percentage to each transaction record. The file is rewritten on completion of the calculations, and the menu again displayed after the "adjustment has been made" message and timing loop (line 520) execute.

Selecting menu option 5 unceremoniously ends the program by branching to line 220.

Operation

As a very specific approach to investing, dollar cost averaging is quite easily understood. With basic knowledge of the principles, operation of this program is a very straight forward process. Each data entry routine requests readily available information and the displays are clearly labelled.

A certain amount of data is necessary for the program to function at all. When first using the program, only the directory file is created. Transaction, as entered, create or expand the individual stock files. At least one current quote for each stock in the system must be present to obtain a display of results obtained. It is important to use the correct symbol for each stock transaction, since the symbol becomes the name of its file.

In actual practice, this program closely follows the method of using dollar cost averaging as an investment technique. It is interesting to track the individual stock cost per share figures to readily judge the long term results of this approach. As your holdings increase, the portfolio summary provides a means of conveniently comparing results obtained with various stocks as well as overall performance.

Adapting To Other Versions Of BASIC

Most of the individual statements used in this program have been used in the previous sample programs and discussed before. Some new twists have been added, however, and may require modification to function in your BASIC.

Notice the stock file names are defined as the string variable S$. If your disk operating system requires a different file name configuration, conversion may be required. If a file number, rather than name, is needed, numeric variables consisting of the stock symbol assigned the appropriate value could be used.

The conversion and string manipulation used to justify the displays could require some syntax modifications to run in your system. If the conversion is too cumbersome, consider using the justification routine demonstrated in The Fundamental Analyst. If your BASIC accepts longer variable names, consider assigning more descriptive terms to the variables for clarification of each operation.

Program Modifications Possible

This program was designed with some built-in limitations as noted in the initial description. By adding line counting capability to the displays, along with the appropriate prompts to scroll as desired, capacity for data will increase to the limits of available memory. The necessary routines were included in The Fundamental Analyst.

With minor modification, hard copy prints of the displays could be produced. In most cases, this will involve adding a printer activation command and slight format revision to the printer line width. If your printer is capable of more than 40 characters per line, the data display could be made much more attractive by expanding the spacing between columns.

Obviously, the data used in this program could be helpful in other than dollar cost averaging applications. With some revision of the display routines, for instance, this program could very easily become a portfolio management system for all stock transactions.

As in the other two sample programs, there is considerable room for user modification and improvement here. By combining parts of this and the other programs listed, a relatively sophisticated investment system could be constructed. It's up to you!

SAMPLE OR SYSTEM?

Only three sample programs are contained in this chapter, yet a wide range of programming techniques have been used. Each of the programs listed will indeed work as advertised in a 48K Apple II with Applesoft in ROM and a single disk drive, since that is the configuration on which they were written and tested. They will also run on most other personal computers by carefully following the suggestions given for adaptation to other versions of BASIC.

Is it possible to assemble an investment management system using just these three programs? Yes. Would such an approach represent efficient use of both your own and your computers time and abilities? No. For purposes of illustration, let's consider the pros and cons of such a system.

If you have carefully followed the suggestions made in earlier chapters, it is possible that your method of selecting stocks is reflected in The Fundamental Analyst. Perhaps moving average analysis, used in Stock Trend Analyst, is your method of choice for timing purchases and sales of stocks. As a method of building further investment capital, you have decided to follow a program of dollar cost averaging, making the Dollar Cost Averaging Analyst of more than passing interest. Let's assume you, the hypothetical investor, have decided that our three sample programs will constitute the majority of your investment approach.

Under the circumstances, two choices are open to you. First, you could type in the programs exactly as they are listed and use each one individually. Second, the sample programs could be modified to form a single master program. The first choice obviously demands the least initial effort, the second could markedly reduce the amount of effort expended over a period of time. Even if results obtained through either choice are identical, why sentence yourself to long term drudgery?

By opting to type and use the sample programs verbatim, you have provisions to select, time and track results of investment transactions. What's missing? A lot! Each of the programs requires data to be entered, although much of the data used is common to all three. Stock name or symbol, current quote, date and split divisor are some of the common items. Files for each program are separate and incompatible with the others. The Fundamental Analyst and Dollar Cost Averaging Analyst both use a file named DIRECTORY. Storing and using these programs on the same disk would cause some interesting things to happen to the files! Each of the programs contains subroutines that could be shared by one or both of the others if the programs were not run separately. Of course, the quality most obviously missing is personalization.

Even the most cursory study will show areas of potential improvement, particularly if the programs are to be combined in some fashion. Slight revision of variables and file structure would dramatically reduce the number of disk files required. Subroutines with similar functions (display justification, for instance) could be made to serve all three applications. Manipulation of display and computation parameters, along with data procedure changes, may result in more efficient operation. Menu selection of additional functions can cut down the number of disk operations required.

More detailed analysis would point out the need for extensive personalization of the total system, especially in the area of programming logic alternatives. Modifying The Fundamental Analyst to generate a list of stocks considered purchase candidates, for instance, would be a good starting point.

Hopefully, you have seen the potential problems inherent in attempting to use the sample programs as an adequate investment system. By their very natures, cyclical timing approaches as outlined in the Stock Trend Analyst and dollar cost averaging are incompatible. Using these, or any other programs, without extensive examination and testing is virtually begging for problems to happen.

SUMMARY

In the preceeding section, we discussed some reasons not to combine the sample programs and call the result a system. There are several reasons to consider using them singularly, however:

☐ To "get your feet wet" by using a program for handling a predefined investment application that may become a part of your total approach.

☐ To see for yourself the results of various programming techniques that could be used in your own programs.

☐ To test the manipulation of specific variables and parameters used in your own system.

☐ To actually handle a specific chore in your total investment management approach.

☐ To provide a library of subroutines that can be readily incorporated into your own programs.

☐ To establish a foundation upon which more personalized programs can be constructed.

Personally, I have used programs roughly similar to the three presented here as parts of a total investment management system for some time. More importantly, however, I have used many of the techniques outlined in numerous programs developed for my own applications.

As promised earlier, we have intentionally avoided using some of the Apple II's unique capabilities in these programs. By concentrating primarily on those features and commands found in most versions of BASIC offered for personal computers, conversion of programs listed here should be considerably simpler. In developing your own programs, use all the capabilities your system possesses. Color graphics, for instance, are an especially effective way of generating interesting graphs and tables for investment applications using the Apple II.

I hope some of the programming techniques, subroutines or actual programs presented here have enhanced your understanding of personal computer potential. While you may never have the desire to become a super programmer, some knowledge of programming techniques is essential to being an informed consumer of others programs. The importance of developing (or purchasing) programs appropriate for your specific applications cannot be overemphasized!

Program Listing 7-1

```
10   REM   FUNDAMENTAL ANALYST 3.0
20   REM   BY L. SCHMELTZ
30   D$ = CHR$ (4): REM   CHR$(4) I
     S CTRL-D
40   DIM A(28),B(28),C(28),K$(29),
     A$(100),E$(100)
50   GOSUB 5000
60   CALL  - 936: VTAB (6)
70   PRINT  TAB( 5);"1.   INPUT DAT
     A FOR NEW STOCK": PRINT
80   PRINT  TAB( 5);"2.   DISPLAY D
     IRECTORY OF DATA FILE": PRINT

90   PRINT  TAB( 5);"3.   DELETE DA
     TA FOR ANY STOCK": PRINT
100  PRINT  TAB( 5);"4.   DISPLAY
     RAW DATA": PRINT
110  PRINT  TAB( 5);"5.   DISPLAY
     COMPUTED DATA": PRINT
120  PRINT  TAB( 5);"6.   EXIT THE
     PROGRAM": PRINT : PRINT
130  PRINT  TAB( 5);"WHICH?": GET
     Z$
140 Z = . VAL (Z$)
```

```
150    IF Z < 1 OR Z > 6 THEN  PRINT
       "SELECT NUMBER 1-6 ONLY": GOTO
       60
160    ON Z GOTO 4000,3000,3300,100
       0,500,5230
500    REM   ROUTINE TO DISPLAY COMP
       UTED DATA
510    PRINT : PRINT : INVERSE : PRINT
        TAB( 25);"1"; TAB( 31);"2";
        TAB( 37);"3": NORMAL
520    GOSUB 2000
530 K$(18) = "OP.PROFIT MARGIN (%
       ):"
540 K$(19) = "        CURRENT RATI
       O:"
550 K$(20) = "        LIQUIDITY RAT
       IO:"
560 K$(29) = "CAPITALIZATION RATI
       OS"
570 K$(21) = "    LONG TERM DEBT (
       %):"
580 K$(22) = "   PREFERRED STOCK (
       %):"
590 K$(23) = " COMM. STOCK+SURP.(
       %):"
600 K$(24) = "SALES TO FIXED ASSE
       TS:"
610 K$(25) = " SALES TO INVENTORI
       ES:"
620 K$(26) = "NET INCOME--NET WOR
       TH:"
630 K$(27) = "ASSET VALUE PER SHA
       RE:"
640 K$(28) = "   PRICE VARIATION (
       %):"
650    FOR I = 18 TO 28
660    GOSUB 1500
670    IF Z > 1 THEN  GOSUB 1560
680    IF Z > 2 THEN  GOSUB 1610
690    IF I = 21 THEN  PRINT K$(29)
700    IF Z = 1 THEN  PRINT K$(I); TAB(
       L);A(I)
```

```
710   IF Z = 2 THEN  PRINT K$(I); TAB(
      L);A(I); TAB( M);B(I)
720   IF Z = 3 THEN  PRINT K$(I); TAB(
      L);A(I); TAB( M);B(I); TAB(
      O);C(I)
730   NEXT I
740   PRINT
750   PRINT "PRESS:"
760   INVERSE : PRINT  TAB( 2);"ES
      C";: NORMAL : PRINT "-DISPLA
      Y RAW DATA FOR ABOVE STOCKS"
      : INVERSE : PRINT  TAB( 2);"

      RTN";: NORMAL : PRINT "-RETU
      RN TO PROGRAM MENU"
770   GET Z$
780   IF Z$ =  CHR$ (13) THEN  GOTO
      60
790   IF Z$ <  >  CHR$ (27) THEN  GOTO
      770
800   VTAB (Z + 2): HTAB (1): CALL
       - 958: GOTO 1030
1000   REM  DISPLAY RAW DATA ROUTI
      NE
1010   GOSUB 2000
1020   INVERSE : PRINT  TAB( 25);"
      1"; TAB( 31);"2"; TAB( 37);"
      3": NORMAL
1030 K$(0) = "        OPERATING PRO
      FIT:"
1040 K$(1) = "           TOTAL SA
      LES:"
1050 K$(2) = "         CURRENT ASS
      ETS:"
1060 K$(3) = "   CURRENT LIABILIT
      IES:"
1070 K$(4) = "       CASH & EQUIVAL
      ENT:"
1080 K$(5) = "          LONG TERM D
      EBT:"
1090 K$(6) = "PAR VALUE ALL PF ST
      OCK:"
```

168

```
1100 K$(7) = "PAR VALUE ALL CM ST
     OCK:"
1110 K$(8) = "        CAPITAL SURP
     LUS:"
1120 K$(9) = "        RETAINED EARNI
     NGS:"
1130 K$(10) = "VALUE-PLANT,EQUIP,
     LAND:"
1140 K$(11) = "  YEAR END INVENTO
     RIES:"
1150 K$(12) = "              NET IN
     COME:"
1160 K$(13) = "  NUMBER COMMON SH
     ARES:"
1170 K$(14) = "MKT VALUE ALL PF S
     TOCK:"
1180 K$(15) = "  12 MO, HIGH-CM S
     TOCK:"
1190 K$(16) = "   12 MO, LOW-CM S
     TOCK:"
1200 K$(17) = "        TOTAL AS
     SETS:"
1210  FOR I = 0 TO 17
1220  GOSUB 1500
1230  IF Z > 1 THEN  GOSUB 1560
1240  IF Z > 2 THEN  GOSUB 1610
1250  IF Z = 1 THEN  PRINT K$(I);
     TAB( L);A(I)
1260  IF Z = 2 THEN  PRINT K$(I);
     TAB( L);A(I); TAB( M);B(I)
1270  IF Z = 3 THEN  PRINT K$(I);
     TAB( L);A(I); TAB( M);B(I);
     TAB( O);C(I)
1280  NEXT I
1290  PRINT "PRESS:";: INVERSE : PRINT
     "ESC";: NORMAL : PRINT "-VIE
     W COMPUTED DATA FOR ABOVE": PRINT
     TAB( 7);: INVERSE : PRINT "
     RTN";: NORMAL : PRINT "-RETU
     RN TO PROGRAM MENU"
1300  GET Z$
```

```
1310   IF Z$ =  CHR$ (13) THEN  GOTO
       60
1320   IF Z$ <  >  CHR$ (27) THEN
       GOTO 1300
1330   VTAB (Z + 2): HTAB (1): CALL
       - 958: GOTO 530
1500   REM  ROUTINE TO JUSTIFY DAT
       A FIGURE DISPLAY
1510   IF A(I) < 1.0 THEN L = 26: RETURN

1520   IF A(I) < 10.0 THEN L = 25:
       RETURN
1530   IF A(I) < 100.0 THEN L = 24
       : RETURN
1540   IF A(I) < 1000.0 THEN L = 2
       3: RETURN
1550  L = 22: RETURN
1560   IF B(I) < 1.0 THEN M = 32: RETURN

1570   IF B(I) < 10.0 THEN M = 31:
       RETURN
1580   IF B(I) < 100.0 THEN M = 30
       : RETURN
1590   IF B(I) < 1000.0 THEN M = 2
       9: RETURN
1600  M = 28: RETURN
1610   IF C(I) < 1.0 THEN O = 37: RETURN

1620   IF C(I) < 10.0 THEN O = 36:
       RETURN
1630   IF C(I) < 100.0 THEN O = 35
       : RETURN
1640   IF C(I) < 1000.0 THEN O = 3
       4: RETURN
1650  O = 33: RETURN
2000   REM  ROUTINE TO SELECT DATA
       FOR DISPLAY
2010   CALL  - 936
2020   PRINT
2030   PRINT "YOU MAY EXAMINE DATA
       FOR 1, 2 OR 3"
2040   PRINT "STOCKS AT ONE TIME."
```

```
2050  PRINT
2060  PRINT "EACH STOCK YOU SELEC
      T MUST BE"
2070  PRINT "IDENTIFIED BY ITS DI
      RECTORY NUMBER."
2080  PRINT
2090  PRINT "DO YOU NEED TO SEE T
      HE DIRECTORY"
2100  PRINT "TO OBTAIN YOUR NUMBE
      RS? (Y/N)"
2110  GET Z$
2120  IF Z$ = "Y" THEN  GOTO 3000
2130  IF Z$ < > "N" THEN  PRINT
      "PLEASE ANSWER Y OR N": GOTO
      2090
2140  PRINT
2150  PRINT "DISPLAY HOW MANY REC
      ORDS? (3 MAX)"
2160  INPUT Z
2170  IF Z < 1 OR Z > 3 THEN  PRINT
      "SELECT 1, 2 OR 3 ONLY": GOTO
      2150
2180  INPUT "STOCK NUMBER 1?";F
2190  IF Z > 1 THEN  INPUT "STOCK
      NUMBER 2?";G
2200  IF Z = 3 THEN  INPUT "STOCK
      NUMBER 3?";H
2210  PRINT D$;"OPEN DATA-L205,L2
      05"
2220  PRINT D$;"READ DATA-L205,R"
      ;F
2230  INPUT A$: INPUT E$
2240  FOR I = 0 TO 28: INPUT A(I)
      : NEXT
2250  IF Z > 1 THEN  PRINT D$;"RE
      AD DATA-L205,R";G: INPUT B$:
      INPUT F$: FOR I = 0 TO 28: INPUT
      B(I): NEXT
2260  IF Z = 3 THEN  PRINT D$;"RE
      AD DATA-L205,R";H: INPUT C$:
      INPUT G$: FOR I = 0 TO 28: INPUT
      C(I): NEXT
```

```
2270    PRINT D$;"CLOSE DATA-L205"
2280    CALL  - 936
2290    REM  ROUTINE TO CAPTION DAT
        A DISPLAY
2300    PRINT "STOCK#1:";A$; TAB( 3
        0);"DATE:";E$
2310    IF Z > 1 THEN  PRINT "STOCK
        #2:";B$; TAB( 30);"DATE:";F
        $
2320    IF Z = 3 THEN  PRINT "STOCK
        #3:";C$; TAB( 30);"DATE:";G
        $
2330    RETURN
3000    REM  DIRECTORY OF DATA FILE
        ROUTINE
3010    CALL  - 936
3020    PRINT : PRINT D$;"OPEN DIRE
        CTORY"
3030    PRINT D$;"READ DIRECTORY"
3040    INPUT N
3060    FOR I = 0 TO N
3070    INPUT A$(I): INPUT E$(I)
3080    NEXT
3090    PRINT D$;"CLOSE DIRECTORY"
3100    PRINT
3110    PRINT " RECORD"; TAB( 15);"
        STOCK NAME"; TAB( 34);"DATE"
3120    PRINT " ------"; TAB( 10);:
        FOR I = 0 TO 20: PRINT "-";
        : NEXT : PRINT  TAB( 33);"--
        ----": PRINT
3130    POKE 34,4
3140    X = 0:Y = N
3150    IF N > 18 THEN Y = 18
3160    FOR I = X TO Y
3170    PRINT  TAB( 4);I; TAB( 10);
        A$(I); TAB( 33);E$(I)
3180    NEXT
3190    X = X + 18
3200    IF N - X > 0 THEN Y = X + (
        N - X)
```

172

```
3210   IF N - X > 18 THEN Y = X +
       18
3215   IF N - X < = 0 THEN  GOTO
       3230
3220   VTAB (22): HTAB (2): FOR I =
       0 TO 37: PRINT "-";: NEXT : PRINT
       : PRINT TAB( 5);"PRESS ";: INVERSE
    : PRINT "ESC";: NORMAL : PRINT "
       TO CONTINUE LISTING": GET Z
       $: GOTO 3240
3230   VTAB (22): HTAB (2): FOR I =
       0 TO 37: PRINT "-";: NEXT : PRINT
       : PRINT TAB( 5);"PRESS ";: INVERSE
    : PRINT "RTN";: NORMAL : PRINT "
       TO RETURN TO PROGRAM MENU":
       GET Z$
3240   IF Z$ =  CHR$ (27) THEN  CALL
       - 936: GOTO 3160
3250   IF Z$ <  >  CHR$ (13) THEN
       GET Z$: GOTO 3240
3260   TEXT : GOTO 60
3300   REM  THIS ROUTINE WILL DELE
       TE DATA FOR ANY STOCK
3310   CALL  - 936: PRINT
3320   PRINT "THIS ROUTINE ALLOWS
       YOU TO DELETE DATA"
3330   PRINT "FOR ANY STOCK IN YOU
       R FILE."
3340   PRINT
3350   PRINT "YOU WILL BE ASKED FO
       R THE RECORD NUMBER"
3360   PRINT "OF THE STOCK AND DAT
       E TO BE DELETED."
3370   PRINT
3380   PRINT "RECORD NUMBER MAY BE
       OBTAINED FROM"
3390   PRINT "THE DIRECTORY ROUTIN
       E."
3400   PRINT
3410   PRINT "WOULD YOU LIKE TO SE
       E THE DIRECTORY"
```

```
3420   PRINT "TO LOCATE A RECORD N
       UMBER? (Y/N)"
3430   GET Z$
3440   IF Z$ = "Y" THEN  GOTO 3000

3450   IF Z$ < > "N" THEN  PRINT
       "PLEASE ANSWER Y OR N"; GOTO
       3410
3460   PRINT : PRINT D$;"OPEN DIRE
       CTORY"
3470   PRINT D$;"READ DIRECTORY"
3480   INPUT N
3500   FOR I = 0 TO N

3510   INPUT A$(I),E$(I)
3520   NEXT
3530   PRINT D$;"CLOSE DIRECTORY":
       PRINT
3540   PRINT "ENTER THE RECORD NUM
       BER TO BE DELETED"
3550   INPUT Y
3560   IF Y > N THEN  PRINT "NO SU
       CH RECORD NUMBER--TRY AGAIN"
       : GOTO 3550
3570   PRINT
3580   PRINT "RECORD TO BE DELETED
       :"
3590   PRINT  TAB( 5);A$(Y); TAB(
       30);E$(Y)
3600   PRINT "CORRECT? (Y/N)"
3610   GET Z$
3620   IF Z$ = "N" THEN  GOTO 3410

3630   IF Z$ < > "Y" THEN  PRINT
       "PLEASE ANSWER Y OR N"; GOTO
       3600
3640   IF Y = N THEN N = N - 1: GOTO
       3680
3650   FOR I = Y TO (N - 1)
3660   A$(I) = A$(I + 1):E$(I) = E$
       (I + 1)
3670   NEXT :N = N - 1
```

```
3680   PRINT : PRINT D$;"OPEN DIRE
       CTORY"
3690   PRINT D$;"DELETE DIRECTORY"

3700   PRINT D$;"OPEN DIRECTORY"
3710   PRINT D$;"WRITE DIRECTORY"
3720   PRINT N
3730   FOR I = 0 TO N: PRINT A$(I)
       : PRINT E$(I): NEXT
3740   PRINT D$;"CLOSE DIRECTORY"
3750   PRINT "DATA NOW DELETED"
3760   FOR I = 0 TO 2000: NEXT
3770   GOTO 60
4000   REM   DATA INPUT FOR NEW STO
       CK SUBROUTINE
4010   CALL   - 936
4020   PRINT "NAME OF STOCK?------
       --------------"
4030   PRINT : PRINT  TAB( 12);"DA
       TE (MM/YY)?--/--"
4040   PRINT : PRINT  TAB( 13);"OP
       ERATING PROFIT?------"
4050   PRINT  TAB( 18);"TOTAL SALE
       S?------"
4060   PRINT  TAB( 15);"CURRENT AS
       SETS?------"
4070   PRINT  TAB( 10);"CURRENT LI
       ABILITIES?------"
4080   PRINT  TAB( 8);"CASH & ITS
       EQUIVALENT?------"
4090   PRINT  TAB( 15);"LONG TERM
       DEBT?------"
4100   PRINT " PAR VALUE OF ALL PR
       F. STOCK?------"
4110   PRINT "  PAR VALUE-ALL COMM
       ON STOCK?------"
4120   PRINT  TAB( 14);"CAPITAL SU
       RPLUS?------"
4130   PRINT  TAB( 12);"RETAINED E
       ARNINGS?------"
4140   PRINT "  VALUE-PLANT, EQUIP
       . & LAND?------"
```

```
4150   PRINT   TAB( 9);"YEAR END IN
       VENTORIES?------"
4160   PRINT   TAB( 19);"NET INCOME
       ?------"
4170   PRINT " # COMMON SHARES OUT
       STANDING?------"
4180   PRINT " MARKET VALUE-ALL PR
       F. STOCK?------"
4190   PRINT   TAB( 5);"12 MO. HIGH
       -COMMON STOCK?------"
4200   PRINT   TAB( 6);"12 MO. LOW-
       COMMON STOCK?------"
4210   PRINT   TAB( 17);"TOTAL ASSE
       TS?------"
4220   VTAB (1): HTAB (14): INPUT
       A$
4230   VTAB (3): HTAB (24): INPUT
       E$
4240 X = 5: FOR I = 0 TO 17
4250   VTAB (X): HTAB (29): INPUT
       A(I)
4260 X = X + 1
4270   NEXT I
4280   VTAB (24): PRINT "PRESS ";:
       INVERSE : PRINT "RETURN";: NORMAL
: PRINT " IF CORRECT, ";: INVERSE
     : PRINT "ESC";: NORMAL : PRINT
     " TO CHANGE"
4290   GET Z$
4300   IF Z$ = CHR$ (27) THEN  GOTO
       4010
4310   IF Z$ < > CHR$ (13) THEN
       GOTO 4280
4320   PRINT : PRINT D$;"OPEN DIRE
       CTORY"
4330   PRINT D$;"READ DIRECTORY"
4340   INPUT N: IF N = - 1 THEN  GOTO
       4360
4350   FOR I = 0 TO N: INPUT A$(I)
     : INPUT E$(I): NEXT
4360 N = N + 1
4370 A$(N) = A$:E$(N) = E$
```

```
4380   PRINT D$;"OPEN DIRECTORY"
4390   PRINT D$;"DELETE DIRECTORY"

4400   PRINT D$;"OPEN DIRECTORY"
4410   PRINT D$;"WRITE DIRECTORY"
4420   PRINT N
4430   FOR I = 0 TO N: PRINT A$(I)
       : PRINT E$(I): NEXT
4440   PRINT D$;"CLOSE DIRECTORY"
4450 A(18) =  INT ((A(0) / A(1)) *
     100)
4460 A(19) =  INT ((A(2) / A(3)) *
     100 + .5) / 100
4470 A(20) =  INT ((A(4) / A(3)) *
     100)
4480 A(21) =  INT ((A(5) / (A(6) +
     A(7) + A(8) + A(9) + A(5))) *
     100)
4490 A(22) =  INT ((A(6) / (A(6) +
     A(7) + A(8) + A(9) + A(5))) *
     100)
4500 A(23) =  INT (((A(7) + A(8) +
     A(9)) / (A(6) + A(7) + A(8) +
     A(9) + A(5))) * 100)
4510 A(24) =  INT ((A(1) / A(10))
     * 100 + .5) / 100
4520 A(25) =  INT ((A(1) / A(11))
     * 100 + .5) / 100
4530 A(26) =  INT ((A(12) / (A(6)
     + A(7) + A(8) + A(9))) * 10
     0)
4540 A(27) =  INT (((A(17) - (A(3
     ) + A(5) + A(14))) / A(13)) *
     100 + .5) / 100
4550 A(28) =  INT ((A(15) / A(16)
     ) * 100) - 100
4560   PRINT D$;"OPEN DATA-L205,L2
       05"
4570   PRINT D$;"WRITE DATA-L205,R
       ";N
4580   PRINT A$: PRINT E$
4590   FOR I = 0 TO 28
```

```
4600    PRINT A(I)
4610    NEXT
4620    PRINT D$;"CLOSE DATA-L205"
4630    GOTO 60
5000    CALL  - 936: PRINT : PRINT
        TAB( 9);"FUNDAMENTAL ANALYS
        T 3.0": PRINT : FOR I = 0 TO
        2500: NEXT :
5010    PRINT "THIS PROGRAM ALLOWS
        YOU TO ANALYZE": PRINT "FINA
        NCIAL DATA FOR STOCK SELECTI
        ON.": PRINT : PRINT  TAB( 10
        );"*"; TAB( 15);"*"; TAB( 20
        );"*"; TAB( 25);"*"; TAB( 30
        );"*": PRINT
5020    PRINT "RAW DATA OR COMPUTED
        RESULTS FOR UP TO": PRINT "
        THREE DIFFERENT STOCKS, OR T
        HE SAME": PRINT "STOCK OVER
        THREE DIFFERENT TIME PERIODS
        ": PRINT "MAY BE DISPLAYED A
        T ONE TIME."
5030    PRINT : PRINT  TAB( 10);"*"
        ; TAB( 15);"*"; TAB( 20);"*"
        ; TAB( 25);"*"; TAB( 30);"*"
        : PRINT
5040    PRINT "DATA FOR DISPLAY IS
        CONTAINED IN THE": PRINT "DA
        TA-L205 AND DIRECTORY FILES
        ON": PRINT "YOUR DISK.  IF Y
        OU HAVE NOT USED": PRINT "TH
        IS PROGRAM BEFORE, PRESS ";:
        INVERSE : PRINT "ESC": NORMAL
5050    PRINT "TO CREATE THE FILES
        ON YOUR DISK.": PRINT : PRINT
        TAB( 10);"*"; TAB( 15);"*";
        TAB( 20);"*"; TAB( 25);"*";
        TAB( 30);"*": PRINT
5060    PRINT "IF YOU HAVE USED THE
        PROGRAM BEFORE,": PRINT "PR
        ESS ";: INVERSE : PRINT "RET
```

```
          URN";: NORMAL : PRINT " TO C
          ONTINUE."
5070    GET Z$
5080    IF Z$ =  CHR$ (13) THEN  RETURN

5090    IF Z$ < >  CHR$ (27) THEN
          GOTO 5070
5100    PRINT : PRINT D$;"OPEN DATA
          -L205,L205"
5110    PRINT D$;"DELETE DATA-L205"

5120    PRINT D$;"OPEN DATA-L205, L
          205"
5130    PRINT D$;"CLOSE DATA-L205"
5140    PRINT  TAB( 12);"DATA FILE
          CREATED"
5150    PRINT D$;"OPEN DIRECTORY"
5160    PRINT D$;"DELETE DIRECTORY"

5170    PRINT D$;"OPEN DIRECTORY"
5180    PRINT D$;"WRITE DIRECTORY"
5190    PRINT  - 1
5200    PRINT D$;"CLOSE DIRECTORY"
5210    PRINT  TAB( 9);"DIRECTORY F
          ILE CREATED"
5220    FOR Z = 0 TO 2500: NEXT : RETURN

5230    END
```

Program Listing 7-2
Stock Trend Analyst

```
10    CALL  - 936: VTAB (10): PRINT
        TAB( 10);"STOCK TREND ANALY
        ST": PRINT : PRINT  TAB( 9);
        "WRITTEN BY L. SCHMELTZ"
20    DIM A(374):D$ =  CHR$ (4): REM
        CHR$(4) IS CTRL-D
30    PRINT : PRINT "HAVE YOU USED
        THIS PROGRAM BEFORE? (Y/N)"
40    GET Z$
50    IF Z$ = "N" THEN  GOTO 8500
```

```
 60  IF Z$ < > "Y" THEN  GOTO 40
 70  PRINT : PRINT D$;"OPEN DATA F
     ILE"
 80  PRINT D$;"READ DATA FILE"
 90  FOR I = 0 TO 374: INPUT A(I):
     NEXT
100  PRINT D$;"CLOSE DATA FILE"
110  CALL  - 936: VTAB (3): PRINT
     "SELECT PROGRAM OPTION NUMBE
     R:"
120  PRINT : PRINT  TAB( 5);"1.
     DISPLAY FILE DIRECTORY": PRINT
     : PRINT  TAB( 5);"2.  PRINT
     FILE DIRECTORY": PRINT : PRINT
      TAB( 5);"3.  DATA ENTRY ROU
     TINE": PRINT : PRINT  TAB( 5
     );"4.  VERIFY OR CORRECT DAT
     A"
130  PRINT : PRINT  TAB( 5);"5.
     STOCK ANALYSIS": PRINT : PRINT
      TAB( 5);"6.  END"
140  INPUT Q: IF Q < 1 OR Q > 7 THEN
     GOTO 110
150  ON Q GOTO 8020,8010,8500,820
     0,300,9030
300  INPUT "DATE (MM/DD/YY)";A$: PRINT
     "D.J.I.A.": INPUT B: PRINT "
     N.Y.C.I.": INPUT K: PRINT "A
     DVANCES": INPUT E: PRINT "DE
     CLINES": INPUT F
310  X = 0:Y = 14: GOSUB 5800:T$ =
     "DJIA":X = 15:Y = 19: GOSUB
     5000: GOSUB 6000
320  PRINT "PRESS SPACE BAR TO CO
     NTINUE"
330  POKE  - 16368,0: WAIT  - 163
     84,128: WAIT  - 16384,1,1: CALL
      - 936
340  T$ = "NYCI":B = K:X = 55:Y =
     59: GOSUB 5000: GOSUB 6000
350  PRINT : PRINT "AT ? INSERT C
     LOSING PRICE, 'SKIP, OR": PRINT
```

```
            "'SPLIT' FOR EACH STOCK.": PRINT
            : PRINT   TAB( 15);"NYSE STOC
            KS": PRINT
360    INPUT "ABC CORP.?";E$:T$ = "
       ABC":X = 95:Y = 99
370    IF E$ = "SPLIT" THEN  GOSUB
       9000
380    IF E$ = "SKIP" THEN 400
390    CALL  - 936:B =  VAL (E$): GOSUB
       5000: GOSUB 7000
400    PRINT : INPUT "BCD CO.";E$:T
       $ = "BCD":X = 135:Y = 139
410    IF E$ = "SPLIT" THEN  GOSUB
       9000
420    IF E$ = "SKIP" THEN 440
430    CALL  - 936:B =  VAL (E$): GOSUB
       5000: GOSUB 7000
440    PRINT : INPUT "CDE LIMITED?"
       ;E$:T$ = "CDE":X = 175:Y = 1
       79
450    IF E$ = "SPLIT" THEN  GOSUB
       9000
460    IF E$ = "SKIP" THEN 480
470    CALL  - 936:B =  VAL (E$): GOSUB
       5000: GOSUB 7000
480    PRINT : PRINT  TAB( 15);"AME
       X STOCKS"
490    PRINT : INPUT "DEF COMPUTER
       CORP.?";E$:T$ = "DEF":X = 21
       5:Y = 219
500    IF E$ = "SPLIT" THEN  GOSUB
       9000
510    IF E$ = "SKIP" THEN 530
520    CALL  - 936:B =  VAL (E$): GOSUB
       5000: GOSUB 7000
530    PRINT : INPUT "EFG PETROLEUM
       ?";E$:T$ = "EFG":X = 255:Y =
       259
540    IF E$ = "SPLIT" THEN  GOSUB
       9000
550    IF E$ = "SKIP" THEN 570
560    CALL  - 936:B =  VAL (E$): GOSUB
```

```
      5000: GOSUB 7000
570   PRINT : INPUT "FGH STORES?";
      E$:T$ = "FGH":X = 295:Y = 29
      9
580   IF E$ = "SPLIT" THEN  GOSUB
      9000
590   IF E$ = "SKIP" THEN 610
600   CALL  - 936:B =  VAL (E$): GOSUB
      5000: GOSUB 7000
610   PRINT : INPUT "GHI AIRCRAFT?
      ";E$:T$ = "GHI":X = 335:Y =
      339
620   IF E$ = "SPLIT" THEN  GOSUB
      9000
630   IF E$ = "SKIP" THEN 650
640   CALL  - 936:B =  VAL (E$): GOSUB
      5000: GOSUB 7000
650   PRINT D$;"OPEN DATA FILE"
660   PRINT D$;"DELETE DATA FILE"
670   PRINT D$;"OPEN DATA FILE"
680   PRINT D$;"WRITE DATA FILE"
690   FOR I = 0 TO 374: PRINT A(I)
      : NEXT
700   PRINT D$;"CLOSE DATA FILE"
710   PRINT : PRINT "STOCK ANALYSI
      S COMPLETED AND FILES": PRINT
      "UPDATED.": PRINT : PRINT "P
      RESS SPACE BAR TO RETURN TO
      MENU"
720   POKE  - 16368,0: WAIT  - 163
      84,128: WAIT  - 16384,1,1
730   GOTO 110
5000  C1 = 0:C2 = 0:C3 = 0:C4 = 0:
      C5 = 0:C6 = 0:D1 = 0:D2 = 0:
      D3 = 0:D4 = 0:D5 = 0:D6 = 0:
      P = 100
5010   FOR I = X TO Y:C1 = C1 + A(
      I): NEXT :C2 = B + (C1 - A(Y
      )):Y = Y + 10
5020   FOR I = X TO Y:C3 = C3 + A(
      I): NEXT :C4 = B + (C3 - A(Y
      )):Y = Y + 25
```

182

```
5030  FOR I = X TO Y:C5 = C5 + A(
      I): NEXT :C6 = B + (C5 - A(Y
      )):X = X + 1
5040  D1 = C1 / 5:D1 =  INT (D1 *
      P + .5) / P:D2 = C2 / 5:D2 =
      INT (D2 * P + .5) / P
5050  D3 = C3 / 15:D3 =  INT (D3 *
      P + .5) / P:D4 = C4 / 15:D4 =
      INT (D4 * P + .5) / P
5060  D5 = C5 / 40:D5 =  INT (D5 *
      P + .5) / P:D6 = C6 / 40:D6 =
      INT (D6 * P + .5) / P
5070  PRINT : PRINT  TAB( 5);"TOT
      ALS"; TAB( 15);T$; TAB( 22);
      "MOVING AVERAGES": PRINT
5080  PRINT "LAST 5 WK-";C1; TAB(
      20);"LAST 5 WK-";D1: PRINT "
      5 WK--";C2; TAB( 20);"5 WK--
      ";D2: PRINT
5090  PRINT "LAST 15 WK-";C3; TAB(
      20);"LAST 15 WK-";D3: PRINT
      "15 WK--";C4; TAB( 20);"15 W
      K--";D4: PRINT
5100  PRINT "LAST 40 WK-";C5; TAB(
      20);"LAST 40 WK-";D5: PRINT
      "40 WK--";C6; TAB( 20);"40 W
      K--";D6: PRINT
5110  FOR I = Y TO X STEP  - 1:A(
      I) = A(I - 1): NEXT :X = X -
      1:A(X) = B
5120  RETURN
5800  H1 = (E - F) + A(X): FOR I =
      X TO Y:H2 = H2 + A(I): NEXT
      :H3 =  INT (H2 / 15):X = X +
      1
5810  H4 =  INT ((H1 + (H2 - A(Y))
      ) / 15): PRINT "ADV-DEC LAST
      -";H3;"  CURRENT-";H4
5820  IF H4 =  > H3 THEN B$ = "UP
      "
5830  IF H4 < H3 THEN B$ = "DOWN"
```

```
5835    PRINT "ADVANCE-DECLINE LINE
        ";B$
5840    FOR I = Y TO X STEP  - 1:A(
        I) = A(I - 1): NEXT :X = X -
        1:A(X) = H1
5850    RETURN
6000    PRINT : PRINT T$;" MARKET C
        OMMENT--WEEK ENDING ";A$
6010    IF D4 =  > D6 AND D6 =  > D
        5 AND B$ = "UP" THEN C$ = "B
        ULL MARKET-STAY INVESTED": PRINT
        C$: RETURN
6020    IF D4 < D6 AND D6 < D5 AND
        B$ = "UP" THEN C$ = "UNCERTA
        IN--AVOID NEW PURCHASES": PRINT
        C$: RETURN
6030    IF D4 =  > D6 AND D6 =  > D
        5 THEN C$ = "UNCERTAIN-AVOID
         NEW PURCHASES": PRINT C$: RETURN

6040    IF D4 < D6 AND D2 <  = D1 AND
        B$ = "DOWN" THEN C$ = "BEAR
        MARKET-AVOID NEW PURCHASES":
         PRINT C$: RETURN
6050    IF D2 > D1 AND D2 < D6 AND
        D4 < D6 AND B$ = "DOWN" THEN
        C$ = "5 WK UPTURN-BUY STRONG

        EST STOCKS": PRINT C$: RETURN

6060    IF D2 =  > D6 AND D4 < D6 AND
        D6 < D5 AND B$ = "DOWN" THEN
        C$ = "BUY-BEAR RALLY OR EARL
        Y BULL": PRINT C$: RETURN
6070    IF D2 < D6 AND D4 < D6 AND
        D6 < D5 AND B$ = "UP" THEN C
        $ = "BUY-BEAR RALLY OR EARLY
         BULL": PRINT C$: RETURN
6080    IF D2 =  > D6 AND D4 < D6 THEN
        C$ = "BUY-SECOND BULLISH SIG
        N": PRINT C$: RETURN
6090    IF D2 =  > D6 AND D4 =  > D
        6 THEN C$ = "BUY AGGRESSIVEL
```

```
              Y-BULL MARKET AHEAD": PRINT
       C$: RETURN
6100   PRINT "NONE OF THE MARKET S
       UMMARY CRITERIA MET": PRINT
       "MARKET APPARENTLY UNCERTAIN
       ": RETURN
7000   IF D2 = D1 THEN H$ = "NEUTR
       AL"
7010   IF D2 > D1 THEN H$ = "UP"
7020   IF D2 < D1 THEN H$ = "DOWN"

7030   IF D4 = D3 THEN J$ = "NEUTR
       AL"
7040   IF D4 > D3 THEN J$ = "UP"
7050   IF D4 < D3 THEN J$ = "DOWN"

7060   IF D6 = D5 THEN K$ = "NEUTR
       AL"
7070   IF D6 > D5 THEN K$ = "UP"
7080   IF D6 < D5 THEN K$ = "DOWN"

7090   PRINT : PRINT "40 WK ";K$;"
        15 WK ";J$;"  5 WK ";H$: PRINT

7110   IF D4 < = D6 AND D2 < = D
       6 THEN  PRINT "AVOID REGARDL
       ESS OF MARKET TREND": RETURN
7120   IF D4 < = D6 AND D1 < D5 THEN
       PRINT "5 WK JUST PENETRATED
       40 WK": FLASH : PRINT "POSS
       IBLE BUY": NORMAL : RETURN
7130   IF D2 < = D6 THEN  PRINT "
       CONSIDER PURCHASE ON 5 WK MA
       RKET UPTURN": RETURN
7140   IF D2 < = D4 THEN  PRINT "
       HOLD IF BULL MKT, SELL IF BE
       AR": RETURN
7150   PRINT "HOLD IF OWNED. CANDI
       DATE FOR PURCHASE BETWEEN ";
       D6;"--";D2: RETURN
7160   PRINT "NONE OF THE ANALYSIS
       CRITERIA MET. WATCH CAREFUL
```

```
        LY FOR TREND": RETURN
8000  REM --FILE DIRECTORY SUBROU
      TINE
8010  PRINT D$;"PR#1"
8020  PRINT  TAB( 14);"FILE DIREC
      TORY"
8030  PRINT : PRINT  TAB( 5);"NYS
      E DATA"; TAB( 22);"SYMBOL"; TAB(
      32);"LOCATION": PRINT
8040  PRINT "ADVANCE-DECLINE"; TAB(
      34);"0--14"
8050  PRINT "D.J.I.A."; TAB( 33);
      "15--54"
8060  PRINT "N.Y.C.I."; TAB( 33);
      "55--94"
8070  PRINT "ABC CORP."; TAB( 23)
      ;"ABC"; TAB( 33);"95-134"
8080  PRINT "BCD CO."; TAB( 23);"
      BCD"; TAB( 32);"135-174"
8090  PRINT "CDE LIMITED"; TAB( 2
      3);"CDE"; TAB( 32);"175-214"
8100  PRINT : PRINT  TAB( 5);"AME
      X DATA"
8105  PRINT
8110  PRINT "DEF COMPUTER CORP.";
      TAB( 23);"DEF"; TAB( 32);"2
      15-254"
8120  PRINT "EFG PETROLEUM"; TAB(
      23);"EFG"; TAB( 32);"255-294
      "
8130  PRINT "FGH STORES"; TAB( 23
      );"FGH"; TAB( 32);"295-334"
8140  PRINT "GHI AIRCRAFT"; TAB(
      23);"GHI"; TAB( 32);"335-374
      "
8150  PRINT D$;"PR#0"
8160  PRINT : PRINT : PRINT "PRES
      S SPACE BAR TO RETURN TO MEN
      U"
8170  POKE  - 16368,0: WAIT  - 16
      384,128: WAIT  - 16384,1,1
```

```
8180   GOTO 110
8200   REM  VERIFY OR CORRECT DATA
       ROUTINE
8210   CALL  - 936: PRINT "THIS RO
       UTINE ALLOWS YOU TO VERIFY O
       R": PRINT "CORRECT ITEMS IN
       EACH DATA ARRAY": PRINT : PRINT
       "WHICH ARRAY TO YOU WANT TO
       CHECK?": PRINT
8220   PRINT  TAB( 5);"1.  ADVANCE
       -DECLINE": PRINT  TAB( 5);"2
       .  D.J.I.A.": PRINT  TAB( 5)
       ;"3.  N.Y.C.I.": PRINT  TAB(
       5);"4.  ABC CORP.(ABC)": PRINT
       TAB( 5);"5.  BCD CO.(BCD)":
       PRINT  TAB( 5);"6.  CDE LIM
       ITED (CDE)"
8230   PRINT  TAB( 5);"7.  DEF COM
       PUTER CORP. (DEF)": PRINT  TAB(
       5);"8.  EFG PETROLEUM (EFG)"
       : PRINT  TAB( 5);"9.  FGH ST
       ORES (FGH)": PRINT  TAB( 4);
       "10.  GHI AIRCRAFT (GHI)": PRINT
       TAB( 4);"11.  NONE, RETURN
       TO MENU"
8240   INPUT Z
8250   IF Z = 11 THEN  GOTO 110
8260   IF Z < 1 OR Z > 10 THEN  GOTO
       8210
8270   PRINT : PRINT "DATA WILL BE
       PRESENTED ONE ITEM AT A": PRINT
       "TIME, MOST RECENT FIRST.  P
       RESS ANY": PRINT "KEY IF COR
       RECT, 'N' IF INCORRECT.  THE
        ?": PRINT "AFTER AN N ALLOW
       S YOU TO CORRECT THAT": PRINT
       "ITEM"
8280   ON Z GOTO 8290,8300,8310,83
       20,8330,8340,8350,8360,8370,
       8380
8290 X = 0:Y = 14: GOTO 8390
8300 X = 15:Y = 54: GOTO 8390
```

```
8310 X = 55:Y = 94: GOTO 8390
8320 X = 95:Y = 134: GOTO 8390
8330 X = 135:Y = 174: GOTO 8390
8340 X = 175:Y = 214: GOTO 8390
8350 X = 215:Y = 254: GOTO 8390
8360 X = 255:Y = 294: GOTO 8390
8370 X = 295:Y = 334: GOTO 8390
8380 X = 335:Y = 374
8390  FOR I = X TO Y: PRINT A(I)
8400  INPUT "CORRECT?";Z$
8410  IF Z$ = "N" THEN  GOSUB 844
     0
8420  NEXT I
8430  GOTO 110
8440  INPUT A(I)
8450  RETURN
8500  CALL  - 936: PRINT : PRINT
      TAB( 12);"DATA ENTRY ROUTIN
     E": PRINT : PRINT "THIS ROUT
     INE WILL REPLACE ALL DATA": PRINT
     "CURRENTLY IN YOUR DATA BASE
     ,": PRINT "OR CREATE DATA FI
     LES IF NONE EXIST."
8510  PRINT : PRINT "IF YOU WISH
     TO CHANGE OR VERIFY ONLY A":
      PRINT "FEW ITEMS, USE THE '

     VERIFY OR CORRECT": PRINT "R
     OUTINE (MENU ITEM 4)"
8520  PRINT : PRINT "DO YOU WISH
     TO CONTINUE? (Y/N)": GET Z$:
      IF Z$ = "N" THEN  GOTO 110
8525  IF Z$ < > "Y" THEN  GOTO 8
     520
8530  PRINT "INPUT ALL DATA WITH
     MOST RECENT FIRST": PRINT
8540  PRINT "INPUT ADVANCE-DECLIN
     E FIGURES":X = 0:Y = 14: GOSUB
     8710
8550  PRINT "INPUT D.J.I.A. FIGUR
     ES":X = 15:Y = 54: GOSUB 871
     0
```

```
8560   PRINT "INPUT N.Y.C.I. FIGUR
       ES":X = 55:Y = 94: GOSUB 871
       0
8570   PRINT "INPUT ABC CORP.(ABC)
       FIGURES":X = 95:Y = 134: GOSUB
       8710
8580   PRINT "INPUT BCD CO.(BCD) F
       IGURES":X = 135:Y = 174: GOSUB
       8710
8590   PRINT "INPUT CDE LIMITED (C
       DE) FIGURES":X = 175:Y = 214
       : GOSUB 8710
8600   PRINT "INPUT DEF COMPUTER C
       ORP. (DEF) FIGURES":X = 215:
       Y = 254: GOSUB 8710
8610   PRINT "INPUT EFG PETROLEUM
       (EFG) FIGURES":X = 255:Y = 2
       94: GOSUB 8710
8620   PRINT "INPUT FGH STORES (FG
       H) FIGURES":X = 295:Y = 334:
       GOSUB 8710
8630   PRINT "INPUT GHI AIRCRAFT (
       GHI) FIGURES":X = 335:Y = 37
       4: GOSUB 8710
8640   PRINT D$;"OPEN DATA FILE"
8650   PRINT D$;"DELETE DATA FILE"

8660   PRINT D$;"OPEN DATA FILE"
8670   PRINT D$;"WRITE DATA FILE"
8680   FOR I = 0 TO 374: PRINT A(I
       ): NEXT
8690   PRINT D$;"CLOSE DATA FILE"
8700   GOTO 110
8710   FOR I = X TO Y: INPUT A(I):
       NEXT
8720   RETURN
9000   PRINT :P = 100: PRINT "DIVI
       SOR FOR SPLIT": INPUT S:Y =
       Y + 35
9010   FOR I = X TO Y:A(I) = A(I) /
       S:A(I) = INT (A(I) * P + .5
       ) / P: NEXT
```

```
9020    PRINT T$;" ADJUSTED FOR SPL
        IT": PRINT :Y = Y - 35: INPUT
        "CURRENT PRICE";E$: RETURN
9030    END
```

Program Listing 7-3
Dollar Cost Averaging Analyst

```
10    REM   DOLLAR COST AVERAGING AN
      ALYST
20    REM   WRITTEN BY L. SCHMELTZ
30    DIM DT$(16),T$(16),NS(16),C(1
      6),S$(16),CQ(16),VL(16)
40 D$ = CHR$ (4): REM  CHR$(4) I
      S CTRL-D
50    CALL  - 936
60    VTAB (11): PRINT  TAB( 14);"D
      C A ANALYST": PRINT : PRINT
      TAB( 14);"BY L. SCHMELTZ": FOR
      Z = 0 TO 2500: NEXT
70    CALL  - 936: VTAB (12): PRINT
      TAB( 5);"FIRST USE OF THIS
      PROGRAM? (Y/N)": GET Z$
80    IF Z$ = "Y" THEN  GOTO 1600
90    IF Z$ < > "N" THEN  GOTO 70
100   CALL  - 936
110   VTAB (6): PRINT  TAB( 5);"SE
      LECT:"
120   PRINT : PRINT  TAB( 10);"1.
      DISPLAY SUMMARY"
130   PRINT : PRINT  TAB( 10);"2.
      UPDATE CURRENT QUOTE"
140   PRINT : PRINT  TAB( 10);"3.
      ENTER TRANSACTION"
150   PRINT : PRINT  TAB( 10);"4.
      ADJUST FOR SPLIT/DIVIDEND"
160   PRINT : PRINT  TAB( 10);"5.
      EXIT THE PROGRAM"
170   PRINT : PRINT  TAB( 5);"WHIC
      H?"
180   GET Z$
190 Z = VAL (Z$)
```

```
200   IF Z < 1 OR Z > 5 THEN  PRINT
      "SELECT 1-5 ONLY": GOTO 180
210   ON Z GOTO 3000,2000,1000,300
      ,220
220   END
300   CALL  - 936
310   PRINT : PRINT "THIS ROUTINE
      WILL ADJUST FOR STOCK": PRINT
      "SPLITS AND DIVIDENDS PAID I
      N SHARES."
320   PRINT : INPUT "ENTER THE STO
      CKS' TRADING SYMBOL?";S$
330   PRINT : PRINT "PRESS ";: INVERSE
      : PRINT "S";: NORMAL : PRINT
      " FOR SPLIT, ";: INVERSE : PRINT
      "D";: NORMAL : PRINT " FOR S
      TOCK DIVIDEND": GET Z$
340   PRINT : PRINT D$;"OPEN";S$
350   PRINT D$;"READ";S$
360   INPUT T
370   FOR I = 0 TO T: INPUT DT$(I)
      ,T$(I),NS(I),C(I): NEXT
380   PRINT D$;"CLOSE";S$
390   IF Z$ = "S" THEN  PRINT : PRINT
      "ENTER THE DIVISOR FOR THIS
      SPLIT": INPUT D: FOR I = 0 TO
      T:NS(I) = NS(I) * D: NEXT : GOTO
      440
400   IF Z$ <  > "D" THEN  PRINT "
      INPUT S OR D ONLY": GOTO 330

410   PRINT : PRINT "STOCK DIVIDEN
      D PERCENTAGE?": INPUT D
420   IF D < 0 OR D > 100 THEN  PRINT
      "PERCENTAGE MUST BE BETWEEN
      0 AND 100": GOTO 410
430   FOR I = 0 TO T:NS(I) = NS(I)
      + (NS(I) * (D / 100)): NEXT

440   PRINT D$;"OPEN";S$
450   PRINT D$;"DELETE";S$
460   PRINT D$;"OPEN";S$
```

```
470    PRINT D$;"WRITE";S$
480    PRINT T
490    FOR I = 0 TO T: PRINT DT$(I)
       : PRINT T$(I): PRINT NS(I): PRINT
       C(I): NEXT
500    PRINT D$;"CLOSE";S$
510    PRINT "ADJUSTMENT HAS BEEN M
       ADE"
520    FOR I = 0 TO 2500: NEXT
530    GOTO 100
1000   REM   ENTER TRANSACTION SUBR
       OUTINE
1010   CALL  - 936
1020   PRINT : PRINT  TAB( 15);"TR
       ANSACTION": PRINT : PRINT  TAB(
       10);"DATE (MM/DD/YY):--/--/-
       -"
1030   PRINT : PRINT  TAB( 13);"ST
       OCK SYMBOL:-----"
1040   PRINT : PRINT  TAB( 3);"TRA
       NS. TYPE (BUY/SELL):----"
1050   PRINT : PRINT  TAB( 9);"NUM
       BER OF SHARES:-----"
1060   PRINT : PRINT "  TOTAL COST
       (STOCK+COMM):------"
1070   PRINT : PRINT "  ***PRESS "
       ;: INVERSE : PRINT "RETURN";
       : NORMAL : PRINT " AFTER EAC
       H ENTRY***"
1080   VTAB (4): HTAB (25): INPUT
       DT$
1090   VTAB (6): HTAB (25): INPUT
       S$
1100   VTAB (8): HTAB (25): INPUT
       T$
1110   VTAB (10): HTAB (25): INPUT
       NS
1120   VTAB (12): HTAB (25): INPUT
       C
1130   VTAB (18): HTAB (1): PRINT
       "FIRST TRANSACTION FOR THIS
       STOCK? (Y/N)"
```

```
1140   INPUT Y$
1150   VTAB (20): PRINT "PRESS:"

1160   PRINT  TAB( 7);: INVERSE : PRINT
       "RETURN";: NORMAL : PRINT "
       IF CORRECT"
1170   PRINT  TAB( 7);: INVERSE : PRINT
       "ESC";: NORMAL : PRINT " TO
       CHANGE"
1180   GET Z$: PRINT
1190   IF Z$ =  CHR$ (27) THEN  GOTO
       1010
1200   IF Z$ <  >  CHR$ (13) THEN
       GOTO 1180
1210   IF Y$ = "Y" THEN  GOSUB 141
       0
1220   PRINT : PRINT D$;"OPEN";S$
1230   PRINT D$;"READ";S$
1240   INPUT T: IF T =  - 1 THEN  GOTO
       1280
1250   FOR I = 0 TO T
1260   INPUT DT$(I),T$(I),NS(I),C(
       I)
1270   NEXT
1280   PRINT D$;"CLOSE";S$
1290   T = T + 1
1300   DT$(T) = DT$:T$(T) = T$:NS(T
       ) = NS:C(T) = C
1310   PRINT D$;"OPEN";S$
1320   PRINT D$;"DELETE";S$
1330   PRINT D$;"OPEN";S$
1340   PRINT D$;"WRITE";S$
1350   PRINT T
1360   FOR I = 0 TO T
1370   PRINT DT$(I): PRINT T$(I): PRINT
       NS(I): PRINT C(I)
1380   NEXT
1390   PRINT D$;"CLOSE";S$
1400   GOTO 100
1410   PRINT : PRINT D$;"OPEN DIRE
       CTORY"
1420   PRINT D$;"READ DIRECTORY"
```

```
1430   INPUT N: IF N =  - 1 THEN  GOTO
       1450
1440   FOR I = O TO N: INPUT S$(I)
       : NEXT
1450   PRINT D$;"CLOSE DIRECTORY"
1460  N = N + 1
1470  S$(N) = S$
1480   PRINT D$;"OPEN DIRECTORY"
1490   PRINT D$;"DELETE DIRECTORY"

1500   PRINT D$;"OPEN DIRECTORY"
1510   PRINT D$;"WRITE DIRECTORY"
1520   PRINT N: FOR I = O TO N: PRINT
       S$(I): NEXT
1530   PRINT D$;"CLOSE DIRECTORY"
1540   PRINT D$;"OPEN";S$
1550   PRINT D$;"DELETE";S$
1560   PRINT D$;"OPEN";S$
1570   PRINT D$;"WRITE";S$
1580   PRINT "-1": PRINT D$;"CLOSE
       ";S$
1590   RETURN
1600   PRINT : PRINT D$;"OPEN DIRE
       CTORY"
1610   PRINT D$;"DELETE DIRECTORY"

1620   PRINT D$;"OPEN DIRECTORY"
1630   PRINT D$;"WRITE DIRECTORY"
1640   PRINT "-1"
1650   PRINT D$;"CLOSE DIRECTORY"
1660   GOTO 100
2000   REM   UPDATE CURRENT QUOTE R
       OUTINE
2010   CALL  - 936
2020   PRINT : PRINT D$;"OPEN DIRE
       CTORY"
2030   PRINT D$;"READ DIRECTORY"
2040   INPUT N
2050   FOR I = O TO N: INPUT S$(I)
       : NEXT
2060   PRINT D$;"CLOSE DIRECTORY"
2070   PRINT : PRINT "YOU WILL BE
```

194

```
           ASKED TO INPUT THE CURRENT":
           PRINT "QUOTE FOR EACH STOCK
           IN YOUR FILES."
2080   PRINT : PRINT "SPLITS OR ST
           OCK DIVIDENDS SHOULD BE": PRINT
           "ADJUSTED, USING OPTION 4 PR
           IOR TO ": PRINT "UPDATING CU
           RRENT QUOTES."
2090   PRINT : PRINT "CONTINUE? (Y
           /N)": GET Z$
2100   IF Z$ = "N" THEN  GOTO 100
2110   IF Z$ < > "Y" THEN  GOTO 2
           090
2120   PRINT : PRINT "AS EACH STOC
           K IS LISTED, ENTER THE": PRINT
           "CURRENT QUOTE AND PRESS RET
           URN.": PRINT "ENTER A 0 IF N
           O QUOTE IS AVAILABLE."
2130   PRINT : INPUT "CURRENT DATE
           ? (MM/DD/YY)";DT$
2140   FOR I = 0 TO N: PRINT S$(I)
           ;: INPUT " CURRENT QUOTE?";C
           Q(I): NEXT
2150   PRINT D$;"OPEN CURRENT QUOT
           E"
2160   PRINT D$;"DELETE CURRENT QU
           OTE"
2170   PRINT D$;"OPEN CURRENT QUOT
           E"
2180   PRINT D$;"WRITE CURRENT QUO
           TE"
2190   PRINT DT$: FOR I = 0 TO N: PRINT
           CQ(I): NEXT
2200   PRINT D$;"CLOSE CURRENT QUO
           TE"
2210   GOTO 100
3000   REM  DISPLAY SUMMARY ROUTIN
           E
3010   CALL  - 936: VTAB (9): PRINT
           "SUMMARIES AVAILABLE:": PRINT
           : PRINT  TAB( 5);"1.  ALL ST
           OCKS IN PORTFOLIO": PRINT : PRINT
```

195

```
        TAB( 5);"2.   INDIVIDUAL STO
     CK": PRINT : PRINT  TAB( 5);
     "WHICH?"
3020  GET Z$:Z =  VAL (Z$)
3030  IF Z < 1 OR Z > 2 THEN  PRINT
     "SELECT 1 OR 2 ONLY": GOTO 3
     020
3040  PRINT : PRINT D$;"OPEN DIRE
     CTORY"
3050  PRINT D$;"READ DIRECTORY"
3060  INPUT N
3070  FOR I = 0 TO N: INPUT S$(I)
     : NEXT
3080  PRINT D$;"CLOSE DIRECTORY"
3090  PRINT D$;"OPEN CURRENT QUOT
     E"
3100  PRINT D$;"READ CURRENT QUOT
     E"
3110  INPUT DT$
3120  FOR I = 0 TO N: INPUT CQ(I)
     : NEXT
3130  PRINT D$;"CLOSE CURRENT QUO
     TE"
3140  IF Z = 2 THEN  GOTO 3510
3150  CALL  - 936
3160  PRINT  TAB( 4);"D C A PORTF
     OLIO SUMMARY ";DT$
3170  PRINT : PRINT " STOCK SHARE
     S  COST  VALUE NET G/L G/L%"
3180  PRINT " ----- ------ ------
     ----- ------- ---"
3190  POKE 34,5:NS = 0:TC = 0:ST =
     0:CT = 0:VT = 0
3200  FOR I = 0 TO N:NS = 0:TC =
     0
3210  PRINT : PRINT D$;"OPEN";S$(
     I)
3220  PRINT D$;"READ";S$(I)
3230  INPUT T: FOR X = 0 TO T: INPUT
     DT$(X),T$(X),NS(X),C(X): NEXT
     X
```

196

```
3240  PRINT D$;"CLOSE";S$(I)
3245  FOR X = 0 TO T
3250  IF T$(X) = "BUY" THEN NS =
      NS + NS(X):TC = TC + C(X): GOTO
      3270
3260  NS = NS - NS(X):TC = TC - C(
      X)
3270  NEXT X
3280  VL = NS * CQ(I)
3290  GL =  INT (VL - TC):GP =  INT
      ((VL / TC) * 100) - 100
3300  VL =  INT (VL):NS =  INT (NS
      ):TC =  INT (TC)
3310  NS$ =  STR$ (NS):TC$ =  STR$
      (TC):VL$ =  STR$ (VL):GL$ =
       STR$ (GL):GP$ =  STR$ (GP)
3320  T1 = 13 - ( LEN (NS$))
3330  T2 = 20 - ( LEN (TC$))
3340  T3 = 27 - ( LEN (VL$))
3350  T4 = 35 - ( LEN (GL$))
3360  T5 = 39 - ( LEN (GP$))
3370  PRINT  TAB( 3);S$(I); TAB(
      T1);NS; TAB( T2);TC; TAB( T3
      );VL; TAB( T4);GL; TAB( T5);
      GP;"%";
3380  ST = ST + NS:CT = CT + TC:VT
      = VT + VL
3390  NEXT I
3400  VTAB (21): HTAB (1): CALL  -
      958
3410  PRINT  TAB( 8);"------ ----
      -- ----- ------- ---"
3420  ST$ =  STR$ (ST):CT$ =  STR$
      (CT):VT$ =  STR$ (VT)
3430  T1 = 13 - ( LEN (ST$)):T2 =
      20 - ( LEN (CT$)):T3 = 27 -
      ( LEN (VT$))
3440  GT =  INT (VT - CT):GT$ =  STR$
      (GT):PT =  INT ((VT / CT) *
      100) - 100:PT$ =  STR$ (PT)
3450  T4 = 35 - ( LEN (GT$)):T5 =
      39 - ( LEN (PT$))
```

```
3460    PRINT "TOTALS:"; TAB( T1);S
        T; TAB( T2);CT; TAB( T3);VT;
        TAB( T4);GT; TAB( T5);PT;"%
        "
3470    PRINT  TAB( 6);"*****PRESS
        ";: INVERSE : PRINT "RETURN"
        ;: NORMAL : PRINT " FOR MENU
        *****"
3480    GET Z$
3490    IF Z$ < > CHR$ (13) THEN
        GOTO 3480
3500    TEXT : GOTO 100
3510    CALL  - 936
3520    PRINT : PRINT "SELECT A STO
        CK SUMMARY:": PRINT
3530    FOR I = 0 TO N: PRINT  TAB(
        5);I; TAB( 10);S$(I): NEXT
3540    PRINT : PRINT "DISPLAY WHIC
        H STOCK (ENTER BY NUMBER) ?"
        : GET Z$
3550 Z =  VAL (Z$): IF Z < 0 OR Z
        > N THEN  GOTO 3510
3560    CALL  - 936
3570    PRINT : PRINT D$;"OPEN";S$(
        Z)
3580    PRINT D$;"READ";S$(Z)
3590    INPUT T
3600    FOR X = 0 TO T: INPUT DT$(X
        ),T$(X),NS(X),C(X): NEXT
3605    PRINT D$;"CLOSE";S$(Z)
3610    CALL  - 936: PRINT  TAB( 15
        );"STOCK: ";S$(Z): PRINT : PRINT
        TAB( 9);"TRANS."; TAB( 22);
        "TOTAL TOTAL $ PER": PRINT "
          DATE    TYPE SHARES  HELD
        COST SHARE"
3620    PRINT "-------- ---- ------
        ----- ----- ------"
3630    POKE 34,5:ST = 0:CT = 0
3640    FOR X = 0 TO T
3650    IF T$(X) = "SELL" THEN ST =
        ST - NS(X):CT = CT - C(X): GOTO
```

```
           3670
3660 ST = ST + NS(X):CT = CT + C(
     X)
3670 PS =  INT ((CT / ST) * 100 +
     .5) / 100:NS =  INT (NS):ST =
      INT (ST):CT =  INT (CT)
3680 NS$ =  STR$ (NS(X)):CT$ =  STR$
     (CT):ST$ =  STR$ (ST):PS$ =
      STR$ (PS)
3685  IF  LEN (PS$) <  = 2 THEN P
     S$ = PS$ + ".00"
3690 T1 = 21 - ( LEN (NS$))
3700 T2 = 27 - ( LEN (ST$))
3710 T3 = 33 - ( LEN (CT$))
3720 T4 = 40 - ( LEN (PS$))
3730  PRINT DT$(X); TAB( 10);T$(X
     ); TAB( T1);NS(X); TAB( T2);
     ST; TAB( T3);CT; TAB( T4);PS

3740  NEXT X
3750  VTAB (21): CALL  - 958: PRINT
      TAB( 5);"*****PRESS ";: INVERSE
     : PRINT "RETURN";: NORMAL : PRINT
     " FOR MENU*****"
3760  GET Z$
3770  IF Z$ <  >  CHR$ (13) THEN
     GOTO 3760
3780  TEXT : GOTO 100
```

Sample Run 7-3
Each Menu Option Selected in Turn

              D C A ANALYST

            BY L. SCHMELTZ
FIRST USE OF THIS PROGRAM? (Y/N)
SELECT:

        1. DISPLAY SUMMARY

        2. UPDATE CURRENT QUOTE

3.   ENTER TRANSACTION

4.   ADJUST FOR SPLIT/DIVIDEND

5.   EXIT THE PROGRAM

WHICH?
SUMMARIES AVAILABLE:

1.   ALL STOCKS IN PORTFOLIO

2.   INDIVIDUAL STOCK

WHICH?

D C A PORTFOLIO SUMMARY 12/02/80

STOCK	SHARES	COST	VALUE	NET G/L	G/L%
SOT	61	839	1054	214	25%
ABC	100	165	225	59	36%
DEF	125	3375	3562	187	5%
TOTALS:	286	4379	4841	462	10%

     *****PRESS RETURN FOR MENU*****
     SELECT:

1.   DISPLAY SUMMARY

2.   UPDATE CURRENT QUOTE

3.   ENTER TRANSACTION

4.   ADJUST FOR SPLIT/DIVIDEND

5.   EXIT THE PROGRAM

WHICH?
SUMMARIES AVAILABLE:

1.   ALL STOCKS IN PORTFOLIO

2.   INDIVIDUAL STOCK

WHICH?

SELECT A STOCK SUMMARY:

    0   SOT
    1   ABC
    2   DEF

DISPLAY WHICH STOCK (ENTER BY NUMBER) ?

STOCK: SOT

DATE	TRANS. TYPE	SHARES	TOTAL HELD	TOTAL COST	$ PER SHARE
03/21/77	BUY	10	10	177	17.78
09/06/78	BUY	10.819	20	327	15.71
10/06/78	BUY	4.09	24	377	15.65
03/06/79	BUY	4.216	28	436	15.45
06/06/79	BUY	4.952	32	498	15.11
09/06/79	BUY	12.91	44	661	14.72
12/06/79	BUY	14.14	58	838	14.42

*****PRESS RETURN FOR MENU*****

SELECT:

    1.   DISPLAY SUMMARY

    2.   UPDATE CURRENT QUOTE

    3.   ENTER TRANSACTION

    4.   ADJUST FOR SPLIT/DIVIDEND

    5.   EXIT THE PROGRAM

WHICH?

YOU WILL BE ASKED TO INPUT THE CURRENT
QUOTE FOR EACH STOCK IN YOUR FILES.

SPLITS OR STOCK DIVIDENDS SHOULD BE
ADJUSTED, USING OPTION 4 PRIOR TO
UPDATING CURRENT QUOTES.

CONTINUE? (Y/N)

AS EACH STOCK IS LISTED, ENTER THE
CURRENT QUOTE AND PRESS RETURN.
ENTER A O IF NO QUOTE IS AVAILABLE.

CURRENT DATE? (MM/DD/YY)12/09/80
SOT CURRENT QUOTE?15.125
ABC CURRENT QUOTE?2.635
DEF CURRENT QUOTE?27
     SELECT:

            1.   DISPLAY SUMMARY

            2.   UPDATE CURRENT QUOTE

            3.   ENTER TRANSACTION

            4.   ADJUST FOR SPLIT/DIVIDEND

            5.   EXIT THE PROGRAM

     WHICH?

                    TRANSACTION

            DATE (MM/DD/YY):--/--/--

               STOCK SYMBOL:-----

      TRANS. TYPE (BUY/SELL):----

            NUMBER OF SHARES:-----

      TOTAL COST(STOCK+COMM):------

      PRESS RETURN AFTER EACH ENTRY
                        ?12/09/80

```
                              ?SOT
                              ?BUY
                              ?25
                              ?375.25
FIRST TRANSACTION FOR THIS STOCK? (Y/N)
?N
PRESS:
        RETURN IF CORRECT
        ESC TO CHANGE
     SELECT:
                1.  DISPLAY SUMMARY
                2.  UPDATE CURRENT QUOTE
                3.  ENTER TRANSACTION
                4.  ADJUST FOR SPLIT/DIVIDEND
                5.  EXIT THE PROGRAM

     WHICH?

THIS ROUTINE WILL ADJUST FOR STOCK
SPLITS AND DIVIDENDS PAID IN SHARES.

ENTER THE STOCKS' TRADING SYMBOL?SOT

PRESS S FOR SPLIT, D FOR STOCK DIVIDEND

STOCK DIVIDEND PERCENTAGE?
?2.5
ADJUSTMENT HAS BEEN MADE
     SELECT:

                1.  DISPLAY SUMMARY

                2.  UPDATE CURRENT QUOTE

                3.  ENTER TRANSACTION

                4.  ADJUST FOR SPLIT/DIVIDEND

                5.  EXIT THE PROGRAM

     WHICH?
```

Chapter 8

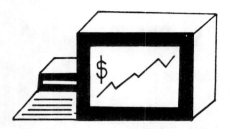

Related Computing

This chapter will cover many of the aspects of personal computing that may or may not become a part of your investment management system. Perhaps if you decided not to use your personal computer in an investment analysis capacity, some of the areas to be covered here will prove of value to you. In keeping with the current trend toward complete honesty in packaging, we will also discuss some of the disadvantages of computer use for investment purposes. Finally, we will attempt to summarize and tie up the loose ends that have been left dangling elsewhere in this book.

KEEPING RECORDS

Virtually every application discussed so far has involved the use of some type of record keeping. Prices, corporate earnings, fundamental analysis data, dollar cost averaging results and moving average information are records that may be necessary to operate your investment management system. In this section, two additional types of records will be added—transaction records and tax data.

Transaction Records

In your stock and bond market dealings, all transactions have most likely been confirmed in writing by your broker. Confirmations range from a very simple statement of what was bought or sold to elaborate analyses of each individual transaction. Once a month or so, you also receive an itemized statement of the activity in your account from the brokerage firm.

With all this information being furnished, is there really a need for you to employ yet another system of keeping transaction records? Well, the answer to that question depends very much on your own situation. If you buy some stock to put in the safety deposit box and forget, additional records will be of little or no use to you. An active trader can accumulate a formidable stack of confirmation slips and would be a good candidate for some type of record keeping system. As we saw in the last chapter, those employing a dollar cost averaging approach can benefit from the kinds of information rarely furnished by your brokerage firm. If you maintain and use accounts with more than one brokerage firm, a transaction record keeping system can help keep your sanity!

There are several advantages to using a transaction record system in conjunction with your other personal computer applications:

☐ Records can be structured to provide exactly the information you require. Depending on your application, this may involve more or less detail than confirmation slips and account statements.

☐ Immediate availability of pertinent data. While a stack of paper records could provide the same information, any computerized system should have a definite edge in this area. Most transactions are confirmed first by phone, then by a confirmation slip sent by mail. If your broker can supply the necessary information by phone, you can have the data in your system long before the mailed form reaches you. Active traders will find this immediate access far more valuable than will those with limited market activity.

☐ Transaction records can be integrated into other areas of your personal investment system. Going back to the dollar cost averaging example, transaction information provides the basis for determining overall results. Maintaining a longitudinal base of transaction data allows the program to operate much more efficiently than if the same data had to be reentered each time it is used.

☐ Much paperwork can be eliminated by maintaining open orders in a pending transaction type file. If you have more than just a few limit or stop orders currently active, keeping track of them manually can become a real headache.

Designing and using a transaction record system is a relatively simple process. With minor modifications, as noted, the dollar cost averaging program described in the last chapter would do very nicely. Writing a program to maintain records and produce reports will provide a good background in programming for other applications. Some of the subroutines used in the sample programs will provide help in file management, justification, data input, output and error trapping.

There are many data base management and business record keeping programs available commercially. Some of the more capable commercial programs allow the user to custom design input and output formats, produce reports sorted by virtually any record in the file, add or delete data easily and incorporate error trapping to keep you from going too far astray.

Tax Records

As mentioned earlier, I am not a qualified tax advisor! That does not prevent me, however, from keeping records needed for use by someone who is. Transaction information, as mentioned in the last few paragraphs, should be the foundation for your tax records. Your accountant (or you, if you do your own taxes) will need to know dates of transactions, price paid or received, brokerage fees incurred and dividends involved for every stock you buy and sell to determine tax liability.

Expenses directly related to producing investment income are generally tax deductible and should be part of your records. Such things as toll charges for phone calls to your broker, certain investment oriented publications, advisory service charges, interest on your margin account and numerous other items should be discussed with your tax advisor. Providing proper documentation with your personal computer can be a lot easier than digging through a large stack of receipts at the end of the year trying to determine what is or is not pertinent to your tax situation.

A word of caution should be inserted here—the records generated by your computer program can be invaluable to whoever prepares your tax returns, but the original documentation for the expense (cancelled check, receipt, statement, etc.) should be easily located in case you are called on to produce it. By making your computerized records complete as possible, your tax advisor should be better able to help you pay only the necessary amount of taxes.

A transaction record keeping system, with only minor expansion, can also serve your tax related needs. By adding a file to accept descriptions and amounts of investment related expenses, you will be well on your way to "killing two birds with one stone".

Systematic Record Keeping

A good record keeping system, regardless of the information contained, must be designed for accuracy, user convenience and safety. The amount of importance you attach to the records involved will determine the time and expense devoted to the system used.

Accuracy, of course, must be the primary measure of acceptability of any record keeping system. Once defined by the user, a record keeping system must be able to maintain the desired degree of accuracy. You may decide, for instance, that cost figures rounded to the nearest whole dollar amount are adequate for one particular application but another requires amounts correct to the fractional penny. If your record keeping system will handle the greater accuracy, the rounding process can be done for one application while the records maintain the fractional amounts. Record keeping systems that regularly drop bits of information, mismanage memory and peripherals or have built-in "bugs" that cause unpredictable crashes are obviously unsuited to any application.

User convenience becomes an important factor if more than occasional use of the record keeping system is planned. Input prompts should clearly state what information is expected and the format for entering the data. This is especially important for data not shown by example on the screen, such as expense codes or abbreviated descriptions. Somewhere in the program or accompanying documentation, a directory of unusual codes should be provided. Error trapping, even in its simplest form, helps the user to know what is acceptable in each field. By providing a "second chance" to examine and verify the accuracy of data before committing it to a file, the program can avoid many potential problems.

Similarly, output from the program should be logical and easy to interpret. Providing a limited and well defined set of output options allows the user to easily obtain the desired results.

Safety of records has always been an important consideration in large data processing applications. It is indeed a rare commercial data processing operation that does not have a complete set of duplicate records locked away in the vault. Personal computing applications have been woefully negligent in this regard. If you have ever had to go back and reconstruct a large body of data because your tape deck curled a cassette or your disk got scratched, safety has certainly entered your mind! Including provision in a program for making a duplicate data file, recording a back-up tape, or transferring records to another medium is not at all difficult. Keep at least two current copies of any and all information that is important to you!

The considerations just discussed should be part of any record keeping program you write yourself. Commercial programs vary widely in these areas and should be thoroughly tested for accuracy, user convenience and safety before routine use. Testing may be accomplished by using dummy data that can be easily verified. Try inputting some erroneous information, press the wrong keys, insert the wrong disk and do whatever else you can think of to see how the program reacts. Sometime, somehow you will commit a serious error in program use. It's better to find out what will happen during this testing phase than after you have loaded six months worth of data. If nothing else, your own programming efforts will benefit greatly from this experience!

TELECOMPUTING

For those who knew something about computers before the personal computer explosion, telecomputing used to be called time-sharing. I guess those who know, have attempted to differentiate the use of personal computers in a time-share mode from the age old practice of using remote terminals in a time share mode by coining a new phrase. Whether you prefer telecomputing or time-sharing, the process boils down to linking multiple terminals to a computer for shared access.

The Missing Link

Without delving deeply into the actual mechanics of the linkage, telecomputing is accomplished by transmission of data over telephone lines. The lines may be specially conditioned for the high speed transmission of data, but standard "voice grade" circuits are adequate for lower speeds. Both ends of the line are terminated in a modem which either encodes or decodes data from the tone combinations used for transmission. Terminals needing continuous access to the computer are most often connected to lines leased for that purpose. Most personal computing applications function quite well by first establishing communication by standard telephone methods and then putting the modems on line. See Fig. 8-1.

So why are we discussing this topic in a book related to investments? Well, as attorneys are fond of stating, we are preparing a foundation for evidence about to be introduced!

If you own or have access to a personal computer or terminal and a modem (similar to that shown in Fig. 8-1), telecomputing is well within your grasp. All that you need now is access to a computer set up for telecomputing applications. Where do you find these computers?

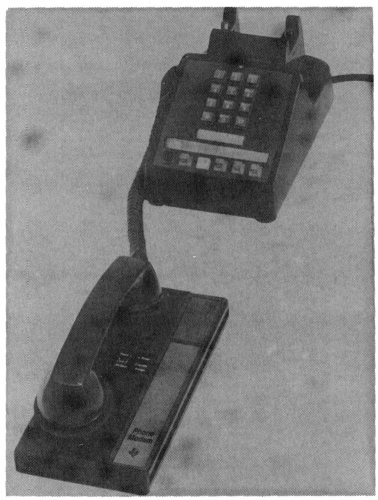

Fig. 8-1. Modems provide the necessary link between a personal computer and telecomputing network. Acoustic coupling, as shown here, or "hardwire" coupling by plugging direct into a telephone line are used to transmit and receive data. In addition to the modem, a serial communication interface and application software are needed for telecomputing (courtesy of Texas Instruments, Inc.).

□ Some corporations allow personal use of their computer during non-business hours. If permitted at all, this is usually limited to employees.

□ Many cities have commercial time-share corporations who may be willing to rent time for personal computing applications.

□ Some personal computer owners and clubs have established computerized bulletin board and limited time share systems.

□ Several large computer networks have been designated and marketed specifically for personal telecomputing applications (more on these later).

□ Even CATV systems are getting in to the act. Our local cable company is presently offering sophisticated game type computers which receive data transmitted on their lines.

Who Needs Another Computer?

The owner of a "bare" terminal obviously needs a computer, whether it is located on the premises or some remote location. For those who have purchased a personal computer system that operates entirely on its own, the answer is far less obvious. Adding the modem, software and computer access are all additional expenses that must be balanced against the potential benefits offered by the telecomputing system.

Communication with another computer can be limited to simple applications such as exchanging programs, getting the latest computer club information, sharing a game of chess or merely chatting. Sophisticated applications, more cost effective to the investor, may include:

□ Increasing the capacity of your system by accessing large blocks of memory, more extensive disk files and faster processing of some types of data.

□ Using your computer as an intelligent terminal to obtain data not readily available from other sources, or to provide significant time savings in gathering necessary data.

□ Sharing ideas with other computer users through "electronic mail" capabilities.

□ Purchase or rent programs which can be "downloaded" into your own system. This can be especially attractive for the occasional rental of a program that is either too expensive or too large for your own system.

□ Providing access to data bases not usually available to the personal computer user.

With a little thought, I'm sure you could come up with several more potential applications for telecomputing in your own situation. All of the applications mentioned above are commercially available today, many more are planned for the future.

The Telecomputing Investor

Gathering up to the minute data on stock prices, market trends, financial news and related activities can be nearly impossible for the average investor. Having almost immediate access to sizable data bases containing all the necessary information could certainly benefit most of us.

Picture, if you will, the following scenario. You sit down at your personal computer and want to see the latest price, volume, earnings and dividend information on the hundred or so stocks you follow. Further, you want to read any pertinent news releases from your hundred companies. Finally, the computer is to process this data in your own investment management program and provide a list of those stocks that meet your criteria as potential purchase candidates. After a few minutes the list of stocks and printed news items pops out of the printer. Farfetched? Hardly! The hardware, software and telecomputing capacity is available right now. A resourceful programmer could construct such a system with little difficulty.

A few commercially available investment management programs are designed to handle portions of the above scenario. With new software being introduced almost daily, it is only a matter of time before all the capacities described above are offered.

At least two major computer networks presently offer an impressive array of services to the personal computer user. For an initial fee and on-going charges based on time used plus the telephone charges, services ranging from electronic mail to financial data base access are available. More and more large time-share operations are considering offering services to personal computer users as a way to fill in the slack typically experienced during non-business hours. Look for some very recognizable name corporations to be added to the list very soon. You will find more information regarding telecomputing systems and software in the Appendices.

RELATED INVESTMENT VEHICLES

As you have no doubt noticed, our emphasis in this book has been on common stock as a primary investment vehicle. The vehicle is not nearly as important as the direction in which it is pointed, however. By developing an investment philosophy and approach that is compatible with your personal goals and objectives, the foundation for expansion into other areas of financial risk has been laid.

Rest assured you have not wasted any time or effort by developing the type of approach recommended. There are many aspects of trading in common stocks that we have not even broached in this admittedly limited introduction. You may want to investigate more sophisticated techniques such as short sales, leverage through margin accounts, day trading, new issues, etc., etc.

Gaining a reasonable understanding of activity and trends in the stock market makes the selection of alternate investment vehicles that much easier. In fact, a thorough background of information about common stocks will dramatically increase your chances of success with most of the alternatives presented here.

Options

One of the most highly leveraged forms of investment, options grant the right to control the fate of a specified number of shares of a stock for a limited amount of time. There are two basic types of options—put and call.

A call option allows the buyer to purchase stock (in multiples of 100 shares) at a designated price for a specific amount of time. The seller of the option receives a premium related to the amount of risk he is assuming that his stock will be sold at that price during the time involved. Let's say, for example, the stock of DEF is selling for $17.00 a share. Investor A owns 100 shares of DEF and would like to incresse his immediate income. He sells a call option for 9 months which will allow his stock to be sold for $15.00 a share. In return he receives an immediate return of $200.00 plus any time premium paid for the option. Investor B has a feeling that DEF will be selling for $25.00 a share before the 9 months expire, so he happily purchases the right to buy 100 shares of the stock at $15.00 a share. If B is correct and the price rises, his option is obviously worth far more than the $2.00 or so he paid. If the price of DEF decreases or stays the same, A's stock will not likely be called, the option expires worthless and he has received additional income.

Put options are exactly the opposite of calls. The buyer is paying a premium for being able to sell his stock at a particular price, and the seller is paid for offering to buy the stock. In this instance, the buyer hopes the price of the stock will decline during the term of the option. Sophisticated option traders often deal in complex combinations of puts and calls known as spreads, strips, straps and straddles. Combinations are constructed based on the traders opinion of which way the short term trend of the market will be going.

Option prices (premiums) are, in large part, determined by the price of the underlying stock. Time value and the degree of enthusiasm exhibited by traders make up the rest of the premium. As leveraged vehicles, option premiums tend to fluctuate far more widely than do the prices of the underlying stock on which they are based. Since the total investment involved is only a small percentage of what would be required to purchase the same amount of stock, opportunities for sizable gains (and losses) are easier to identify than in the stock market.

Buying options is generally regarded as speculation. Your potential loss is limited to the premium paid for the option, potential profits are unlimited. Selling options can significantly increase the rate of return on stocks owned, thus qualifying as a prudent investment procedure.

Since options are written for a maximum life of 9 months, your investment approach must take a very close look at short term market trends. In ordinary stock transactions, maximum profits are often realized by holding the shares for a relatively long period of time. Options, unless the price of the underlying stock changes dramatically, decrease in value as they approach expiration.

I suspect every investor, at some time or other, longs to take a fling in the options market. Stories of fortunes being made with little capital required can be downright appealing at times. If your investment approach has proven sensitive to relatively short term movements of particular stocks, perhaps some of your funds designated for speculation could provide some action in the options market. The faster pace noted in options makes doing your homework and carefully constructing a plan of action doubly important. See Fig. 8-2.

Stock Rights

Corporations seeking to raise additional capital often issue rights to their shareholders. Rights give the stockholder an option to purchase stock in the corporation ahead of the general public, usually at a more favorable price and without brokerage commis-

TREND OF OPTION PREMIUM LEVELS

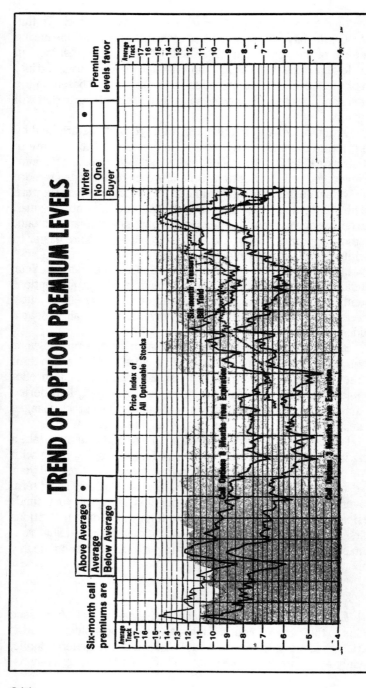

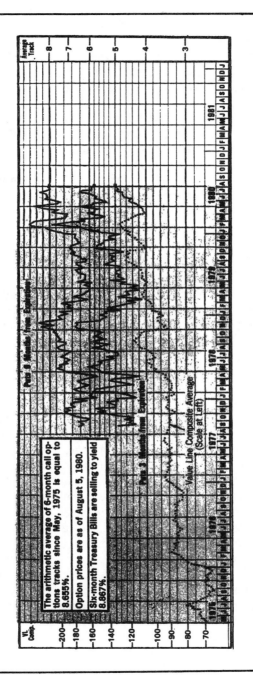

Fig. 8-2. Premiums for put and call options often fluctuate more widely than the prices of stocks on which they are based. An interesting comparison of premiums and stock prices is shown by this trend chart from *Value Line Options & Convertibles* (courtesy of Arnold Bernhard & Co., Inc.).

sions. Most rights offers have relatively short time limits, so rapid action is required.

You can, of course, exercise any right received and purchase the stock at a slight discount. Unexercised rights can be bought and sold in the open market, with prices determined by supply and demand.

The determination of whether to exercise, buy or sell rights must be made on the basis of your assessment of the issuing company. If the stock involved is one your investment approach has indicated is worth considering, rights can provide a slight savings in purchasing the stock. When buying and selling rights, carefully consider the costs involved. Although no brokerage fees are involved when exercising rights, buying and selling them is quite another story.

Warrants

A warrant is an option to buy a specific number of shares of a security at a set price for a specified length of time. The price at which the warrant can be exercised is fixed above the market price of the security at the time the warrant is issued. Time periods specified are relatively long, usually ranging from 5 years to perpetuity. Most often warrants are issued as an inducement to purchase other securities of a corporation. Bonds, for instance, packaged with warrants can often be sold at a lower interest rate than just the bond alone.

Warrants sound, in many ways, like call options and indeed are similar. The major differences are only one set exercise price and the length of time involved. Like options, buying warrants is pure speculation. Unless the price of the stock is above the exercise price set, warrants expire worthless. The real value of warrants is simply the difference between the exercise price and the current market price of the stock involved. Market value of warrants reflects the real value, if any, plus or minus the general consensus of traders as to whether or not the price of the stock will exceed the exercise price.

For the investor, warrants offer the attraction of leverage. In many cases, limited capital can be used to good advantage through trading in warrants. If you have developed an effective common stock system, you should be able to identify characteristics of corporations whose warrants may be wise investments. The decision is simple—buy only the warrants of common stocks that you would purchase if more capital was available!

The financial world abounds in investment vehicles, many of which we have not even mentioned here. Preferred stocks, debentures, mutual funds, T-Bills, GMAs, futures, commodities—the list is endless. We have neither the space nor expertise to discuss them here. Bonds, mentioned only in passing, are an excellent investment vehicle during certain types of market conditions.

There is literally an investment vehicle to suit every taste. A quick look through the investment section of your local bookstore or library will give you some idea of the amount of information available. Specialty magazines, newsletters and advisory services are all sources of information not to be overlooked in your search for a suitable method of increasing your wealth.

Some methods of investing are better suited to personal computer use than others, but application software is woefully lacking. By carefully applying the methodical steps outlined throughout this volume, you should be able to develop relevant programs for use in whatever investment medium you select.

CAN COMPUTER USE BE UNPROFITABLE?

Yes, indeed! Simply having the use of a computer for your investment program is no guarantee of success. In spite of all its capability, your computer is inherently stupid! What other machine can you think of that does nothing on its own but sit there and wait for instructions? It is the quality of instructions, rather than stupidity of the computer, at the root of most unprofitable situations.

Let's "bite the bullet" and consider, over the next several paragraphs, some situations that can clearly contribute to unprofitable use of your computer.

The computer itself can become an end rather than the means to accomplish your goals and objectives. Getting mired in the mechanics of your system is an understandable part of initially learning the care and feeding of a computer. Each time a new peripheral or capacity is added to your system, more learning is necessary. Before useful work can be done, however, this learning must have taken place and primary consideration given to the task at hand.

Badly underusing the capacity of your computer system implies that you overbought initially. Spending $5000 on a deluxe four-color word processing quality high speed line printer to produce a once a week list of ten stocks to buy is definitely overkill! If your primary computer use is investment management, be objective in determining the capacity you need and closely monitor cost effectiveness.

Failing to take into account all the expenses involved can compound losses. Not only the computer related expenses of hardware, software and materials should be considered. Taxes, brokerage fees, publications, advisory services, and other related expenses must be also be added to your investment program overhead.

Over-complicating your investment program so that you no longer understand every detail can lead to disaster. This usually results from trying to change program parameters to fit every small shift in market conditions. You must be able to recognize when your computer is leading you astray. When that happens, carefully re-examine your basic approach and the program before attempting to make any changes.

Depending too much on the computer instead of your own common sense can be a real danger. On the other hand, making subjective dicisions in the "heat of battle" that are completely incompatible with your carefully outlined and tested objective approach can be worse. Learn to walk the fine line between these two extremes and you may reverse the profit picture rapidly.

Failing to recognize clear cut, objective signs of inadequate preparation and bad judgement can be costly. There is little excuse for not testing a program as thoroughly as possible prior to use. Unexpected problems may surface later and must be recognized quickly. Similarly, bad stock selection methods, poor timing decisions, and other unforseen complications must be constantly anticipated.

You may be one of the primary reasons for the problem. Have you lost the motivation to maintain records and use your approach as it was designed? Do you jump from one approach to another at every shift in the market? Has the novelty of using your computer worn off? Do you need to start over and completely redesign your investment approach? Would you? Would your approach be more successful without the use of a computer?

The question asked at the beginning of this section may be a little misleading, since your computer is utterly incapable of making or losing money on its own. The actions you take as the result of using your computer are final determinants of whether or not profits are obtained. There are times in any investment program when profits are nonexistent and a defensive posture of limiting losses must be adopted. The secret of remaining on the plus side of the profit picture is recognizing whether losses are a relatively temporary or chronically permanent state of affairs.

WHEN AND WHY TO REVISE YOUR THINKING

There are times and reasons to change your investment approach regardless of profit and loss considerations. In the last section we explored some reasons for unprofitability and will take a more positive tone here. There are many investors who subscribe to the philosophy, "If it works, don't touch it!". Since we are dealing with a very personalized approach and more computer capability than we are likely using at the moment, perhaps the more appropriate philosophy would be, "How can I make a good able use of your computer?"

Over the next few paragraphs, some legitimate situations for revision will be identified. No doubt you will be able to think of several others that would prompt you to change your own thinking.

A significant change in investment goals and objectives may be noted. The happiest of these is, of course, that all your original goals have now been achieved and you are determined to reach for bigger and better things. Changing interests may also require a different approach. Going from common stocks to options or bonds may not require as radical a change as switching from stocks to commodities or futures, but in either case your approach will have to be altered. Periodic reassessment of investment goals and objectives is necessary if you are to prevent your program from stagnating.

Your personal situation may also have changed. If you have, for instance, spent some time building up capital through dollar cost averaging and are now prepared to assume more risk, a change is in order. Family demands, income requirements and other factors related to you, as an investor, may cause some serious revision of your approach. As mentioned earlier, anticipating changes in your personal situation early enough can make revision of your investment program much easier than trying to adjust at the last possible minute.

Additional sophistication can be added to your investment program when your computer skills have grown sufficiently. Actual investment experience allows you to be more sensitive to subtle condition changes. Hardware and software capability of your system may also have grown significantly, allowing much more involved application programs to be run.

Your investment approach is not consistently producing the anticipated results. After insuring that enough time has been allowed to prove or disprove the effectiveness of your system, revision may be necessary. Perhaps you are receiving an overall return of 10% when at least 20% was anticipated. A little fine tuning may be just what is needed to remedy the problem. Perhaps you can increase the overall yield to a more acceptable figure by selling call options on stock you plan to hold, switching stock group emphasis or investing in more volatile issues. If your approach is consistently providing the desired rate of return, how can even better results be achieved?

If you can identify a specific area in your investment program where a problem has surfaced, definitely revise your thinking there! Other areas where your approach could be strengthened will become evident from time to time and should be considered. Change for the sake of change should be avoided. By carefully considering all the implications of a planned improvement to your system and thoroughly testing the improvements made, positive results will usually come from strengthening the weak areas in your system.

Finally, a radical change in your thinking is needed when everyone else agrees with you! Granted, this may happen occasionally, but if it gets to be a chronic problem—start all over again. Keep in mind that most thundering herds are on their way to slaughter! One of your primary investment goals should be to get in ahead of the crowd and out just as they are arriving.

SUMMARY

Summarizing an entire volume in just a couple of pages can be difficult, at best. Rather than attempt to repeat the information already presented, let me outline a few thoughts on what we have covered and relate them to the whole picture of what we are all trying to accomplish.

As I told you in the first chapter, my efforts at computerized investment management have not yielded (as yet) any great fortunes. They haven't lost any, either! By proceeding slowly and deliberately, each new program and revision has been a valuable learning experience for me. My own investment program has benefited greatly by the writing of this book, since I have been forced to follow my own suggestions and define my goals and objectives much more carefully than I ever had before.

Since we have discussed at great length a concept that can be reduced to three words, let's summarize on the basis of those three words—*Personal investment approach*.

Start by learning more about yourself. Judging your own reactions in a particular situation is difficult unless you have been there before. Normally level-headed people have been known to succumb to the excitement of chasing a stock price upward in a big rally, only to sell at a loss when the rally has fizzled. Not me, you say? Are you sure? I thought so too, but suffice to say I speak from experience! Take full advantage of your personal strengths and build compensations for your weaknesses into the system. In order to construct a personal investment approach, you must know all about the person!

The word personal was also attached to the computers we discussed. A computer becomes truly personal as the result of your selecting the appropriate hardware and learning to use it effectively. Dedicating a computer to personal use implies that the user has decided to go through the trials and tribulations necessary to consummate the partnership. The single most effective way to learn about your computer is to *use it*! Reading about how a computer works, watching it work, making it work and finding out why it won't work are separate and distinctly different learning experiences. Of the four, the latter two will prove most valuable.

Investment vehicles have been pretty much limited to common stocks, more as an example than a recommendation. If your preference lies in related areas such as bonds, options, or commodities many of the same principles apply. Hopefully, you will have built enough flexibility into your selection process that alternate forms of investment can be easily accommodated. As a starting point and solid foundation for further growth and development, the area of simple buying and selling of common stocks will prove a worthy challenge.

And then there's the approach. There is no shortage of people willing to share their method of making millions with you. The bookshelves are loaded with $9.95 keys to the secret of becoming filthy rich with little capital and no effort. Many of the methods described did indeed work—for that individual, under those conditions and involved some pretty gigantic lucky breaks. We've all read at least one of those books, right? Keep in mind that fortunes can also be made $9.95 at a time! If I knew how to make millions in the market, I sure as hell wouldn't waste my time writing books!

Perhaps the most noteworthy thing that can be said of the approach outlined here is that it puts the responsibility clearly where it belongs—on you. The process of constructing a viable approach has been presented, and methods of incorporating computer use have been suggested.

Constructing your own investment approach is not an easy process, as you have seen. Don't expect 100% success from the start, but learn to view each failure as a learning experience and obstacle that will not be encountered again. You are developing a unique system that needs to be fine tuned for maximum effectiveness. Start with your best effort and build from there. Study, learn, read and try every possible alternative. Use whatever you can find that has already been done by someone else if it fits your specific application. Or, as Don Lancaster succinctly put it in a recent issue of *Microcomputing,* "Don't reinvent the wheel—steal the plans instead".

Accepting mediocrity in your investment approach is quitting prematurely. Sure, it's difficult to rewrite a marginal program or make major changes in your system. The tedium of acquiring more data or carefully reviewing historical figures can be overwhelming at times. Isolating the causes of mediocre performance require a careful examination of all the parameters of your approach, an ambitious project indeed. Sound the charge, load your guns and attack the villians of mediocrity at every opportunity!

Document, document, document! Extensive notes of where you have been and what was done are an absolute necessity. Programs that seem clear today may not be as obvious to you a year from now. Learn to keep records on every aspect of your investment approach. Jot down possible revisions, thoughts for subsequent programs and the minutest details of what you are doing. Invariably, good documentation proves sooner or later to be worth its weight in gold!

The tone of this book has been quite serious throughout, a rather unavoidable state of affairs when trying to pack as much information as possible into one volume. I would hasten to remind you, however, that a good sense of humor will be your best ally throughout your investment experience. Being able to laugh at dumb mistakes we all make, seeing the humor in little disasters and enjoying what you are doing will go a long way toward relieving the inevitable tensions that develop.

The path we are attempting to tread by integrating personal computers into investment management approaches has been travelled by precious few so far. No doubt many others will follow as hardware and software become more available. There's no time like the present to get moving and beat the crowd! Good Luck!

Chapter 9

The Nuts And Bolts
of Computer Operation

For those unacquainted with personal computer use, this chapter will cover some of the "nuts and bolts" items that need to be considered. If you have owned your computer for some time, some of the hints noted here may help to solve problems you have experienced.

SETTING UP YOUR COMPUTER

Most of the information needed to properly plug in the cables and get your computer running is contained in the manuals received with your system. We will not attempt to duplicate that here, but will instead concentrate our efforts on what the manuals don't cover.

Location is an important consideration. Using the kitchen table may be convenient at times, but either the computer is moved regularly or it ends up with a screen full of lasagna! For infrequent use it may be acceptable to assemble the system from storage each time, but regular users need to have the computer in a readily accessible location. If you have the space, the computer should be left fully assembled and ready for use at a moments notice. Look carefully around your house or apartment— chances are there is some suitable location at hand.

If you have a choice of locations, there are several factors that should be considered. Avoid areas near windows because of the problems created by glare and strong sunlight. Ideally, there should be sufficient space to allow for some storage of books and materials. If you have small children, an out of the way spot may discourage using your system as a toy. For night owls, like myself, it is advisable to locate your computer as far from the family sleeping area as possible.

Once you have selected a location, certain facilities must be provided. First, of course, is a desk or table of sufficient size to hold your computer and all the associated paraphernalia. At least part of the surface should be a convenient typing height for your keyboard. There are some attractive commercial desks with cutouts for keyboards, cable tracks, disk drive spaces and monitor shelves made especially for personal computers. The manufacturer of your system may offer such a desk, others can be located in magazine ads or mail-order catalogs. Most any desk or table of sufficient size can be pressed into service for your computer. A handy formula for estimating the size needed is to take the area you think is sufficient for now and double it!

A file or storage cabinet should be available to hold supplies of paper, disks, manuals, etc. Bookshelves may be constructed inexpensively and will definitely help solve some of your storage problems. A comfortable chair is a definite plus, particularly when you are at the keyboard for an extended period of time. I find the adjustable height secretarial chair works best for me. Lighting should be sufficient for easy reading, but not so harsh as to cause a glare on the video display screen. Overhead flourescent or one of the adjustable arm desk lamps should work very well.

If the number of outlets available in the immediate area is limited, consider adding one of the multiple outlet power strips available. Most of these have a separate fuse or circuit breaker and allow you to turn on all your equipment with one switch. Be sure your electrical service is grounded and of sufficient capacity to carry whatever current your system demands. Most computers and accessories do not consume huge amounts of power, so ordinary household circuits usually suffice.

Many accessories are available for added convenience. Printer stands, for instance, often offer paper storage and baskets to catch printouts before they have a chance to tangle in your lap. Disk or cassette storage files offer the advantages of protection and easy accessibility of programs. Extension cables allow separation of components as needed. Readability of your display may be enhanced by a shade or filter, both readily available. Dust covers are worth their weight in gold and should be one of the first accessories you consider. For traveling, custom fitted carrying cases will protect your investment.

In summary, your computer should be located in a spot that is both convenient and readily accessible. Facilities should be such that both you and the computer have whatever you need to function efficiently.

GETTING ACQUAINTED

As mentioned earlier in this book, one of the best ways to get acquainted with your computer is to use it! Sit down with the manuals in hand and immediately apply what you are reading. Reading about a procedure is one thing, doing it is quite another. Actually seeing the results of each step you take is very effective reinforcement of what is explained in the manuals. Press all the buttons, try some new steps, see what happens if you do this or that. The chances of your breaking anything are miniscule compared to the amount of learning that will take place!

Once you have reached the end of the manuals, try running some programs. Chances are that some programs were furnished by the manufacturer. If not, a visit to your local computer store is in order. Buy a few simple programs that look interesting and run them often enough to be comfortable with the operation of your computer.

The next step is writing a simple program or two of your own. No need to be elaborate at this stage of the game, just a few lines will do for a start. If you have had no prior programming experience, just creating a simple program that will run is quite a thrill. As your programming experience grows, more elaborate and complex programs will certainly follow. For now, the object of this exercise is to get acquainted with both the computer and languages you have.

Until you feel comfortable with both your computer and its primary programming language, avoid adding accessory peripherals. Learning to use the computer alone is enough for anyone at one time. Life can get unduly complicated if you are trying to absorb too much at once. If you have purchased accessories such as a printer, disk drive, modem, etc., add them to your system one at a time following the same learning procedure for each.

No doubt you are anxious to put your computer system to work helping you to manage your investment program. Rest assured you are not wasting time by getting well acquainted with your computer and accessories. The background provided by this process will be a definite help when you are trying to run, or write, your investment application software.

USING PERIPHERAL DEVICES

There are many peripherals commonly added to basic personal computer systems. Some, like a video display, are necessary to begin operation of the unit. Others can provide capabilities that will be of great help in your own applications.

A printer, regarded by some as a necessity, can greatly enhance your operational capabilities. Just the ability to list programs on paper can be a big help in your programming efforts. My first printer was a Teletype(tm) ASR-33 which did an admirable job of providing program listings and simple correspondence. Presently I am using a dot-matrix unit that prints bidirectionally at 125 characters per second, has upper and lower case characters and offers form feed. New and better printers are being introduced for the personal computing market almost daily. It is now possible to puchase a very capable printer for well under $1000.

In operation, most printers are remarkably simple. Output from the computer is directed to the printer instead of, or in addition to, the video display. The Apple, for instance, uses a PR# command to direct output to a printer interface card. Adding printing capability to your programs is just a matter of inserting the proper command wherever you would like hard copy printed. A few minutes spent getting acquainted should familiarize you with any special features of your printer and the codes necessary to use them. My printer, for example, can change print sizes, vertical format, skip over perforations and vertical tab all under program control. Simple commands from within a program or switch selection on the printer itself will allow you to access any of the options offered by your own unit.

Disk drives, if purchased from the manufacturer of your computer, almost always include a Disk Operating System (DOS). The DOS provides the additional commands necessary for proper operation of the drive, and may include its own version of BASIC or some other language. Multiple drive systems share the same DOS and, in some cases, controller hardware. This accounts for the lower price tags noted for additional disk units.

Operation of disk drives is quite simple, in fact it is easier than most cassettes. A magnetic disk, enclosed in a sheath, is inserted into the door of the drive and the door is closed. Once you have properly initialized the DOS, reading from and writing to the disk is controlled entirely from the keyboard or program. DOS locates and reads or writes the necessary files without having to rewind, count revolutions or handle the disk at all! About all you have to do is change disks once in a while to locate a particular program or file.

Typical commands added for disk operations include CATALOG, LOAD. SAVE, LOCK, UNLOCK, OPEN, CLOSE,

READ, WRITE, DELETE, INITIALIZE, VERIFY, APPEND, RENAME and EXEC. For an explanation of these commands, see the glossary.

Cassette tape storage units are much more reasonable in cost than are disk drives. While operations are somewhat more limited and slower than disk, tape storage does still have a place in your computer operations. Initially, all your programs and files may be stored on tape. Later, as you go to disk storage, tape can provide valuable back-up capability for your files and programs.

Operational commands for tape storage, at least in the Apple, are very simple. Programs are stored and retrieved by the SAVE and LOAD commands. Data arrays use the STORE and RECALL commands for input and output to tape. It remains the responsibility of the operator to locate the proper data on the tape and handle physical operations of the recorder. Unless you are using these commands in the immediate mode from the keyboard, prompts to direct tape operations must be added to your programs or the computer will "hang" for no apparent reason.

While the printer and mass storage unit are the most commonly added peripherals, the list of possibilities is virtually endless. As you add additional peripherals to your system, take time to get well acquainted with each. Often, a peripheral device will affect operation of not only your computer, but also the other peripherals you already have connected. Learning the procedures and obtaining the software necessary to use multiple peripherals can be a time consuming process, but will provide rewards once you have assembled a well integrated system that performs all the functions you have in mind.

ENTERING PROGRAMS

The process of entering programs from the keyboard of your computer is as simple as typing a business letter. If you never make a typographical error, have all the commands in your program completely debugged and know exactly how the computer will react, more power to you. For those of us with ten thumbs on the keyboard and prone to more than occasional error, the next few paragraphs may be of interest.

In writing your own programs, try to format the lines in exactly the same fashion as listings produced by your computer. This means line number on the left, several spaces and then the appropriate commands. Lines intended for video display are more easily constructed on forms designed for that purpose. I use a 24 ×

40 grid outlined on graph paper. Also, commercial forms are available. Clearly include, with exaggeration if necessary, all the required punctuation and syntactical markings. Print or write clearly! By the time you sit down at the keyboard, your program should be completely written and ready for entry. While entering the program, stay alert for any obvious errors and correct them on the written listing while entering them on the keyboard. Proceeding in this fashion allows you to examine all your material twice and significantly reduces the chances of minor errors creeping into your programs.

One of the simplest forms of insurance against losing valuable programs and time is multiple saves during entry. This process is often overlooked by beginners, but rarely by those of us who have lost the fruits of several hours of typing due to unforseen developments. The process couldn't be simpler—just save the material you have entered regularly to tape or disk. For my own purposes, I save a copy to disk about every 25 program lines, deleting the previous copy only after verifying the accuracy of the latest. The copy then insures that I can lose no more than 25 lines of work if the power fails momentarily, I press the wrong keys or some other disaster occurs. It's cheap protection that every programmer should use regularly!

TESTING AND DEBUGGING YOUR PROGRAMS

Identifying and correcting problems in your programs can be made much simpler if you can isolate each subroutine and test it as you go. Plugging in dummy values for variables and actually running each subroutine will point out errors that may not have been obvious during your writing of the program. Identifying problems is much easier in a short subroutine than an entire program. Once you have thoroughly tested and, if necessary, debugged the subroutine, save it on tape or disk and continue the same process for the rest of the program. All the subroutines can then be assembled into a workable program using EXEC, CHAIN or similar commands in your system.

Complex program operations are often difficult to follow on paper. Applesoft, like many other BASIC language variations, allows the user to monitor several parameters during program execution. TRACE, for instance, causes the line number of each statement to be displayed as the statement is executed. MON, in Apple DOS, allows display of commands, input and output from the disk. The BASIC used by your computer probably has similar commands. If you are doing any amount of programming at all, the monitor and trace capabilities of your system will help your problem solving efforts considerably.

Program Editing

The process of modifying, deleting or adding material to a program is known as program editing. Most personal computers have some editing capability, a few have rather extensive systems. Adding new lines or deleting existing ones is the simplest form of editing. New lines may be added at any point in program entry and will appear in proper line number sequence in the listing. Deleting lines is simply a matter of typing the line number and RETURN or ENTER. Modification of or addition to material already contained in program lines gets more complex.

Commands to move the cursor to any desired position on the screen allow modification of whatever is in that position by typing over what is presently there. Deleting or adding characters to program lines can be accomplished in any of several ways, depending on your system. The Apple, for example, requires several cursor moves and a good memory to accomplish these tasks. TRS-80 Level II BASIC has a very capable editing system which allows modification of program lines to be accomplished much more easily.

If your computer has limited program editing capabilities, you may want to consider adding them by using an external editing system. One of the best I have seen for the Apple is the *Program Line Editor* for *Synergistic Software*, 5221 120th Ave. S. E., Bellevue, WA 98006. PLE adds numerous editing and function commands to the Apple without affecting normal operation of the computer in any significant way. Many other editing programs are available for the Apple and most popular personal computers. Check with your dealer, other users of similar systems, or the ads in computer oriented periodicals to find the best editor for your computer. The additional programming flexibility afforded by a good editing program will more than justify the cost involved.

Programming Hints

In Chapters 6 and 7 we discussed some of the background necessary to develop your own investment oriented computer programs. This discussion will be limited to ways to make your programming more efficient and effective. If you have not yet taken the time to write a few programs, do so. As mentioned earlier, the best way to learn programming is to do it!

The importance of documentation cannot be overemphasized. In addition to the written documentation mentioned earlier, liberal use of REM (remark) statements in your program will help follow program logic. Unless you have unlimited memory in your computer, however, REM statements must often be limited to a few words. Developing a set of keyword REMS that you can use in all your programs is well worth the effort. REM JUSTIFY X, for example, can be as meaningful to you as REM PRINT ALL THE VALUES OF X WITH DECIMAL POINTS ALIGNED. If a program with REMs will not fit in the memory you have available, consider deleting the REM statements from the program and storing them in a separate file or in written form.

In addition to deleting REM statements, efficient use of memory available can be enhanced in several ways. Use multiple statements per line wherever possible. Variables are more space efficient than constants, particularly when the same variable is reused several times during the program. Subroutines or user defined functions are preferable to having several sections of the program perform identical operations. Your tape or disk storage can be utilized for storage of information not constantly needed in memory during program execution. If the last few bytes are crucial, consider deleting END if not required in your BASIC, using the zero element of matrices, shortening variable names, etc.

Most likely your efforts at efficient memory utilization will pay an unexpected bonus—an increase in execution speed. Although it will not decrease memory utilization, putting frequently used subroutines at the beginning of your program rather than the end will also significantly increase execution speed. Using common files for several programs, keeping as much data in memory as possible and using variables wherever you can will also speed things up.

Is there a price to be paid for increasing memory efficiency and execution speed? Indeed, there is. Program readability suffers from each of the steps suggested. Modifying or debugging a program that has been "crunched" to use minimal memory space is a very trying process at best. I would suggest that two versions of your program be kept—one heavily documented with REM statements and the other pared to fit memory limitations. If a problem develops, the documented version will be your prime source of helpful information to enable you to modify the abbreviated program. Keeping printed listings of both versions of a program enables you to cross reference them and, in addition, provides back-up insurance in case one or the other of the programs is lost or destroyed.

ADVANCED PROGRAMMING TECHNIQUES

Once you have mastered the fundamentals of using BASIC or other high level language with your computer, advanced programming techniques may be considered. Although we will certainly not exhaust the list of possibilities here, perhaps this section will give you a few ideas of things to include in future programs.

Machine language programming offers advantages of flexibility and speed over higher level languages. Each instruction used by the microprocessor can, and must, be specified in machine language programs. Actually, higher level languages are machine language routines which must execute not only the user instruction, but also the process for accomplishing the process designated in that instruction. It is apparent that machine language programs will execute much faster due to their having to handle only one level of commands. Memory efficiency is also a real strength of machine language programs.

A proficient machine language programmer can get around the constraints imposed by higher level languages. Constructing machine language subroutines to accomplish specific tasks that are difficult, lengthy or impossible in higher level languages is getting increasingly popular in commercial programs. Recently, magazine articles describing ways to augment your BASIC by adding features in machine language have been published. I have noticed, for instance, that procedures for adding a PRINT USING command, screen printing and extended editing capabilities to Applesoft have been published recently.

If it is such a simple process, why are we considering machine language programming in an advanced techniques discussion? Learning to use machine language effectively is a rather complex process that requires initimate knowledge of both the processor and programming techniques. For those willing to make the necessary effort, machine language programming opens exciting new vistas in computer capability.

Graphics is another area ripe for use in investment oriented programs. Stock charts, visual comparisons of results, trend lines and interaction of various factors are all good possibilities for the enterprising graphics programmer. Some personal computers have outstanding graphics capability which is fairly easy for the user to program. All computers are capable of limited graphic displays, although more resourcefulness is needed to program them.

Color graphics capability further expands the range of possibilities. Color coded moving averages on a graph, for instance, are much easier to identify than those merely labelled. If you have a color capable computer (Apple, TI-99/4, etc.) and video display, experiment with color coded data or graphic displays. Try it, you'll like it!

Often, programming graphic displays is a relatively complex process. Commercial programs and hardware to make the job easier are available. Several graphic utility programs are described in the software directory, many others are available. Graphic input tablets and light pens offer a way of directly inputting shapes and data for later display. Both accessories are presently offered for most popular personal computers.

Graphic overlays can also be very helpful at times. If your computer can be programmed to construct two or more "pages" of graphic display, superimposing one on the other is extremely effective in visualizing comparison data. A logical extension of graphics is animation. There are some circumstances where being able to see dynamic interaction between factors is a distinct advantage. Comparing price action of a stock against a market average, for instance, can be vividly portrayed by actually seeing the curves interact in real time.

Sound (usually a nondescript beep) is used in many computers for advising the operator of errors, verifying keystrokes, storage prompts, etc. The presence of a speaker and sound routines leads to many other interesting programming possibilities. With a little programming ingenuity, these computers can literally talk back to you. Commercial programs and add-on hardware, if necessary, can be combined with your programs to create voice and music routines.

FUN AND GAMES

For the most part, our approach to investment management programs has been on the serious side in this book. Beginning programmers tend to take their efforts seriously and create no nonsense programs that do little more than get the job done. This is as it should be, since the primary goal in designing an investment system is to create a businesslike approach. More advanced programmers, having adequately fulfilled the initial goals for their programs, tend to embellish them with more finishing touches. There is nothing to prevent a program from being both effective and fun to use.

If you feel the urge, why not enclose your screen displays in a fancy filigree? An animated character on the screen to give you a round of applause for a market coup or an emphatic thumbs down for a disaster may be just what you need to maintain the proper perspective! How about a rousing chorus of *We're in the money* or a "raspberry" from the speaker to reinforce profits and losses respectively? Let your imagination run wild and add some fun touches to your programs. In addition to helping maintain interest in using the program, these little extras will certainly impress the next friend who asks, "What can you do with a little computer?" If you are concerned with maintaining decorum when others are present, add an option to turn off the frivolity when it is not needed.

PLANNING FOR THE FUTURE

Your programming efforts should be designed for future expansion and modification as interests and capabilities change. The prospect of having to completely rewrite a lengthy program to accommodate a new peripheral or technique is downright unappealing at times. This section will discuss some techniques for making the inevitable future changes easier.

Line numbering in relatively large increments, or leaving periodic gaps in line number sequence makes adding new lines a simple process. Instead of the usual 1,2,3, or even 10,20,30 sequence, consider using 100,200,300 for those programs subject to later change. If necessary, most programs can be renumbered by the computer. The renumbering process becomes cumbersome, however, in relatively sophisticated programs with referenced line numbers in program statements.

Variables are much easier to redefine when their initial use and function are carefully documented, either by REM statements in the program or in written form. Similarly, it is much easier to modify user defined functions than recurrent mathematical operations. Maximum possible use of subroutines for recurrent program operations is not only good programming technique, but provides an opportunity to easily modify portions of the program. If memory permits, each subroutine should be preceeded by REM statements explaining its function.

Stretching the limits of available memory with a program makes later expansion nearly impossible. It is far better to have some free memory left for future development. Often it is possible to break a lengthy program into two or three smaller programs which share common data files and are selected by a short menu program. Similarly, data files should be structured with an eye toward future expansion. Leaving a few extra bytes in random access records, not completely filling a disk or tape with data files and making data formats as universal as possible are some ways future applications can be accommodated.

The process of writing an investment management system program is one that really never ends. Although the initial effort may perform up to your expectations, advances in programming knowledge and hardware sophistication have a way of raising expectations. If you have been diligent in providing for modification of your system, the program sophistication can be raised to meet these new expectations. After each program modification, take some time to make a list of capabilities you would like to see in your system at some future date. Periodically refer to that list and add those items as hardware and software become available.

KEEPING UP

The entire field of personal computer use is literally flooded with new and important information. Numerous publications are devoted to specific computers or application interests. It is nearly impossible to keep up with the constant flow of material. On the other hand, as a computer owner and user it is important that you be aware of new developments.

User groups may be found in many areas and provide a good source of information and ideas. Subscribing to one or more of the periodicals listed in Appendix B can also be of great value. The common denominator I find most valuable is contact with other computer owners, either face-to-face or through articles and books. Whether your computer is only an investment tool or used for many other purposes, information must flow to prevent stagnation of ideas.

SUMMARY

We've discussed some of the "nuts and bolts" of computer use and neglected many others. By the time you read this, advancement of both hardware and software technology will have taken another leap forward. Not to worry! In every field of human endeavor, there will always be experts and beginners. It is safe to assume that every expert was a beginner at some time. Whether you are an expert or just beginning to learn about personal computers, don't let the technology intimidate you.

If there is a message to be gleaned from this section, it is this—don't be afraid to try! Using a computer is a process completely foreign to most of us initially. Managing investments with a computer, particularly when designing your own approach, compounds the problem. We all have a lot yet to learn about this whole business. Learning takes place with experience, and experience is gained by doing.

Take your computer in hand and gain some experience. Failures that take place along the way are every bit as valuable as learning experiences as successes. In a surprisingly short time, you will feel comfortable with the computer and be ready to take on new and exciting application projects. If you have a sound investment concept in mind, the mechanics of transforming that approach into a computerized system will surely follow.

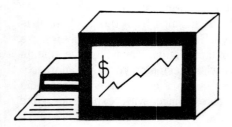

Glossary of Computer Terms

In this glossary, we will discuss some of the terminology associated with personal computers. Most of the terms included will be those actually discussed or referred to in the text. The terms printed in all capital letters are abbreviations or statements used in BASIC programming. Wherever possible, the simplest definition of each term will be used.

access—The process of obtaining data from or placing data in storage. Also used to denote the process of gaining the use of another computer or program via remote linkage.

accuracy—Used in the context of a record keeping system, accuracy refers to the ability of the system to maintain the desired degree of precision.

adaptibility—The degree to which a program or system can be easily modified to suit the requirements of differing applications.

alpha—A term used to denote alphabetical characters. Often expanded to Alphanumeric, in which case it includes both alphabetical and numeric characters.

AND—When used to join conditions in a conditional branching statement, both expressions must evaluate as true in order for the branch to take place. For example, IF X=0 AND Y=0 THEN STOP. Both X and Y must be equal to 0 for the STOP statement to execute.

APPEND—In most disk operating systems, this command allows the user to add information to the end of a sequential text file. Using APPEND opens a file and sets the pointer to the next byte beyond the last one presently in the file.

APL—A Programming Language developed by Iverson. Features an extensive set of operators and data structures in a flexible, powerful and concise arithmetic procedural language.

Applesoft (tm)—A floating point, extended BASIC developed for the Apple II computer. Enhancements have been added to take advantage of the Apple's sound and graphics capabilities. Available on tape, disk or ROM for use in various configurations.

applicability—The extent to which a program or system actually does what it is proportedly intended to do. One of the better ways to evaluate applicability is using the program or system with known data and results, comparing the output obtained with the known results.

application software—Programs designed to perform certain functions in a specific application. Investment management programs, payroll systems and word processing programs are a few examples of application software.

array—A block of subscripted variables. May be one, two or multi-dimensional in most systems. Most commonly, one or two dimension arrays are used to provide convenient access to tables of numbers. DIM A(15), for instance, sets aside room in memory for an array containing elements A(0) through A(15).

ASCII—American Standard Code for Information Interchange. Specific bit patterns are assigned for numbers, letters, symbols, signs and operations.

assembler—A computer program which generally translates symbolic input codes into machine instructions, item for item.

back-up—A second copy of a program or file created for the express purpose of insuring continuity of operations if the original copy is lost or destroyed.

BASIC—Beginners All-purpose Symbolic Instruction Code, a programming language developed at Dartmouth College in 1963. BASIC is relatively easy to learn and use. Available in many versions, this language has become the mainstay of the personal computing world. Presently, some version of BASIC is available for virtually every personal computer on the market.

bidirectional print—Printing not only in the normal left to right sequence, but also on the return right to left travel. Bidirectional capability increases the throughput of most printers by eliminating the wasted return travel of the printhead or carriage.

binary digit—A numerical representation in the binary (base 2) scale of notation. The digit may be only 1 or 0 (on or off, yes or no). All numbers used internally by a computer are binary digits. Often abbreviated to Bit.

block—Used to describe input/output or working areas in main memory of a computer (memory block). Also applied to a group of consecutive characters considered or transferred as a unit (data block).

bomb—A slang expression describing the complete failure of a program or system, usually with disastrous results.

boot—A technique for initiating entry into programs or operating systems. Also used in the context of "bootstrap," which describes a program or system that automatically loads other information necessary to obtain the desired operation.

bootleg—Refers to the copy of a program under less than honorable circumstances. An unauthorized copy of a commercial program is usually considered in this category unless it is created by the program purchaser for the singular purpose of having a back-up copy for his own use. Bootleggers are those who make and distribute unauthorized copies of commercial programs, usually at a price substantially below that of the original program copied.

branch—Departure from the normal sequence of executing instructions in a computer program. Also a sequence of instructions executed as a result of a decision instruction (conditional branch).

bug—A mistake in the design or coding of a program which interferes with proper operation. Also known by several unmentionable names, especially if encountered in expensive commercial or complex, lengthy user generated programs.

bus—A circuit used for the transmission of data or power in a computer. Several different bus designs are found in personal computing systems, few of which are compatible with each other. The S-100 bus is probably the closest approximation of a standard at the present time.

byte—A measurable portion of consecutive binary digits (bits). Most personal computers recognize 8 bit bytes.

CALL—A statement that causes execution of a machine language subroutine located at the memory address specified following CALL. For example, CALL -936 causes the Apple to clear all text in the video display window and return the cursor to the upper left (home) position.

capability—Refers to the operational potential of a computer system in terms of memory size, execution speed, peripherals attached, etc. Graphics capability, for instance, means a computer has the hardware and operating system which enables it to produce graphic displays.

card—A printed circuit board used for mounting of electronic components. Often the complete board with components is referred to by function, such as serial interface card.

carrier—A tone used to convey information in telecomputing applications. The carrier tone is transmitted by the host computer to an acoustic coupler, received by an acoustic coupler on the users end.

cassette tape—Mass storage for personal computing applications is often accomplished with tapes and recorders as used for audio applications. The computer transmits data by tones to the tape recorder for storage, and converts these tones back to data on input from the tape unit.

CATALOG—In disk based systems, this command displays the names of files contained on the specified disk.

CHAIN—A command used from within a BASIC program to call another program for immediate execution.

chip—A slang expression used to denote integrated circuits. Usually used with a qualifier to indicate the function of the circuit, i.e., memory chip, etc.

CHR$(X)—Returns the ASCII character corresponding to the numeric value specified by X. Of course, X must be within the range of 0 to 255 which encompasses all the ASCII codes.

CLEAR—In Applesoft, sets all variables to zero and strings to null values. TRS-80 Level II BASIC resets the variables to zero and can set aside the number of bytes specified by a constant or expression following CLEAR.

clock/calendar card—A printed circuit card which may be installed in a computer for the purpose of providing real time information. Data from the card is retrieved with a machine language or BASIC subroutine for insertion into various operations.

CLOSE—A command indicating termination of read or write operations in a particular file, usually on a disk based storage system. When CLOSE is executed, memory buffer space for operations to that file is deallocated by the disk operating system.

COBOL—COmmon Business Oriented Language. A relatively sophisticated programming language not yet generally available for personal computing systems, although it is commonly used in larger systems.

communication—As used in the text, refers to the process of exchanging data between two computers, or terminals and a host computer. Communication circuits may be hardwired (connected permanently) on site or accomplished remotely through telephone line or radio linkage.

conditional branch—A sequence of instructions executed within a program as the result of a decision instruction. IF-THEN commands in BASIC are one way of initiating a conditional branch.

conditioned line—A telephone line which has been modified for computer communications. Modifications may include frequency response, background noise and close control of transmission levels.

connect time—The actual time that communication has been established between two computers, or a computer and terminal. This figure is used to determine user charges in telecomputing systems and may differ considerably from CPU time.

CONT—BASIC abbreviation for continue, causes program execution to resume after being halted by STOP or a similar instruction.

cost effectiveness—The extent to which a personal computer, in this context, amortizes its initial and operating expenses by providing significantly greater profits or time savings.

countdown timer—A circuit or program that measures the progress of actual time between two events. May be part of a real-time clock system that measures in time of day units or an independent system that measures in specified units of time.

CPU—Central Processing Unit. The principle and most basic unit of the computer where actual manipulation of data occurs. Although it can, the CPU does not necessarily consist of only one chip. In most personal computers, the CPU is identified by the type of microprocessor chip it contains, i.e., 6502, Z80, etc.

CPU time—The actual amount of time the central processing unit was engaged in operations for a particular program or user. Although it is rarely used in personal computing applications, this figure becomes important in telecomputing and time share applications where billing is done on the basis of hours, minutes or seconds of CPU time used.

crash—Similar to bomb, this expression is often used to describe the dynamic failure of a computer or peripheral. Another of the few socially acceptable words one can use in that type of situation.

CRT—Abbreviation for Cathode Ray Tube, used in computer applications to describe the video display of computer output on a television type screen.

CTRL—The Control key. Used in conjunction with other keys on a computer keyboard to generate distinctive ASCII codes for functions.

cursor—A distinctive block or line on a video display which is used to indicate the current screen position being addressed.

DATA—Creates a list of elements to be used by READ statements in a program.

data base—Information stored as data items, usually in the form of records in a file.

data base management—A systematic approach to the updating, retrieval and storage of information stored in a data base. In larger systems, many on-site or remote users may share the same data base and management programs.

debug—The process of locating and correcting any operational errors in a program, operating system or computer hardware.

DEF FN(X)—Allows the user to define functions to be used in a program. Once a function in defined, it may be used repeatedly throughout a program.

deferred execution commands—Operational statements which will be executed during program operation.

DELETE (DEL)—When followed by a line number or two numbers separated by a comma, deletes the specified line or range of lines from a program in memory. Deleting a single line may also be accomplished by typing the line number followed by return. In disk based systems, DELETE followed by a file name deletes that file from the disk. Some versions of BASIC allow the abbreviation DEL, others require the full term be typed.

DIM—Sets aside space for arrays with subscripts specified in the dimension statement. Some versions of BASIC also require the maximum length for each string variable used in the program to be specified in dimension statements.

directory file—A specific file which describes the layout of other records within a file or on a disk.

disk—A storage device on which information is recorded on the revolving surface of a magnetized disk. Most personal computer disk systems are known as "floppy disk", as opposed to the rigid disk packs used in large systems. Floppy disks are thin, magnetized disks encased in a sheath which may be readily inserted and removed from a disk drive. Also classified as to size, floppy disks are eight inches in diameter, mini-floppies five and a quarter inches in diameter.

documentation—In personal computing usage, refers to the information accompanying a program. If a commercial program is being considered, documentation is usually provided in the form of a users manual which contains instructions, description of operations, possible modifications, etc. User generated programs also require careful documentation in the form of notes, program listings, sources of data, etc. Documentation can also be provided within a program itself through the liberal use of remark (REM) statements.

DOS—Disk Operating System. A group of programs designed to handle input and output functions, keep track of files and manage all other operations associated with the use of a disk based storage system.

Some DOS routines are supplied in ROM, others must be loaded from the disk itself.

dot-matrix printer—An electrostatic, photographic or wire printer in which characters are formed from individual dots, usually a 5 × 7 dot matrix.

downloading—The process of transferring programs or information from a host computer to a user unit capable of running the program or manipulating the data received.

duplex—A method of operating a communications circuit so that each end can simultaneously transmit *and* receive (full duplex), or either end can transmit *or* receive at one time (half duplex).

editor—A program or system used to add, delete, modify, rearrange and test data or information. Many types of editors are available for use with personal computers. Simple screen editing functions are built in to most microcomputers. The Program Line Editor, mentioned in the text, provides extensive editing functions for programs written in Apple Basic. Similar systems are available for most other popular computers and languages.

efficiency—The degree to which program utilizes fully the operational and memory capacity of a computer during its operation. Also the savings in time and increased work capacity provided by the use of a particular program or system.

EIA interface—A set of standards specified by the Electonic Industries Association for signal characteristics necessary to successfully connect pieces of equipment.

electronic mail—The transmission of correspondence by electronic, rather than written, means. Several telecomputing systems offer the personal computer user the opportunity to address messages to other users and receive messages addressed to him through electronic means. Corporate computers operated by a network of remote terminals are routinely used in the same fashion.

element—An item contained in an array. Elements in array are identified by subscripts which describe their location in terms of the number of dimensions in the array.

ELSE—Followed by a statement or line number, ELSE specifies an alternative action in case the IF test fails in an IF-THEN statement. Some versions of BASIC permit the use of ELSE, others automatically skip to the next program line if the IF test fails.

END—Causes a program to cease execution and returns control of the computer to the user. Not all versions of BASIC require END at the conclusion of a program, but only a few bytes are saved by its exclusion.

EPROM—Erasable Programmable Read Only Memory. A form of memory chip that can be both programmed and erased by following specific procedures outlined for the type of device. One form of EPROM uses electrical charges for programming and ultra-violet light exposure for erasure.

ERROR—A message displayed by a computer upon encountering an unacceptable condition in program or peripheral operations. Most personal computers will display error messages related to syntax, memory full, input/output operations, lack of data, illegal processes, undefined statement or functions.

error trapping—The process of examining, by decision statements, the data input to program prompts with the intention of allowing the user an opportunity to correct the error condition. Simple error trapping includes type of data, number ranges, excessive or inadequate responses, etc. Error trapping must be incorporated in the design of a program, since many program related errors will not cause the computer to display an ERROR condition. Good programming technique calls for consideration of all the possible input responses and trapping for the inappropriate possibilities.

ESC—The Escape key, usually used in conjunction with some other key to accomplish a desired control function. ESC does generate a distinctive ASCII code which can be used, despite the fact that it does not print, for various program operations. Many personal computer programs use the ESC key as an input trigger to end the program, print a page, etc.

execution time—The sum total of time required to complete one or a set of instructions.

exponential notation—Also known as scientific notation, refers to the display of numbers as a fractional part followed by a power of ten scaling factor. For example, 200 could also be written as 2E+02. Most personal computers will display numbers beyond their range of accuracy in exponential form.

expression—A series of constants, variables or functions that may be connected by operational symbols and punctuation to cause a desired computation to take place.

file—A collection of related information treated as a unit. A program file is one which contains all the statements necessary to execute a program. Text files contain data which is used in the course of executing a program. See also Random Access File and Sequential Access File.

FLASH—Sets the Apple video display mode to alternately change from normal to inverse video (white on black to black on white).

floating point—A system of number representation in which quantities are represented by a number multiplied by the number base raised to a power. (Also known as Exponential or Scientific Notation.)

floppy disk—A flexible plastic disk which is coated with a magnetic material and enclosed in a sheath. In size designation, usually refers to an eight inch flexible disk.

flowchart—A graphic representation of a sequence of operations by using symbols to represent the operations. Programs are often outlined in flowcharts for ease of understanding fully the options involved in actual operation. Flowcharts are also helpful to programmers designing the necessary conditional branching and flow of control statements.

FOR—NEXT—Used to construct a loop which will perform any instructions between FOR and NEXT a specified number of times. STEP may be added, if desired, to increment the loop at a rate other than the implied +1 contained in most BASICs. For example, FOR I = 1 TO 10: PRINT: NEXT I, will execute 10 print statements and then pass control to the next statement following NEXT.

foreground/background processing—The ability to process a high priority foreground program and a subsidiary program during the times the foreground program is not using the CPU. An example of this might be an investment program which is used in the foreground and a temperature control system which uses the CPU only infrequently for minor adjustments of a thermostat in the background. In this instance, the temperature control system could generate an interrupt which would allow it access to the CPU only when status of a sensor changed.

form feed—The capability of a printer to handle paper produced on continuous fan-folded strips or rolls. Also a control character which causes such a printer to begin printing on a new sheet.

format—A predetermined arrangement of characters, lines, fields, etc. Refers to the display capabilities of a video display and the arrangement of printed information on a page. Video display formats are usually expressed in terms of the number of lines vertically and the number of characters horizontally that may be displayed at one time, i.e., 24 × 40. Format mode, in a video display terminal, refers to the ability to construct a screen display that prompts user input in a certain sequence and remains on the screen until cleared by exiting the format mode. Some word processing programs use a format line to designate all the variables for left margin, right margin, paragraph indentation, etc. Printed pages may also be set up in any number of formats to match pre-printed forms, align columns, etc.

FORTRAN—FORmula TRANslator, a language originally developed for IBM, now widely adapted for business and personal programming. Several versions of FORTRAN are offered for personal computers.

friction feed—In a printer or typewriter, refers to the movement of paper by the action of a rolling cylinder to which paper is held by smaller friction rollers. Generally acknowledged to be somewhat less precise than tractor, or pin, feed.

function—A way of referring to a type or sequence of calculations within an arithmetic statement. Most programming languages have a certain number of predefined mathematical functions, such as square root derivation, logrithmic functions, etc. Also a special purpose or characteristic action, such as an editing function.

game paddles—On the Apple and several other personal computers, game paddles are compact hand-held controls containing a potentiometer and switch. The term comes from the usual application of these controls, namely the real time control of graphic figures used in entertainment programs.

GET—Accepts the input of a single character from the keyboard. On most computers, RETURN or ENTER need not be pressed and the character entered does not appear on the video display. Often used in programs to input the response to a yes or no question, press key to continue, etc.

GOSUB—Must be followed by a line number. Causes program execution to branch to the line number following the GOSUB statement. Upon encountering a RETURN statement, program execution resumes at the next statement following GOSUB. Each GOSUB statement used in a program must have an accompanying RETURN in order to prevent termination of program operations at the conclusion of a particular subroutine.

GOTO—Causes an unconditional branch to the line number following the GOTO statement. Like GOSUB, must be followed by a line number.

GR—In the Apple II, sets the low resolution graphics mode to on.

graphics—Sophisticated pictures that show the results of computations in a form that is easy to interpret and remember. Also refers to the ability of a computer to display data in the form of pictures, graphs, animation, etc. Simple graphics are within the range of all computers, sophisticated graphics capabilities are incorporated into many popular personal computers. An increasing number of computers are offering numerous graphics capabilities, including color displays, for sophisticated business applications.

graphic input tablet—A peripheral device which allows the user to input data to a computer by drawing or reproducing a shape on the face of the tablet. Personal computer graphic input tablets consist of a flat surface tablet to which a stylus is applied when input is desired. Most also have an area of the tablet set up for transmitting predefined commands to the computer to store data, save a shape, etc. At least one, and possibly other, commercial investment programs allow the user to input historical data by reproducing a stock or market chart on a graphics input tablet.

hard copy—Printed permanent copy of machine output, as opposed to soft copy which is usually a perishable display on a video screen.

hard disk—A rigid disk coated with a magnetic material used for data storage. Hard disks are used singularly or in "disk packs" in drives which have a separate read/write head for each disk. Although they are relatively difficult to insert and remove, hard disks offer advantages in terms of rapid access and increased storage capacity over floppy disks.

hardware—A slang expression used to denote any piece of computer or related equipment. Also used to denote routines or capabilities contained in a separate circuit capable of operating directly. Some computers, for instance, require separate boards to rapidly handle floating point arithmetic operations. Opposite of programs and operating systems which are referred to as software. To further confuse the issue, some programs which are contained in ROM are called firmware.

header record—A record, usually the first, in a file which details the types and characteristics of the balance of the records in that file.

help file—A direct self-teaching facility or program provided to assist inexperienced users. A help file usually explains the nature of the program, any special commands used and techniques necessary to insure proper operation of the program or system. Although usually found only on larger systems, some personal computer programs are incorporating help files.

HGR—In the Apple, activates the high resolution graphics mode. In this mode, the screen resolution capability is 280 × 160 points. Similar commands are used in other systems with high resolution display capability.

high level language—A language designed for programming ease and conciseness which produces many machine level instructions for each statement. BASIC is considered to be a high level language.

HIMEN—Designation for high memory. In the Apple, the number following HIMEM sets the address of the highest memory location available to a user program, including variables.

HOME—Refers to the starting position of the cursor, usually the upper left corner of a video display screen. As a command, returns the cursor to the home position and, in some systems, clears the display.

IC—An abbreviation which refers to an integrated circuit. See also Chip.

IF—THEN—A logical statement used to initiate a conditional branch of program execution to instruction following THEN only if the expression following IF evaluates as true. If the expression evaluates as false, most versions of BASIC continue program execution at the next numbered line. Some systems permit the use of ELSE to specify an alternative instruction to be executed if the IF statement is not true.

immediate execution commands—Statements which may be executed directly from the keyboard of a computer, as opposed to deferred execution commands which can be executed only from within a program.

IN#—Used in the Apple to designate the slot number of the peripheral which will be providing subsequent input.

increment—In one usage, defines the amount by which the values specified in a FOR-NEXT loop will be changed following each iteration of the steps specified following next. Designated by STEP(X) following NEXT. If no increment value is defined, BASIC uses a default value of +1.

INPUT—In BASIC, a command which prompts and accepts input of data. When used to prompt input from the keyboard, an optional string expression can be printed to describe the type of input called for. Requires RETURN or ENTER to be pressed at the conclusion of keyboard input. Also used in some systems to read data from tape or disk files.

INT—An abbreviation for integer. As a command, returns the largest whole number which is less than or equal to the expression following INT.

intelligent terminal—A printing or video display terminal possessing memory and processing capacity which is connected to another computer. Opposite is a dumb terminal, which depends on the host computer for all except input and display functions. Personal computers may serve in either capacity for a particular (usually telecomputing) application.

interactive—Refers to programs which accept user input and act immediately on that input. Courses of action are entirely dependent on user input. Also known as conversational processing, since the user in a sense is actually conversing with the computer.

interface—A common boundary provided between pieces of equipment in a data processing system.

interrupt—A break in the normal flow of program operation such that operation can be resumed from that point later on. Interrupts are events that divert the attention of the computer from the primary program being executed because of the occurence of some sequence of events related to a particular address, usually a signal from an external device.

inverse—For video displays, refers to the printing of letters or characters in a mode opposite of that normally used. For most displays, normal operation prints white on a black background and inverse prints black on a white background.

iteration—A process or procedure designed to successively execute a series of statements until some condition is satisfied. Also known as looping. FOR-NEXT statements are the primary means of producing iteration in BASIC programs.

justification—The process of aligning a set of characters horizontally or vertically to predetermined margins. Also, perhaps more commonly, the rationale you provide your spouse when the bill arrives for your computer system!

K—Commonly used abbreviation for kilo, a prefix meaning one thousand. In reference to computer devices, it means 1024. For example, 4K memory means 4096 bytes.

keyboard—The portion of a terminal or computer equipped with a typewriter—like arrangement of switches. Used as a primary input and control device for most personal computers.

language—A system of vocabulary and rules of syntax used to enter instructions to a computer. May be either low level, such as machine language, or high level, such as BASIC, FORTRAN, etc.

LEFT\$(X\$,I)—Returns the leftmost number of characters specified by I of the string expression X\$. For instance, LEFT\$("INVESTMENT",6) would return INVEST.

LEN(X\$)—Prints the number of characters contained in the string expression X\$. LEN("INVESTMENT"), for example, would return 10.

LET—In BASIC, assigns the value of the expression on the right of the equals sign to the variable specified on the left. Use is optional in most versions of BASIC, since the equals sign (=) serves exactly the same purpose whether or not LET is present.

light pen—A high speed photo-sensitive peripheral which can be used as a direct input device for computer operations. In practice, the light pen is touched to a particular area of the video screen to produce data input.

line number—An integer preceeding a program line which determines the order of storage and execution of lines. BASIC begins program execution at the lowest line number and proceeds sequentially unless flow of control is directed elsewhere by either a conditional or unconditional branch statement.

LIST—Causes an entire program to be displayed on a video screen or printed. Some BASICs permit displaying portions of a program by specifying beginning and ending line numbers to be listed. LIST followed by a single line number displays only the line specified.

LOAD—Reads a program or file from disk or tape into the computer's memory.

LOCK—In a disk or tape storage system, LOCK prevents accidental over-writing or deletion of a file. Also used to describe unique features incorporated into a program to prevent unauthorized copying or listing, hence the term Program Lock.

logic diagram—A graphic system used to illustrate the flow of a program as a result of decision statement alternatives.

loop—The repititious execution of a series of instructions by having the last statement in the series direct program operation to the first. Exiting from an accidental loop involves generating a priority interrupt from the keyboard or external device. Controlled looping, such as that produced by a FOR-NEXT command, is an effective way to handle repititious operations within a program.

machine language—The basic operating language of a computer. Machine language instructions are recorded in a form which is directly usable by the computer. Programming in machine language offers significant advantages in terms of memory utilization and speed of execution.

mainframe—The main part of a computer. Commonly used to describe computers which support the use of multiple remote terminals and peripherals.

mass storage—Usually refers, in personal computing applications, to tape or disk data storage. In a broader sense, mass storage is any means of storing data outside the main memory of the computer.

matrix—A tabular arrangement of numbers or variables that is subject to mathematical operations. Also refers to a tabular arrangement of circuit elements designed to perform a certain function. The wires in a printhead, for instance, are described as producing a dot-matrix used to print various characters.

medium—In one usage, refers to a specific material on which data can be stored. Magnetic tapes or disks are both common storage media.

memory—A device into which information can be copied, held and retrieved at a later time. The term is synonomous with storage, although common usage of memory relates to actual memory in the computer rather than mass storage devices. There are several types of memory devices used in personal computers which can be described in the two broad categories of random access memory (RAM) and read only memory (ROM). Random access memory, as the name implies, can be easily read from or written to by the computer user. Read only memory is programmed through specialized techniques and usually contains programs or routines necessary to the operation of a

247

computer. User access to read only memory is limited to reading the contents without being able to modify them during normal operations of the computer.

menu—The display of a number of options from which the user may select a desired alternative. Program menus are used for numerous purposes in personal computing software. In many programs, the main menu determines which subroutines will be executed and allow the user an opportunity to exit the program in a logical fashion. More complex programs may have several menus, each providing the opportunity for the user to specify exactly the operations desired.

microcomputer—Any computer which uses a microprocessor chip for a central processing unit. More commonly, a description of any small computer.

microprocessor—An integrated circuit containing a complete central processing unit (CPU) which is limited, by design, to handling significantly smaller words (bytes) than a full sized CPU. Most microprocessors used 8 bit bytes, whereas full sized computers use 16, 32 or even 64 bit bytes.

MID\$(X\$,A,B)—In BASIC, returns a substring specified by the variables following the string expression. In the example above, the substring returned would be B characters long and begin with the Ath character of expression X\$. To illustrate, MID\$("INVEST-MENT",7,4) would return MENT.

mini-floppy disk—Refers to a flexible disk slightly over five inches in diameter used as a mass storage medium. Most disk drives used with personal computers are designed to handle mini-floppy disks rather than the larger (eight inch diameter) floppy disk.

modem—Abbreviation for modulator/demodulator, a device which converts data from a form compatible with computers to a form compatible with transmission facilities and vice versa.

module—In one usage, a program segment which is intended for use as a component of a number of larger programs, i.e., a routine or subroutine which is treated as a unit. Also refers to an interchangable, plug in device, containing components or programs in read only memory.

monitor—A supervisory program capable of invoking system function programs, or a specific supervisory program which controls the execution of a user program. Also refers to a type of CRT unit that will accept and display composite video output from a computer.

motherboard—The major circuit board in a computer, usually contains the central processing unit and provisions for adding peripheral devices or circuit cards. The Apple II motherboard, for instance, contains all the basic operational components of the computer and is capable of accepting a total of 48K RAM. Slots provided on the motherboard allow eight peripheral controllers or devices to be added to the basic configuration.

nested loop—A loop imbedded within another, larger loop. Most BASICs support several levels of nesting loops. To properly execute, each imbedded loop must complete its iterations before the next larger loop can operate. Improper nesting will cause the program to lose knowledge of imbedded loops and, in many cases, terminate due to a NEXT WITHOUT FOR error.

NEW—Deletes the current program and all variables from the computer's memory. SCR (scratch), in some versions of BASIC, accomplishes the same function.

NEXT—Used in conjunction with FOR to construct a loop. See FOR—NEXT for further details.

NORMAL—In the Apple II, sets the video mode to display the usual white characters on a black background. Opposite of INVERSE, which produces black characters on a white background.

null—An absence of information, i.e., a string which contains no characters. Often used in BASIC programs to initialize a string variable or to deallocate storage space which was used by a non-null string variable.

number base—Refers to the quantity and type of characters designed for use in the digital positions of a numbering system. Four systems of numbering are commonly used for computer applications—Binary (base 2), Octal (base 8), Decimal (base 10) and Hexadecimal (base 16).

ON—In a programming application, used to construct ON—GOTO and ON—GOSUB statements. Both these statements cause a branch to the line number indicated by the value of the expression following ON. For example—ON Z GOTO 100,200,300. If Z=1 the program will branch to line 100, if Z=2 the branch will be to line 200, etc.

ONERR GOTO (X)—Used to avoid an error message that halts program execution when an error is encountered. When an error does occur, program execution will branch to the line number specified by X. Good programming technique calls for an error handling routine to be located beginning at line number X.

operating system—A collection of service routines for supervising the operation of a computer. There are also operating systems for the operation of peripherals. Disk Operating Systems, for instance, handle the operation of a disk based mass storage system.

OPEN—In disk based systems, OPEN allocates a memory buffer for operations involving the file named and prepares to read from or write to that file. If the named file is not located on the disk, a file by that name is created. Syntax and use of the OPEN command vary with the type of file involved and the requirements of the particular version of BASIC and DOS in use.

operator—A symbol which designates what operation to perform. In BASIC, there are five basic arithmetic operators—addition (+), subtraction (−), multiplication (×), division (/) and exponentiation (↑). Arithmetic and string logical operators are also included in most versions of BASIC.

options—In a program, the flexibility provided the user to personalize the program to his particular application and system capabilities. Usually displayed by a menu, options can easily be overdone by overzealous programmers. Thoughtful inclusion of options, such as providing for the use of a printer or changing base parameters of the program, can greatly enhance the usability of a program.

OR—An arithmetic logical operator. One of the uses of OR can be illustrated by IF X=0 OR Y=0 THEN. If either X or Y evaluates as true, the instruction following THEN is executed.

output—Data received from the computer as a result of program manipulation of input data. Also used in some versions of BASIC in the form OUT, which sends a specific byte value to a designated port.

OVERFLOW—An error message which denotes the result of an arithmetic calculation is too large to be represented in a BASICs number format.

page—A unit used to allocate memory or partition programs. Usually denotes the amount of data that can be displayed on the video screen at one time.

parallel—One usage refers to the simultaneous storage or transmission of all bits in a storage location comprising a character or word. Parallel interface, primarily referring to printers, is one which transmits or receives data character by character rather than bit by bit.

parameter—As used in the text, this refers to a definable characteristic of a system, item or device.

Pascal—A programming language, named after Blaise Pascal, that stresses a structured approach to programming. Features local variables, an easy method of passing parameters and versatile data structures. Pascal is rapidly gaining acceptance as a logical alternative to BASIC for programming personal computers.

PEEK(X)—Returns the contents of the memory location specified by the address X. Both the address and contents are displayed in decimal form in the Apple.

peripheral—A device intended to serve a specific function which is attached to a personal computer. Common peripherals include printers, modems, disk drives, etc.

personal computer—As defined in the text, a personal computer is one devoted primarily to personal use. Although the term is widely used to denote microcomputers, any computer can certainly qualify if it meets the personal use criteria.

personalization—Used in the text in two connotations—personalizing both computer capacity and programs. Hardware capacity of a system is personalized when the user's operational requirements are within the range of the computer's ability. With the wide variety of computer systems and peripherals on the market today, an objective determination of requirements is necessary before trying to assemble a personalized system. Programs also must be personalized to meet the user's requirements. The thrust of the majority of this book is devoted to just that topic—construction and use of a personalized investment management system.

POKE(address), value—Stores the binary equivalent of the designated value into the memory location specified by address.

POP—In Applesoft, causes program execution following a RETURN

250

command to continue at the statement following the second most recently executed GOSUB.

PRINT—A command which causes the characters of expressions following PRINT to be displayed on the video screen or printed. PRINT by itself generates a line feed. Numerous variations of PRINT are used to direct output to various devices, reproduce a specific format, etc.

PRINT USING—One of the most useful variations of the PRINT statement, PRINT USING allows the programmer to predefine a format in which data will be printed.

printer—A peripheral device which produces hard copies of a computer's output. In some cases, a printer is combined with a keyboard to form a terminal. The variety of printers available to the personal computer user is indeed vast, ranging from extremely inexpensive used teleprinters to super-sophisticated graphic reproduction units.

PR#—In the Apple, directs subsequent output to the device contained in the slot number designated following #. For instance, in my system PR#1 outputs to the printer.

program—A set of instructions that tells the computer exactly how to handle a complete problem. When used as a verb, program means the actual process of assembling the necessary instructions into a form usable by the computer.

PROM—An abbreviation designating Programmable Read Only Memory. This type of memory chip can be programmed using specialized procedures and equipment. Once programmed, modification of the contents is not possible during the normal course of computer operations.

prompt—A statement printed by a program at the appropriate time to inform the user that some specific action is now required on his part. Prompts are used to describe the nature of data input requested, remind the user to prepare a peripheral device for use, etc. Most often, the prompt is displayed until the desired action has been accomplished. Effective use of prompts within a program greatly reduces the possibility of errors during its execution.

question mark—Aside from its obvious grammatical uses, the question mark is used by the Apple as an acceptable input abbreviation for PRINT. Most versions of BASIC use the question mark as a prompt for data following the INPUT statement.

quotes—Refers to quotation marks (" "). Used in BASIC to designate the boundaries of a string expression or characters to be printed by a PRINT statement.

RAM—Abbreviation for Random Access Memory. As the term implies, RAM may be readily written to or read from during the course of normal computer usage. Most of the "main memory" contained in personal computers in RAM.

random access file—A file containing a number of equal sized records. Primarily used in applications requiring convenient access to specific parts of the file.

READ—Assigns the variables specified in the READ statement successive values from elements contained in DATA statements within the program. In disk based systems, READ(file name) causes subsequent INPUT and GET statements to take response characters from the designated disk file.

real-time clock—A circuit or peripheral which generates periodic signals which allow the computer to measure actual time between events.

RECALL (X)—In the Apple, retrieves a real or integer array which has been stored on cassette tape. The variable designated by X must have been predimensioned in the program to receive the data.

reliability—Used in the text as a means of evaluating software. In assessing reliability, the user must determine first if the program works at all. If that criteria is met, how well does the program do what the supplier said it would? Finally, does the program continue to function adequately over a period of time? In a somewhat broader sense, reliability is a measure of the ability of a program or system to function without failure.

REM—A statement that allows non-operational text to be inserted into a program in the form of remarks. Self documentation of programs is possible (and advisable) through the extensive use of REM statements wherever memory capability permits.

RENUMBER—A capability included in some versions of BASIC which allows the user to change the line numbering of a program automatically.

RESET—A key which, when pressed, causes the immediate and unconditional termination of any program in progress, enters the native language of the system and returns control to the user. Among personal computer users, referred to by many unflattering terms which reflect the frustration of accidently pressing RESET and losing a long evenings work!

resolution—In graphics applications, refers to number of points or lines per square inch that may be plotted. Often the total number of addressable points on a video display will be used instead of the square inch figure to describe computer graphics capabilities. The Apple, for instance, has two graphics modes—standard or low resolution (1880 points) and high resolution (54,000 points).

RESTORE—In BASIC, resets the data list pointer to the first element of DATA contained in a program. A READ command, following restore, begins reading (or re-reading) data from the first element.

RESUME—Used in conjunction with an error handling routine, causes program execution to continue at the statement where the error occurred or branch to a specified line number. Various versions of BASIC implement RESUME differently—check your manual for the options available in yours.

RETURN—As a program statement, causes execution to continue at the next instruction following the most recently executed GOSUB command. Also used to designate the RETURN or ENTER key common to all computer keyboards.

RF converter—(Also known as RF Modulator). In computer usage, takes the composite video output from the computer and converts it to a modulated radio frequency (RF) signal that may be received by a standard television set tuned to the proper channel. The television set then functions as a video display device for the computer.

RIGHT$(X$,A)—In BASIC, returns the specified number (A) of rightmost characters from a string expression (X$). For example, RIGHT $("INVESTMENT",4) would return MENT.

RUN—A statement which clears all variables, resets system pointers and stacks and begins execution of a program at the lowest numbered line. If a line number is specified following RUN, execution will begin at that line. In a disk based system, RUN may be followed by a program name which instructs the DOS to find, load and begin execution of the program named.

SAVE—In the Apple, stores the current program in memory on cassette tape. In disk based systems, SAVE (name) stores the program in memory in a file designated by the name assigned in the SAVE statement.

scale—A ruler-like drawing placed on a graph to aid in determination of values represented by the graphic data. Many commercial investment programs automatically scale graphic plots of price or other data by computing the maximum and minimum values represented and constructing the plot to fit within the range of these values.

scrolling—One process by which lines are displayed on a video screen. A scrolling display is one that adds new lines, usually at the bottom of the screen, moving each line previously displayed up one position. The topmost line disappears from the screen as a new line is added at the bottom. Some systems scroll in the opposite direction, or special applications sometimes call for horizontal scrolling.

sector—The smallest addressable portion of a track on a disk. In the Apple DOS, each sector can contain up to 256 bytes of information. In most instances, several sectors are used to store program or text files. Allocation of sectors for operating system, text and program files is done automatically by the DOS.

self-documentation—The use of REM statements through a program to denote both original and subsequent modifications of program logic or operation.

separator—Refers to the punctuation necessary to construct program lines with more than one statement. In both Apple and TRS-80 BASIC, the required separator is a colon (:).

sequential-access file—A disk or tape file that is arranged so that each item of information (field) is stored immediately after the preceeding item. Access to data stored in sequential-access files requires the reading of all information in a linear fashion. Also known as Serial-access files.

serial—Refers to items in a sequential order. A serial printer, for instance, is one that prints one character at a time. Serial interfaces transmit or receive data one bit at a time.

software—A general term which encompasses all the programs used to operate a computer. Opposite of hardware, which refers to actual mechanical or electrical components of a computer system.

SPC(X)—In some versions of BASIC, inserts X number of spaces between items printed by a PRINT statement. Similar in operation, SPACE$(X) creates a string expression X spaces long which may be inserted into PRINT statements of BASICs which allow the command.

statement—Refers to a meaningful expression or instruction used in programming to cause the computer to perform some sequence of operations.

STEP—A command used to specify the amount by which the values specified in a FOR-NEXT loop will be incremented or decremented following each iteration of the loop. See also Increment.

STOP—Causes a program to cease execution and, in most BASICS, to display a message indicating the line number which contained the STOP command. Once STOP is executed, control of the computer is returned to the user. Program execution may be resumed from the STOP command by using CONT or CONTINUE.

STORE(X)—The Apple uses this command to save the array X to a cassette tape. No subscript need be indicated to store an array to tape, although only the values of X which are subscripted will be saved.

string—A connected sequence of characters enclosed in quotation marks. String variables are differentiated from numeric variables by the use of $ following the variable designation.

**STR$(X)**—Returns a string variable equal to the argument X. For example, if X=125.75 then the statement X$ = STR$(X) would set the string variable X$ equal to "125.75". Often used to manipulate decimal places and format of numbers. See also VAL.

subroutine—A sequence of instructions used to execute repetitive operations within a program. Often accessed from more than one location in a program by the GOSUB(X) command, where X designates the line number which begins the subroutine. A program will continue executing line numbered statements serially in the subroutine until a RETURN is encountered. RETURN instructs the computer to continue program execution at the next statement following the GOSUB most recently used.

subscript—A number (or numbers) enclosed in parenthesis following a variable name which describe a specific data array location. A(1), A(1,2) and A(1,2,3) are examples of subscripted variables.

syntax—In computer applications, the rules governing the structure of program statements. Both vocabulary and punctuation are considered in evaluating syntax.

system—In a broad sense, the hardware, software, personnel and procedures necessary to accomplish a desired data processing operation. Since the personal computer owner is usually also the operator, system commonly refers to the combination of hardware and software capability used for a particular operation. An investment management system, word processing system and home entertainment system can, for instance, all use exactly the same hardware. What differentiates one system from the other in this instance is software.

TAB(X)—Used in conjunction with a PRINT statement, moves the cursor or printhead to the print position designated by X. Some versions of

TAB(X)—track

BASIC also permit the use of HTAB(X) and VTAB(X) to move the cursor horizontally and vertically to a specified position on the screen.

telecomputing—A technique whereby numerous terminal devices can utilize a central computer concurrently for input, processing and output functions. The most common way of accessing a central computer is through the use of telephone line coupling, hence the term Telecomputing. Personal computer users may equip their systems with a modem and the software necessary to operate within a telecomputing network. Several commercial and numerous user group telecomputing systems are presently available.

terminal—In the text, refers to an input-output device capable of transmitting data to and receiving data from the computer system of which it is a part. A terminal may be directly connected (hardwired) to a personal computer or used with a modem to access telecomputing networks. Personal computers can serve as either intelligent (memory and processing capable) or dumb (input-output only) terminals in either application.

TEXT—A command used by the Apple to set the screen to the usual non-graphics mode and reset the text window to full screen display (24 × 40).

text file—Also known as a Data File, used to store non-program information in a mass storage medium. Text files are created and retrieved through the use of appropriate commands in a program. See also file, random access file and sequential access file for further details on some of the types of text files.

THEN—Used in conjunction with IF to create a conditional branching statement within a program. See IF—THEN for further information.

thermal printer—A type of printer that makes impressions on specially coated paper through the use of heat. Most thermal printers use a dot-matrix arrangement of wires which apply an instantaneous burst of heat to form characters, rather than the traditional ribbon used by other impact printers.

timesharing—In personal computing applications, this term is used interchangably with telecomputing. Also refers to the use of any computer or peripheral device by several users concurrently. Very few personal computers are capable of performing as host units for timesharing operations, but almost all can be configured to be users of such a system.

TRACE—In a broad sense, TRACE is an interpretive diagnostic technique that provides an analysis of each instruction executed and writes the analysis to an output device. TRACE, as implemented in the Apple and other popular personal computers, causes the line number of each statement to appear on the screen as it is executed.

track—On a disk used for mass storage, a specific number of concentric circles have been defined by the DOS. Each of these circles is called a track and consists of a specific number of smaller units called sectors. In one version of the Apple DOS (3,2), there are 35 tracks on a disk. Each track has a storage capacity of 3328 bytes, and is divided into 13 sectors which have a storage capacity of 256 bytes each. The read/write head of the disk drive moves to the various tracks and provides access to the sectors contained in a specified track.

tractor feed—Commonly used to designate a printer paper handling system which provides for the use of forms which are perforated on both sides and supplied in continuous, folded sheets separated by perforations. Pin feed is often used to describe the same type of system. More properly, a form tractor and pin feed mechanism are two distinctly different pieces of hardware used to accomplish essentially the same operation.

tutorial—In computer applications, commonly refers to a program of interactive instruction about a certain topic. See also help file.

UNLOCK—In a disk operating system, allows the user to remove the previously imposed restriction against writing to or deleting a specific file on the disk.

update—Refers to procedures used to modify a file for the purpose of incorporating current information. Frequently used as a verb to designate the process of using the modification procedures.

user's group—An organization comprised of individuals that share a common interest either through owning similar computer systems or using their computers in similar applications. Most user's groups are formed for the purpose of exchanging information and user generated programs. Your local dealer may be able to help you locate user's groups in your immediate area. If no such group exists, there are several large user's groups that publish newsletters as a means of exchanging programs and information.

utility program—A standard routine which is used to assist in the operation of a computer system. Disk utility programs, for instance, provide additional features that may not have been included in your computer's DOS. Other examples of utility programs include sorting routines, number base conversion programs, upper to lower case conversion routines, etc.

**VAL(X$)**—Interprets the string expression X$, up to the first non-numeric character, as a real or integer and returns the value of that number. For instance, $X = VAL(\text{"3.1415PI"})$ would set the value of the numeric variable X equal to 3.1415.

variable—A data item that assumes different values during the execution of a program. Most versions of BASIC are capable of handling real, integer and string variables. Rules for variable names and designations vary from version to version. Values may be assigned to variables by several different methods including INPUT, GET, READ, and LET.

VERIFY—A command available in some versions of BASIC which allow the user to check the accuracy of information contained in mass storage systems. Apple DOS, for instance, verifies information by comparing a computed checksum byte against one originally stored along with the information in the file.

video display—The display of the output from a computer on the face of a cathode ray tube. Video display may be accomplished through the use of a specially constructed terminal, composite video from the computer displayed directly on a monitor, or RF modulated signals received by a standard television receiver.

voice grade line—Refers to a telephone circuit which has been judged to meet specifications for standard voice communication. In most instances, voice grade lines may be used for low speed (up to 300 baud) data communications with good reliability. High speed communications often require the use of a conditioned line. See conditioned line for details.

voice synthesizer—A hardware and/or software system used to generate digital approximations of the sounds of human speech.

volatile memory—Memory in which data becomes lost or erased when power is removed. RAM, unless protected by a back-up battery system, is usually volatile.

WAIT—A command, used by Apple, which allows the user to insert a conditional pause into a program. A similar action can be initiated in other versions of BASIC through the use of PAUSE or STOP and CONTINUE commands.

window—Usually refers to a text window, the area on a video screen which is used to display and scroll text. Some personal computers allow user modification of the text window parameters, providing capabilities similar to the format mode mentioned earlier.

WRITE—In Apple DOS, all PRINT statements following WRITE direct their output to a specified disk file instead of the video display until cancelled by another DOS command. In a broader sense, write refers to various procedures used to transfer information, usually from main memory to a mass storage device.

X-Y plotter—A hard copy device capable of plotting points along either or both of two axes. Used in conjunction with a computer, the X-Y plotter may be used to plot coordinate points in the form of a graph or line drawing.

zap—What your computer system can do to you if you fail to adequately ground it, shield exposed cables and observe the reason for interlock switches on hardware. A shocking experience, to say the least!

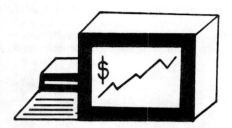

Glossary Of Investment Terms

The terms described in this glossary will be generally limited to those actually used or referred to in the text of this book. In many cases, the definitions offered here are merely one or two of the many possible uses for a specific term. Often we will deviate somewhat from the more complex, complete definition in order to explain only the usage outlined in the text.

account—One form of general usage defines account as a record of business transactions. Account, in our application, refers to the handling and financial arrangements made with your broker to handle investment transactions, i.e., cash account, margin account, etc.

advance/decline line—A cumulative total of the difference between the number of stock prices that advanced and the number that declined on a particular exchange for the period of interest. Initially, the difference between advances and declines is added (or subtracted) to an arbitrary figure. Subsequent differences are then added to the cumulative total from the previous period. In this book, the A/D line is used as a weekly moving average which is useful as a non-price indicator of market trends.

advisory service—Individual or organization that studies a specific area of investments for the purpose of recommending a particular course of action to its subscribers.

amortization—To write off expenditures by prorating their cost over a fixed period.

AMEX (American Stock Exchange)—The smaller of the two major stock exchanges, typically lists stocks of smaller corporations with fewer shareholders than does the New York Stock Exchange.

analyst—One who studies a specific stock or group of stocks for the purpose of determining investment suitability. There are many other types of analysts, but our prime usage of the term here refers to stock analysts.

assets—Things of value that may be used to pay off debts. For corporations, these usually include cash, securites, buildings, machinery, land, inventory, etc.

258

balance sheet—A report of the financial condition of a company as of a given date, usually the end of the accounting year. Interim reports are often issued on a quarterly basis.

bear market—Period during which the primary trends of the market are declining. Usually this downward trend is reflected in the prices of individual stocks.

bellweather theory—This theory relies on the market action of one or several leading stocks, averages or indexes to predict future trends. In a rising market, a bullish signal is generated when the selected leader reaches a yearly or cyclical high. If this leader fails to reach a new high for several months, a market top is predicted. Opposite signals are generated in bear markets. General Motors (GM) is probably the single most popular bellweather stock.

big board—Slang expression which refers to the New York Stock Exchange.

blue chips—Expression denoting the stocks of established, financially strong corporations that are generally acknowledged as leaders within their industry group.

book value—The net worth of a corporation to common shareholders. Usually expressed on a per-share basis obtained by dividing the corporate net worth by the number of common shares outstanding.

bond—Legal expression of the fact that money has been loaned to a corporation or governmental unit. The bond states that the issuer will pay interest at a specified rate until the debt is repaid at face value some time in the future. There are numerous types and variations of bonds.

bottom—The point at which a general market decline reverses and key indicators begin to advance.

break-even point—The price at which an investment instrument, if sold, would fully reimburse all costs connected with its acquistion and subsequent sale.

broad market index—An index constructed in an effort to reflect accurately the price action of the majority of issues on any stock exchange, i.e., the New York Common Stock Index.

broker—Firm or individual holding a seat on the exchange of interest employed by an investor to execute securities transactions. Most brokerage firms offer far more than just this basic service. Broker is also a loose term used by many investors to describe a registered representative employed by a brokerage firm.

bull market—A period during which primary market trends are advancing, economic growth is good and stock prices generally are rising.

buy order—An order placed by an investor directing a broker to purchase a specified number of shares of stock, options, bonds, etc. Limits or conditions specifying price, time or numerous other factors may be imposed, if desired.

call—The date, before maturity, on which all or part of a bond issue may be redeemed by the issuing corporation. Definite conditions are imposed for a bond to be called.

call option—An option to buy a specific number (usually 100) shares of a stock at a fixed price for a specified period of time. Call options are often sold by stockholders seeking to increase the return from their shares and purchased by investors hoping for a price increase in the stock (and option premium) prior to the expiration date. Many other combinations of selling and buying calls are used by proficient option traders.

capital—The amount of money or property needed by an individual or corporation to carry out their normal business activities.

capital gain—In the usual sense, refers to an increase in the value of an investment vehicle relative to the purchase price. For income tax purposes, holding period is used as a determiner of whether a capital gain is long term or short term. Long term capital gains receive some preferential tax treatment, while most short term gains are taxed at the same rate as ordinary income. Similar considerations are made for long and short term capital losses.

capital surplus—The amount of money or property held in excess of that needed to carry out normal business activities.

cash account—Account established by an investor with a brokerage firm in which all transactions are settled in cash during a specified period following execution of the transaction. In many cases, proceeds from sales are credited to the account which may or may not contain funds from previous transactions. Funds necessary for purchases are then taken from the balance and the investor is expected to remit any balance due promptly. Any or all funds remaining in a cash account may be withdrawn as needed.

cash flow—Reflects the actual cast available for use by a corporation. Consists of after tax earnings plus charges levied against income (depreciation, for instance) that do not involve real cash outlays.

central average—An arbitrary range of stock prices used in variable ratio formula plans to determine whether current prices are relatively high (above the central average) or relatively low (below the central average). Determining the central average involves the use of some market indicators the investor feels adequately reflects or anticipates the level of stock prices.

chart—Graphic representation of selected data. Stock charts, for instance, usually include prices, volume, moving averages and price/earnings data.

churning—Refers to an excessively high precentage of turn-over in a securities account. This process is sometimes used by unscrupulous brokers to generate additional commissions.

commodity—In a dictionary sense, refers to anything that is bought and sold. Investment usage refers to futures contracts bought or sold for delivery of specific quantities of corn, wheat, metals or some 30 other tangible goods.

commission—The fee paid to a broker for executing a securities transaction. Usually a percentage of the dollar amount involved, subject to a minimum fee established by the brokerage firm. In most instances, the commission percentage is inversely proportional to the dollar amount involved.

common stock—An ownership interest purchased in a corporation, entitling the holder to a share in any profits realized and some voice in the management of the company.

confirmation—This word has several connotations. For purposes of this book, we have operationally defined confirmation as the verification by a brokerage firm, in writing and/or by telephone, of a securites transaction executed as a result of an order placed by an investor.

constant dollar—An investment formula plan in which a specific dollar figure to be invested in stocks is predetermined. At regular intervals, holdings are totaled and compared to the predetermined figure. Stocks are bought or sold to keep the two figures equal. Profits from sales and funds awaiting investment are assumed to be placed in fixed return savings accounts or bonds.

constant ratio—A formula plan in which a set ratio of stocks to fixed return investments is determined. Total holdings are periodically reevaluated and a second ratio determined. Under this plan, stocks are bought and sold to maintain the set ratio regardless of the current level of stock prices.

convertible—A bond or preferred stock which may be exchanged for common stock or other security, usually of the same corporation. Terms for conversion are set at issue.

cost per share—A figure determined by totalling all the costs connected with the acquisition and ownership of stock, then dividing the resultant total by the number of shares held. This figure is particularly helpful in determining the results of a dollar cost averaging approach and projecting potential profits or losses from a transaction.

CUSIP—Committee on Uniform Security Identification Procedures. Has established a numbering system to identify securities.

cyclical stocks—Stocks of corporations whose earnings are sensitive to business cycles and, most often, accentuated by the peaks and valleys of the cycle. Prices of these stocks fluctuate widely over a complete business cycle.

day order—An order which expires at the end of the day which it is issued.

day trading—Establishing and closing an investment position within the same trading day. Usually practiced only by extremely active traders.

debentures—Refers to convertible bonds. These are debt instruments of the issuing corporation which may be exchanged for shares of common stock at a specified ratio.

defensive stocks—Shares of those companies likely to fare best with earnings and dividends during a period of deteriorating business conditions. Opposite of cyclical stocks.

degree of risk—The amount of uncertainty an investor is willing to withstand in order to obtain a profit. In general, those investment vehicles carrying the highest degree of risk also offer the greatest potential returns.

depreciation—An amount charged against earnings to write off the cost, less salvage value, of an asset over its estimated useful life.

diluted earnings—Earnings stated to reflect per share profits if all outstanding securities that can be exchanged for common stock were exercised.

discount—The amount which a preferred stock or bond sells below its par value. Also means to "take into account", i.e., the news of a stock split was discounted by investors.

discount broker—Term applied to a brokerage firm that offers reduced commissions made possible by providing limited services. Can offer significant savings to investors who do not need the additional services offered by a full service firm.

dividend—A portion of corporate profits received by shareholders. May be paid in cash and/or additional shares.

dividend reinvestment—A plan in which all dividends due the shareholder are automtically reinvested in the companies stock. Additional full or fractional shares are purchased, usually with little or no commission charges, and credited to the shareholder's account.

diversification—Investing funds in several different industry groups in an attempt to hold securities that do not fluctuate in a similar fashion. The premise is that a well diversified portfolio will fluctuate less than any of the individual stocks it contains.

dollar cost averaging—A method of investing in which a set amount of money is invested in a selected stock at regular intervals. It is presumed that this amount of money will buy more shares when prices are low, fewer shares during periods of high prices. Averaged over a long enough period of time, cost per share should be less than if all the shares held were purchased at any one time.

Dow theory—A timing technique, advanced by C. H. Dow, which attempts to signal the beginning and end of both bull and bear markets. Primary concentration is on broad market trends, with little or no emphasis on day to day fluctuations or individual stock selection.

Dow Jones averages—There are three Dow Jones Averages commonly quoted. They are designed to reflect market action of specific stock groups. Each is constructed by totalling the closing price of all stocks in the group and dividing the total by a divisor which compensates for stock splits and stock dividends. The averages are:

Industrials—Made up of the stocks of 30 major industrial corporations. Probably the most commonly quoted of the Dow Jones Averages.

Transportations—Contains the stocks of 18 major airline, railroad, trucking and freight companies.

Utilities—Made up of 15 utility stocks representing diverse geographic locations.

electric approach—Used in this book to refer to a stock selection process that combines the best of many approaches in an effort to identify stocks with good profit potential.

equity—The ownership interest of all classes of stockholders in a corporation. Also, the difference between the value of securities and the debit balance in a margin account.

ex-dividend—Stock is said to be trading less or ex-dividend during the period from the record date to the time dividends are actually paid. Dividends declared are paid to the shareholder as of the record date.

exchange—An auction market for stocks, bonds and other securities. The largest are the New York and American Stock Exchanges.

exercise rights—Take advantage of the privilege granted by rights to purchase stock ahead of the general public, usually at a favorable price and without commission charges.

financial report—A corporate report of financial condition which may be issued annually, semi-annually or quarterly. Contains a balance sheet, income statement and cash flow data. May also contain extensive amounts of other information of interest to shareholders, combined into what is usually called an annual report.

fixed return—An investment where the rate of return is fixed in advance for the designated period, i.e., savings certificate, bonds, etc.

formula plan—A method of investing designed to minimize the effects of timing on a portfolio. Often rely on automatic signals to buy, sell or revise holdings and/or require periodic investments of either money or time. Reasonable returns can be obtained if stocks suitable for long term commitment are selected and the formula plan selected is given sufficient time to produce results. Popular formula plans include Constant Dollar, Constant or variable Ratio and Dollar Cost Averaging.

full service broker—A brokerage firm which offers more than just transaction execution services and charges commensurately higher commissions to cover the cost of the extras. Additional services offered include research publications, stock analysis, account management, specialized types of accounts, etc.

fundamental approach—A method of stock selection which emphasizes value, quality and either yield or growth. Also referred to as the value approach or margin of safety method.

futures—Refers to contracts for commodities. See commodities for further details.

gain—An increase in the value of an investment relative to the purchase price. See also capital gain.

GMA—Fixed return securities backed by the Government National Mortgage Association representing single family VA and FHA mortgages. Commonly referred to as "Ginnie Maes", The investor receives monthly payments consisting of the interest due and a portion of the principal.

goals—Detailed, specific, measurable and reachable units which are components of broad investment objectives. Generally, goals must provide the when, how, where, what and why direction necessary to attain the overall objectives of an investment program.

growth stocks—Ideally, the stock of a corporation that gets bigger and better each year, causing the price of its stock to move up. In practice, the criteria used for defining a growth stock vary with an investors ultimate objectives and perception of what is significant growth. One usable definition—stock in a corporation that shows profit growth through both prosperous and difficult economic cycles.

hedge—When dealing in options, a hedge involves buying one call option and selling another on the same stock with the goal of realizing at least the difference in premiums as profit.

historic data—Data gleaned from a specific time period in the past. Generally used in an attempt to identify trend sequences likely to be repeated at some time in the future. One common application involves comparing the historical price action of a stock with specific market indices in an effort to properly time buy and sell transactions.

hot tip—A piece of information received by an investor, usually requiring immediate action. More often than not, hot tips have little foundation in fact and could result in inappropriate hasty reaction. Some hot tips are valuable, but should be carefully verified prior to committing funds at the suggestion of a tipper.

income stock—A stock that yields generous current returns, often purchased by investors who have an immediate need for income combined with some assurance of capital preservation. Prior to purchasing an income stock, the investor should carefully investigate the reason for uncommonly high yields. Often, stocks have high yields because their shares sell at low prices due to investor concern, the companies ability to maintain yield rate and poor prospects for future growth.

index—An indicator constructed in such a fashion as to reflect the market performance of a specific group of securities or identify general market trends. See also Dow Jones Indexes, New York Common Stock Index, S & P 500.

investment—In this book, we have operationally defined investment to mean any financial instrument purchased in the anticipation of selling that same instrument at a later time for a significantly higher price.

leading indicator—Index or economic group whose changes in basic trend or direction tend to precede and signal cyclical changes in the economy as a whole. Stock prices, for instance, are generally regarded as an indicator which preceeds general business cycle changes by about six months. There are also indicators described as coincident (change with the business cycle) and lagging (change after a shift in the business cycle).

leverage—The degree to which a corporation or individual uses borrowed funds as opposed to equity. If the anticipated return is significantly greater than the cost of borrowing money, leverage can markedly increase gains. Maximum leverage, and risk, is obtained with the smallest possible use of equity. Margin buying, options, warrants and rights are all ways for an individual investor to obtain leverage in his investment program.

liabilities—Monies or debt obligations for which an individual or corporation is responsible. Usually defined in terms of current liabilities (due in less than one year) and long term debt. May include money owned to suppliers, debt retirement, taxes due, dividends payable, etc.

limit order—An order placed with a broker which calls for a securities transaction to be executed upon certain conditions being satisfied. Price and time of execution are only two of the many limits that may be imposed.

liquidity—Refers to the ability to convert to cash or its equivalent any investment instrument. Stocks and bonds are regarded as having good liquidity because disposing of them in the open market is readily accomplished. Some other forms of investment holdings may show significantly less liquidity. Real estate or collectibles, for instance, may take a long time to convert to cash.

list—In this application, list refers to groups of stocks or bonds compiled for a specific purpose. Investment advisory services, for instance, often publish lists of stocks recommended for purchase.

long—A term which signifies ownership of securities. Opposite term is short, which implies securities have been borrowed for a specific purpose.

long term—Generally used as a qualifier, such as long term debt, which implies a period in excess of one year. Long term capital gains, the holding period for which is defined in the tax codes, receive different treatment than short term gains.

margin—Buying on margin, using your securities as collateral for a loan from your broker, is a form of increasing an investors leverage. Margin accounts are subject to strict limits for minimum equity as established by the Federal Reserve Board, although the limits may be set higher by brokerage firms.

market—A broad term used to encompass securities exchanges, although usually "the market" implies the New York Stock Exchange. Commonly applied to both stocks and bonds, i.e., the stock market and money markets.

market cycle—A period of time, usually four to six years, during which stock prices and economic indicators vary from expansion to recession.

market order—An order placed with a broker directing execution of a securities transaction as soon as possible at the going market price. Limit orders, once the conditions imposed have been satisfied, take on the effect of a market order.

market value—The total amount investors would be willing to pay for all the common shares of a corporation. If XYZ corporation, for instance, has ten million common shares outstanding and the stock is presently selling at $5.00 a share, the market value of XYZ would be fifty million dollars.

minimum charge—The smallest commission fee set by a particular brokerage firm. This charge applies to all transactions below a set number of shares or transaction dollar value. For transactions involving only a few shares of stock, the cost per share can be significantly increased when this charge is applied. In selecting a brokerage firm, the minimum charge should be considered if you anticipate much odd-lot trading.

moving average—An average which moves with the unit of time considered. Primarily used as trend indicators, moving averages tend to smooth out short term fluctuations and react slowly, particularly to swift market declines. Often three moving averages are used to indicate short (4-6 week), intermediate (12-16 week) and long (39-42 week) trends.

multiple—A term used to describe price to earnings ratio of a stock or the market in general.

mutual fund—A form of investment company which sells shares for the purposes of providing investors diversification, professional management and maximum liquidity of funds. All funds received for shares are comingled and invested in securities (or other forms of investment, depending on the purpose of the fund). The price of each share reflects the net value of its holdings at the time of purchase or redemption. Mutual funds are open-ended in that there is no limit to the number of shares that may be sold. In operation, closed end funds are quite similar except that only a limited number of shares are available and those shares are traded like regular stocks.

NASDAQ—National Association of Securities Dealers Automated Quotation system. See OTC (Over-The-Counter) for more detailed explanation.

net income—The amount remaining when all the expenses of doing business are subtracted from the total sales or revenues of a corporation, i.e., profit. Used as an indicator of management effectiveness, the best companies are those who increase their profits in total, in percentage of revenues and in relation to stockholders equity each year. Average net income expectations depend on the type of business. Food chains, for instance, average 2-3% while manufacturing corporations average about 6%.

net worth—A figure derived by subtracting from total assets all liabilities. Personal net worth is an important tool for measuring progress of your investment and financial management programs. Corporate net worth is used in a similar fashion by many investment analysts.

new issues—Stocks or other securities being offered to the general public for the first time. May be those of corporations converting from private to public ownership, a new class of security from an existing corporation or shares of a newly formed company. Detailed information about the company and its finances is provided in a prospectus, which must be provided with a new issue.

NYSE (New York Stock Exchange)—The major auction market for common stocks and bonds. Lists shares of corporations who meet strict standards for total revenues, number of shares available, etc.

NYSE common stock index—Also known as the New York Composite Index, this is a composite index covering price movements of all common stocks listed on the New York Stock Exchange. Based on December 31, 1965 closing prices, the index is weighted according to the number of shares listed for each issue. Considered by many to be a good representation of broad market trends.

objectives—Broad, general statements of the focus of your investment program. Examples might be preservation of capital, maximum capital appreciation, etc. Goals are constructed to provide measurable progress in meeting these objectives.

odd lot—An amount of stock less than the established round lot unit. Small investors are often referred to as "odd lotters" because of the relative size of their transactions. Odd lot trading data is generally regarded as a good clue of what not to do in the market, since the average investor has a history of buying most heavily at market tops and selling at market bottoms.

option—See call option, put option and warrants for detailed explanations of the various types of options available.

outstanding—One usage of this term refers to the number of shares of a stock actually issued by a corporation. The number of shares authorized is defined in the corporate charter and may be considerably greater than the number actually outstanding at any one time.

over-the-counter (OTC)—Transactions in securities which do not take place on an exchange are referred to as over-the-counter transactions. The phrase is a carry-over from the past when securities were literally sold over the counter of banking houses. There is no centralized place for trading, virtually any type of security may be listed and brokers may act as principals or agents in transactions. NASDAQ, the National Association of Securities Dealers Automated Quotation system initiated in 1971, is a computerized data base that collects, stores and displays current over-the-counter market information from the network of NASD members.

par value—A dollar amount assigned to each share of stock or bond by a corporation charter. It is common practice to exclude assigning par value to shares of common stock, but preferred stock and bonds usually carry a par value.

peak—Usually refers to the highest point reached prior to a decline. Market peaks may be measured in several ways, individual security peaks are commonly stated in terms of price and/or price to earnings ratio.

point-and figure charting—A method of constructing stock charts to display a compressed picture of significant price changes. These charts contain no time scale and plots are made only when price changes by a predetermined amount. Now horizontal columns of price plots are started each time the direction of price reverses. Small price fluctuations produce areas of congestion. A new trend is indicated by a significant departure from the area of congestion (breakout). When a new trend is indicated, advocates of this approach maintain the eventual level of the trend can be accurately predicted by counting the number of horizontal columns covered by the most recent congestion area and adding this figure to the price level of the congestion area if the trend is upward, subtracting if the trend is down.

portfolio—A term denoting the total securities holdings of an individual or company. Although actually keeping stock certificates in a real portfolio is rare, the label is still used to describe ones holdings. Sample portfolios for various investment goals are also described in many publications.

preferred stock—A security halfway between common stocks and bonds which has fixed dividends and preference on all corporate income available after payment of bond interest and amortization. Most preferred stocks are cumulative, meaning that any unpaid dividends accumulate and must be paid prior to any distribution to the common stockholders. Convertible preferred stocks may be converted to common shares of the same corporation at a specified ratio.

premium—The cost of an option. Quoted in eighths for options selling over $2.00, sixteenths for those priced lower. Also refers to a charge which may be applied for borrowing the stock involved in a short sale.

price to earnings ratio (P/E)—Derived by dividing the price of a share of stock by the companies twelve month earnings per share. Also referred to as multiple.

price goal—A price level for a security that will trigger some action in your investment program. Typically, this price level is set so that a security is sold once your profit has been reached. Particularly important when dealing in short term investments such as options.

projection—Operationally defined in the text as the forward extension of various trends for the purpose of evaluating, modifying or confirming decisions. Most predictions use projection of historic trends combined with the predictor's opinion of what is likely to happen in the future.

profit margin—The ratio of corporate profits to sales or total revenues, expressed as a percentage. This percentage should increase with sales increases and may be used as a comparison among corporations in similar industries. Profit margins are typically low for corporations with heavy plant investments and retailers. Higher profit margins are usually found in marketing firms.

put option—An option to sell a specified number of shares of stock at a fixed price for a designated length of time. Opposite of a call option.

pyramiding—Increasing profits by using the higher value of your holdings in a margin account as collateral for additional loans during periods of rising prices. This can be a very effective way to increase profits, but can also be dangerous when there is maximum collateral and downside risk at the peak of a bull market. Also used to denote similar methods of increasing profit potential, and risk, with other investment vehicles.

quote—A term used to denote current price level, market volume and other relevant data for a security.

ratio plans—As used in the text, ratio plans are formula based investment methods which use a fixed or variable percentage of total investment funds in stocks and fixed return investments. See constant ratio and variable ratio for further details.

record date—The date on which you must be registered as a shareholder in order to receive a corporation's declared dividends, vote on company affairs, etc.

redemption price—Refers to the price at which a bond may be redeemed before maturity by the issuing company, the price a corporation must pay to call in certain types of preferred stocks and the amount received on liquidating mutual fund shares.

registered representative—An employee of a brokerage firm who takes orders for transactions, furnishes information and deals directly with customers of the firm. In return for providing these services, the representative receives a portion of the commission generated. Also known as account executives, salesmen or customers men (or is it salespeople and customers people?), registered representatives must meet certain training requirements in order to be registered. Often referred to simply, and inaccurately, as brokers.

resistance level—The price at which several price advances of a stock have stopped, or from which declines have started. Often constructed as a line on charts, then known as a resistance line. Generally, penetration of this line on heavy trading volume is regarded as a signal of a potential significant price advance.

reseach report—Detailed information on a corporation or industry group issued by analysts for a specific purpose. Research departments of brokerage firms, for instance, regularly issue reports to inform their clients of significant developments or changes. Most often, these reports are accompanied by a recommendation as to the suitability of the company's stock for various investment programs.

retained earnings—Also known as *earned surplus*, this figure represents the amount of corporate earnings retained and reinvested in the business rather than being paid out as dividends to shareholders.

reward—The result of taking a risk which was successful. In investment applications, this implies making a profit commensurate with the degree risk incurred.

rights—An option granted to its shareholders by a corporation seeking to raise additional capital. Through these rights, stockholders are able to purchase additional shares of stock ahead of the general public, usually without brokerage commissions and at a more favorable price. Usually, rights have short time limits before expiration. Unexercised rights are bought and sold in the open market at prices determined by supply and demand. See also *exercise rights*.

risk—The danger of loss of capital and uncertainty as to the outcome of a course of action faced by an investor. See also *degree of risk*.

round lot—A standard unit of trading securities, usually one hundred shares of stock and $1000 par value for bonds.

sales costs—An amount charged against corporate income for selling, general and administrative expenses. This item varies according to the type of business and may include research and development costs.

securities and exchange commission (SEC)—The agency responsible for administering federal ac regarding securities.

selection—The process of picking specific stocks or bonds to help you meet your investment goals.

sell order—A order placed with a broker directing him to liquidate a specified holding. Similar to buy orders in that execution at the market price or limitations may be specified.

short sale—Selling shares of a stock you do not own in anticipation of a significant price decline. Shares are borrowed and must be replaced by purchasing the same number at a later date, hopefully at a lower price. This is one method used by sophisticated investors to make money during periods of market decline.

simulation—A model constructed to closely approximate the action of a large system with many interacting parts. Flight simulators, for example, are regularly used to teach and sharpen piloting skills without having to actually use an airplane. Stock market simulations allow an investor to try different courses of action without actually risking capital.

specialists—Members of the New York Stock Exchange who have two distinct functions. First, they act as agents or brokers to execute limit orders which other members of the exchange leave with them. Secondly, they are assigned the responsibility of maintaining an orderly market in the small group of stocks assigned to them by acting as dealers or principals for their own accounts. Strict requirements are set for market experience, dealer function and amount of capital specialists must possess.

speculator—An investor who buys and sells frequently with the goal of achieving the largest capital gains in the shortest possible time. The most daring of investors in terms of the degree of risk, speculators are willing to face the possibility of losses on some holdings to achieve their goals. Similarly, speculative investments are those which entail the most risk and greatest potential rewards.

split—A distribution of additional shares of stock to shareholders. A two-for-one split, for instance, gives the investor one additional share for each one he holds. Price of the stock is reduced according to the same ratio. In the two-for-one example, if the stock was selling presplit for $50.00, the price after the split would be $25.00. Primarily used by corporations to broaden the market for their stock. Any historical price data used for analysis of the split stock must be retroactively adjusted to reflect the increase in the number of shares.

spread—In one application, an option position combining a call with a striking price above the current market and a put with a striking price below the current market.

Standard & Poor's Stock Price Index—Commonly referred to as the S & P 500, this index relects the NYSE price action of 500 stocks—425 industrials, 20 transportations and 55 utilities.

stop order—Essentially these are conditional orders which become market orders if a specified turn of events take place. A stop order to buy is usually used to limit losses on short sales and becomes a market order if the price of a stock rises above a certain point. Similarly, a stop order to sell is used to protect paper profits and causes stock to be sold if the price declines to a specified level. Since stop orders become market orders after the specified advance or decline, there is no assurance they will be executed at the exact price specified. Stop orders may be specified as good for a certain length of time or good till cancelled.

street name—A term describing the ownership listing of shares held by a brokerage firm for an investor. In this case, ownership of shares is confirmed by an entry in the investors account rather than actual certificates registered in his name and delivered. All dividends and information from the corporation are delivered by the broker for stocks held in street name. This approach provides secure storage and easy transfer when shares are sold.

striking price—The price at which the holder of an option is entitled to buy or sell the optioned stock.

T-bills—Refers to U. S. Treasury securities which are sold with four varying periods to maturity and at a discount which reflects the yield to maturity. Risk free, very liquid forms of investment which may be used as collateral for loans.

technical analysis—A method of determining what the stock market is doing and how a particular stocks price and volume in relation to past performance and market trends reflects the current interest of investors. Basically concerned with proper timing of buying and selling activity, technical analysis can also be helpful in stock selection. Charts and checkpoints are used extensively.

tender—An offer made by a corporation to buy back its own shares. Also an offer by one corporation, interested in acquiring control, to buy the shares of another. Usually, tender offers are made at a price above that of the going market.

ticker—A term used to describe the information carried on the Stock Exchange Market Data System, reflecting the time in the past when this information was printed on tapes by machines which made a ticking sound. Data includes transactions, indexes, news items, and a final summary at the end of the day.

timing—Determining the most opportune times to buy and sell securities. Involves identification of both market and individual security trends and taking appropriate action to maximize profit potential. This is one of the most difficult tasks for the average investor, who has a record of buying at market peaks and selling at bottoms. A personal computer's ability to handle large amounts of data can make it a valuable ally in the area of timing the market.

total return—A term usually interpreted to denote the income plus capital appreciation from an investment.

trading symbol—The abbreviation used to denote a particular security. Some common trading symbols include S—Sears, Roebuck & Co., GM—General Motors, UTX—United Technologies Corp., etc.

trend—The general direction of movement of the market as a whole or a specific stock price, trading volume or price to earnings ratio. Also applied to many other financial indicators.

trendline—On stock charts, trendlines are formed by connecting the upper points of stock price movement when prices are decreasing and the lower points when prices are rising. The trendline becomes important when the stock price penetrates the line if accompanied by an increase in trading volume.

turn-around—Used to denote corporations which have managed to recover from periods of significant losses and are now profitable. Correctly identifying a turn-around candidate allows the investor to purchase shares when the company is in market disfavor and shares are comparatively cheap. Stock prices usually rise as the profitability picture improves, providing the investor with a good return.

turn over—Refers to the percentage of holdings in a portfolio which were bought and sold over a specific time period, usually one year.

undervalued stock—Shares of a corporation which are selling below book value, provided the company reports good profitability and growth. The primary goal of fundamental analysis is to identify those stocks which are significantly undervalued.

unpopular stock—Shares that have fallen into general investor disfavor. These stocks are often candidates for purchase if the company is likely to recover its popularity in the forseeable future.

value approach—A method of stock selection which emphasizes careful scrutiny of a corporations ability to make money and the basic value of its stock. The primary goal of this approach is to locate undervalued stocks, with little regard for prospects of future earnings or dividend growth. Also known as the fundamental approach.

variable ratio—A formula based investment approach which calls for a percentage of capital to be invested in stocks and the balance in fixed return instruments. The ratio of stocks to savings changes as stock prices fluctuate about a central average which must be determined by the investor.

volatility—The extent to which the price of a stock rises or falls in comparison to others in its industry group or a designated market index. Highly volatile stocks show far greater swings in both directions than most stocks. Can also be applied to securities, particularly options which are often extremely volatile.

volume—The number of shares of stock, bonds or options that changed hands during a particular period. Usually stated in terms of daily volume.

warrants—An option to buy a specific number of shares of a security at a set price for a designated length of time. The price at which the warrant may be exercised is fixed above the market price of the security at the time the warrant is issued. The time period specified is relatively long, usually five years or longer. Most often warrants are offered as an inducement to purchase other securities of a corporation. Warrants included with bonds, for instance, often permit the package to be sold at a lower interest rate than the bond by itself.

yield—The amount in dividends or interest paid by a company, expressed as a percentage of the current stock or bond price. Yield is one component of total return, capital gain the other.

Appendix A

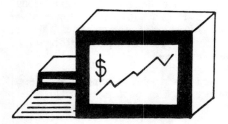

Commercially Available Programs

The programs described in this appendix have been selected to represent a reasonable cross-section of available commercial software that could be of interest to investors. In most cases, descriptive material has been condensed from manufacturers' data sheets or advertising copy. Since the features, specifications and prices on programs are subject to frequent change, it would be advisable to contact the manufacturer or check with your dealer for latest information and prices. Often software designed for one system is later offered for others, so inquire if the program that interests you is not presently compatible with your computer.

The listings that follow are arranged according to this format:

☐ Program name.

☐ Manufacturer or distributor's name and address.

☐ In parentheses, the suggested minimum hardware configuration for use of the program.

☐ Narrative description of program features.

☐ Pricing information, if available.

Listings are current as of the date of this writing. No representation of program suitability or accuracy of descriptive information is being offered here, that must be judged individually by the user. An inquiry directed to most of the suppliers listed will bring more extensive, detailed and current information.

A DAILY STOCK MARKET ROUTINE *Apple II,*
Rainbow Marketware *36K*,
3111 Berkshire Rd. *Disk II*
Baltimore, MD 21214

Introductory programs to establish library files of stock data, key in market data, append long files and view bar charts of stock action.

Price—$49.95 (Disk)

ANA1 (Analysis 1) *Apple II,*
Galaxy *48K,*
P.O. Box 22072 *Applesoft ROM,*
San Diego, CA 92212 *Disk II*

A set of BASIC programs designed for analysis and HIRES plotting of any time series data. Historical data for the Dow Jones Industrial Average

274

since 1897 included. Provision has been made for user to enter his own data.

Once data has been loaded, mathematical functions such as moving averages, least squares linear fit and relationships to any constant may be performed. Results of computations can be plotted individually or in an unlimited series of overlays. Up to 260 points in any one of five user selected colors can be plotted on the screen. Automatic scaling of plots with provision for user modification is included. Graphs and data are maintained on separate "pages", enabling the user to rapidly switch from one to the other. Provisions for drawing straight lines between two points and data fitting are included.

Program disk features a tutorial which demonstrates the capabilities and commands used in the system.

Price—$49.95

APPLE DATA GRAPH
Connecticut Information System Co.
218 Huntington
Bridgeport, CT 06608

Apple II,
36K,
Applesoft ROM

Plots linegraphs (solid, dotted, colored lines) and scattergrams. Up to three 40-point HIRES graphs or scattergrams may be drawn on the same coordinates, with the X and Y axes dimensioned. Plots may be saved to disk and recalled. Hard copy may be obtained with graphics capable printer. Can be used for graphing stocks, business reports and technical data. Custom modifications available.

APPLE PORTFOLIO INTERFACE
Rainbow Marketware
3111 Berkshire Rd.
Baltimore, MD 21214

Apple II,
36K,
Disk II

Conversion program to convert your phone data to the Rainbow system.

Price—$19.95 (Disk)

BEGINNER'S SIMULATED MARKET
Rainbow Marketware
3111 Berkshire Rd.
Baltimore, MD 21214

Apple II,
36K,
Disk II

Simulation program. "Expand our starter program which reads a 3 1/2 year long data file for twelve stocks to devise and test your profitable trading ideas".

Price—$24.95 (Disk)

THE BIG BOARD- A STOCK MARKET GAME
Frank L. Whitsell
P.O. Box 2945
Fayetteville, AR 72701

TRS-80,
Model I,
Level II,
16K

Risk and world events affect stock prices in this market game. The computer/broker tracks players funds, portfolio, margin account, net worth, rate of return, splits, margin calls and more. Hours of fun and practice. Money back guarantee.

Price—$15.00 (Cassette)

BIZDEX—available on The Source Information Utility

Telecomputing Corp. of America *personal*
1616 Anderson Road *computer or terminal*
McLean, VA 22102 *with modem capable*
of accessing The Source

BIZDEX is the general source index to business and financial services which include:

—Investor advisory.

—Tax information.

—American Stock Exchange prices, volumes and most active stocks.

—New York Stock Exchange advances or declines, most actives, odd-lot activity, sales composite, prices and floor volume.

—Stock market information—daily averages, advances and declines, leads, pulse, trends, performance, Dow Jones indexes, D & B index, Standard & Poors and comparisons.

—Financial news and headlines.

—Earnings report.

—Portfolio management through Source files.

—One hundred sixty eight other financial reports.

Current information on investor oriented services may be obtained by writing *The Source.*

BONDS & SECURITIES (990012)

Compucolor Corp. *Compucolor,*
Intecolor Dr. *16K,*
225 Technology Park/Atlanta *disk*
Norcross, GA 30092

Program allows user to change variables and see their effects on bond price and yield. Dates can be entered as real dates or time to maturity. Callable bonds are handled with room for up to five call dates. Single keystroke prints bond amortization schedule.

BULLS AND BEARS

Speakeasy Software, Ltd. *Apple II*
Box 1220 *or*
Kemptville, Ontario, Canada *Apple II*
Plus, 16K

This is a microcomputer game of high finance for up to 5 players. The computer serves as banker and stock broker. You can be a clever speculator or the astute chairman of a powerful corporation. Challenging game which also provides some insights into the workings of corporate finance and the stock market.

Price—$12.00 (Cassette)

BUSINESS PACKAGE II (ED003)

Micro Learningware *TRS-80*
Box 2134 *Model I,*
N. Mankato, MN 56001 *Level II,*
16K

Provides stock market simulation, also loan analysis, annuity calculations and bank reconciliation. Write for further information.

CALCUGRAM CF

Clacugram Co. *TRS-80,*
P.O. Box 3037 *Model I,*
Walnut Creek, CA 94598 *Level II,*
16K, printer

Helps to establish stock option spreads and hedges.

Features:

—Handles up to four simultaneous positions.

—Graphic display of projected gain at any date in the future.

—Easy change of ratios among the entered options, with the effect of the change shown on the display.

—Printer output of gain curves, and tabular future option prices and gains information.

—Computes opening commission and prints table of net profit for any closing date.

CASSETTE BUSINESS PACKAGE (L216)

TRS-80,
Model I,
Level II,
16K

Micro Architect Inc.
96 Dothan St.
Arlington, MA 02174

Contains ten business programs: Data Base Manager, Inventory System, Word Processor, Stock Security Info., Check Balance Program, Deposit Calculator, Sales Analysis, Sort, Linked List Utility and Statistics. Write for further information.

Price—$59.00 (Cassette)

CASSETTE PORTFOLIO SYSTEM

TRS-80,
16K

Radio Shack
obtained at any Radio Shack store

Contains three programs:

—"Buy and Sell" for stocks, mutual funds and bonds.

—"Summary" computes long and short term capital gain information.

—"Options" tracks up to 10 positions, computes returns and unrealized gains.

For actual or imaginary investments, the system will handle 20 current stocks, 10 current bonds, 5 current funds, 10 current option positions. Automatically computes yield, total market value and other key parameters to analyze each security. Graphically compares performance of users portfolio and a selected financial index. Provides a summary (total market value, estimated annual income, and percentage of investments in each type of security) of users total investment program.

Dates, purchase and selling prices are kept and gain or loss computed for easier tax filing. Includes capability to print data seen on the screen.

Price—$29.95 (Cassette)

COLOR BAR GRAPH PROGRAM

Apple II,
16K,
Applesoft

Bill Phmphrey
1633 Kalanjuka Way
Honolulu, HA 96821

This program plots a color bar for each of two to twelve figures the user wants to compare. Bars may be labelled and the graph titled. Includes Double Bar Graph program which compares two sets of data over equal periods.

Price—$7.95 (Cassette)

COMMODITY FILE

Apple II,
32K with Applesoft ROM,
48K with Applesoft RAM,
Disk II,
132 column printer optional

Mind Machine
31 Woodhollow Lane
Huntington, NY 11743

Stores and retrieves information on virtually every commodity traded on all future exchanges. Self-prompting entering of short/long contracts. Computes gross and net profits/losses, maintains a running cash balance. Cash balance may be amended to compensate for deposits or withdrawals from the account. Ready display of contracts on file, cash balances and profit/loss statement. Generates color bar graphs depicting individual and cumulative transactions. Includes routine to proofread contracts prior to filing.

Price—$19.96 (Disk)

CREATE MARKET STRATEGIES
West Coast Consultants
1755 Lincoln Blvd.
Tracy, CA 95376

Apple II,
36K,
Disk II

Advanced programs. Enables the user to create and improve stock trading techniques, build long data files and try point and figure charting.

Price—$49.95 (Disk)

CURVE
Rainbow Marketware
3111 Berkshire Rd.
Baltimore, MD 21214

Apple II ,
48K for full program ,
16K for subroutines

The CURVE program is interactive, fully guiding the user step-by-step through its operation using messages and animated graphics. Once design specifications are entered, a plot is immediately drawn. The 16 CURVE subroutines may be integrated into other programs, providing the capability to add customized hardcopy graphics to existing BASIC programs.

Plotting capabilities include:
—Cartesian, parametric and polar equations.
—Data points or characters entered from the keyboard.
—Shaded bar graphs with either horizontal or vertical orientation.
—A fully scalable alphanumeric character set.
—Linear and logarithmically scaled axes.

Manuals familiarize the user with all required input and operational details. Examples of graphics output resulting from input and program lines are given.

Prices: CURVE program—$50.00, CURVE subroutines—$75.00

DOW JONES
Instant Software
Peterborough, NH 03458

PET,
8K

Financial game in which each player begins with a modest portfolio. Decisions to buy and sell should be based on news bulletins and rumors displayed, and daily trading activity. A computer "broker" offers professional advice (for a fee, of course). Quotes and detailed information on each stock available. Fun, and a good learning experience.

DOW JONES SERIES
Apple Computer, Inc.
10260 Bandley Drive
Cupertino, CA 95014

Apple II
or Apple II Plus,
32K,
Applesoft,
Disk IIV, Modem,

This series consists of three separate program packages, each of which will function independent of the others. All are designed to aid the user in the capture and processing of Dow Jones financial wire service information.

STOCK QUOTE REPORTER allows the Apple to hold a list of stocks and automatically update opening price or bid, closing or asking price, daily high and low, and current volume for each stock. Stock list is easily changed to suit the user. (A2M0022)

PORTFOLIO EVALUATOR analyzes each of up to 50 stocks to provide summaries of short and long term gains and losses, current portfolio value and shares held. (A2D0007)

NEWS REPORTER allows the user to retrieve selected news stories about specific corporations, industries or federal agencies. Once a topic has been selected, the program specifies the number of stories and pages of headlines available and allows for user selection of stories to read. (A2D0011)

To retrieve and use information from the Dow Jones Service, the user must contract directly with the service. Once a password has been acquired, access to the information (delayed 15 minutes) is obtained through a local phone call in most areas of the country.

Available through Apple Dealers.

FFT (Fast Fourier Transform)
TRS-80,
16K

Delta Systems
P.O. Box 1181
Goleta, CA 93017

Set of interactive programs:
—Fast Fourier Transformations.
—Digital Filter Simulator.
—Linear and Exponential Curve Fit.
—Disk or cassette Data and Results File.
—Interactive Graphics.

Documentation provides a tutorial and examples for such applications as plotting stock market values and computed trend lines, etc. Runs in 16K cassette TRS-80, has expanded capabilities for more elaborate systems.

Price—$30.00 (Disk), $25.00 (cassette)

FINANCIAL ANALYSIS (A Tutorial)
or Apple II,
Apple II Plus,
16K

Speakeasy Software Ltd
Box 1220
Kemptville, Ontario, Canada

An interactive learning cassette with sections on risk, Short and Intermediate Term Financing, Financial Statements and Key Business Ratios. The user may then actually use the concepts presented by playing the *Meany Manufacturing Business Game.*

Price—$16.50 (Cassette)

FINANCIAL DECISIONS
H-P 85
Applications
Pac
+00085-13004

Hewlett Packard
1000 N.E. Circle Blvd.
Corvalis, OR 97330

Contains the following programs:
—Compound Interest and Loan Amortization.
—Discounted Cash Flow Analysis.

—Simple Interest and Interest Conversions.
—Bonds and Notes.
—Break-Even Analysis.
—Odd Days Interest.

Includes program descriptions, user instructions and example problems. All programs contain HELP sections with key definition references and GUIDE keys or set of program guidelines which explain unique or potentially difficult concepts in specific sections. Also includes section explaining basic concepts of cash flow diagrams and cash flow sign convention.

Available through Hewlett Packard dealers.

THE FORECASTER
Apple II, 16K,
Applesoft ROM

System Design Lab
121-8th Street Altizer
Huntington, WV 25705

A complete regression analysis is performed and the program gives you an accurate regression equation within seconds. Data is then graphed in HIRES graphics and a trend line is plotted using the regression equation. An excellent tool for important trend analysis.

Price—$16.95 (Cassette), $20.95 (Disk)

FOTOFOLIO—YOUR STOCKS IN BAR GRAPHS
R.E. Packer, Ph.D.
TRS-80,
29-A Estancia Drive
Model I,
Marana, AZ 85238
Level II, 16K

Profit enhancing pictures of each investment. Calculates percent of portfolio, dollar value, dollar and percent gain, approach to price and tax holding goals and precise figure tables. Advanced version indicates profitable stock swaps.

Price—$14.50 (Cassette), $24.50 (Disk), $4.50 (Listing)

INVESTMENT DATA SYSTEM
Apple II, 32K,
Urban Aggregates, Inc.
Applesoft ROM, Disk II,
6431 Brass Knob
Talos or Apple
Columbia, MO 21044
Graphics Tablet

Allows the user to create a complete data base for any stock or commodity. Data charts can be traced from the graphics tablet to create files to the users specifications. Easy update and file display capabilities are included.

Data bases created with this system may then be analyzed by user—generated or other commercially available software. Manual available separately.

Price—$120.00 (System and manual), $20.000 (Manual only)

INVESTOR'S PARADISE
TRS-80

Instant Software
Peterborough, NH 03458

Two stock market simulation programs for your fun and learning:

STOCK TREK—you and five other investors are given the opportunity to transform $5000 into a fortune by buying and selling stocks. Features an automatic ticker tape, stock display board, prospectus for each stock and graphic display of each stock's performance.

SPECULATION—you are asked to enter data on 25 real companies and start playing the market. Shares are bought and sold on net cost, including commissions. Your success is measured by the total value of your portfolio versus investing equivalent funds at a fixed rate of interest. Can simulate up to five years of market activity and save all data for future reference.

LeINVESTOR *Apple II or Apple II*
LeSoftware *Plus, 48K, Applesoft ROM*
3224 Magnolia Ct. *or language system,*
Bettendorf, IA 52722 *Disk II*

Series of interactive programs written by the author of this book. Driven by a master menu, all programs share a common data base which may be expanded if a second disk drive is used. Programs include:

—*CONFIGURE* allows the user to set operational parameters such as length of moving averages, number of indexes and stocks, disk slot and drive numbers, printer slot and width, etc. Once set, parameters become default values until changed by the user.

—*THE FUNDAMENTALIST* analyzes key data from financial reports to aid in stock purchase and sale decisions. Each stock may be analyzed over consecutive time periods and significant changes in key factors signalled. A widely extended version of The Fundamental Analyst 3.0.

—*MARKET MASTER* based on interaction of moving averages which the user may define. Uses advance-decline and selected market index values to construct a Weighted Market Index of general stock market conditions. Analysis of individual stocks is based on moving averages and the WMI. The user can define buy, sell and hold levels for each individual stock in the system. Provision is also made to generate an automatic sell signal when the stock price reaches a user set percentage of its last three week low. Includes capability to adjust for stock splits and distributors, verify/correct data for errors and easy entry of new data. Number of stocks easily adjusted to memory and disk drive requirements.

—*DOLLAR COST AVERAGER* provides a convenient method of determining the effectiveness of a program of dollar cost averaging or dividend reinvestment combined with additional stock purchases. Easy data entry and revision via menu selection. Provides video or printed performance summaries for each stock or a total portfolio. Extended version of The Dollar Cost Averaging Analyst.

—*PORTFOLIO MANAGER* keeps records on all transactions and holdings. Automatically interactive with the other programs in this series to eliminate duplication of data entry. Summaries may be displayed or printed using several optional parameters, i.e., year to date, date to date, etc.

—*HELP* explains the theory and operation of all the programs in this series. A tutorial aids the user in construction of the Weighted Market Index and setting stock signal parameters.

Several additions to this system are presently in progress. Updates and revisions will be compatible with existing programs and supplied for cost of media plus shipping. Write for current information sheet. Documentation available separately, cost applied to purchase.

Price—$125.00 (Disk), $25.00 (Manual only)

LINE GRAPH PROGRAM

Apple II,
16K, Applesoft ROM

Bill Phmphrey
1633 Kalanjuka Way
Honolulu, HA 96821

Uses Apple's HIRES graphics to plot line graphs. Points are labelled with months, letters, numbers on your own codes. Graph title is printed on the bottom line. DELUXE BAR GRAPH program also included.

Price—$7.95 (Cassette)

LOW COST HISTORICAL DATA

Apple II,
36K, Disk II

Rainbow Marketware
3111 Berskhire Rd.
Baltimore, MD 21214

A series of five library files containing data on 60 stocks for a period of 180 days each. The five diskettes cover the period January 1977 to July, 1980. Contact Rainbow for further details.

Price—$14.95 (Each library disk)

MARKET CHARTER(tm)

Apple II or Apple II
Plus, 48K, Applesoft
Rom or language
system, Disk II

RTR Software, Inc.
P. O. Box 12351
El Paso, TX 79912

This system includes CHARTING and MAINTENANCE programs, sample data for three stocks and the users manual.

The CHARTING program will generate color bar graphs or plot any number of simple, weighted and exponential moving averages in the users choice of five colors. Trendlines, trading bands, horizontal support/resistance and speed resistance lines are easily constructed. Volume charts and indicators are also included. Split screen capability allows comparison of the chart with actual data. Automatic scaling feature is designed to utilize the full display screen.

MAINTENANCE allows data entry and updates, correction for stock splits and verify/correct data. Includes disk file utilities to rearrange stocks on data disk, delete unwanted data, create additional data disks and consolidate several disks.

Hard copy of data is available on systems using a PR# command to activate the printer. Printer must have graphics capability.

Up to date weekly data may be purchased from RTR, or you may enter your own. Manual and demo diskette available separately. Contact RTR for prices on various program and data packages offered.

MARKET INFORMATION SYSTEM

TRS-80, Model I,
Level II,
32K,
2 disk drives

Market Information Software
7215 Tod Street
Falls Church, VA 22046

A comprehensive stock market technical analysis information system. Designed to recognize rallies, declines and turnabouts. According to the manufacturer, this system has warned of turnarounds weeks in advance and will pay for itself. Data included.

Price—$49.95 (Disk)

MICROQUOTE—available on MicroNet Personal Computing Service

CompuServe, Inc.
5000 Arlington Centre Blvd.
Columbus, OH 43220

personal computer on terminal
with modem capable
of accessing MicroNet

Provides access to a data base containing trading statistics and descriptive information on more than 32,000 stocks, bonds and options. Data is updated daily and contains price and volume information for most stocks back to January 1, 1974. Dividend dates and history available back to January 1, 1968.

Specific information available:

—*Stocks*—current and historical prices (high, low and closing), volumes, dividends and descriptive data (earnings per share, ratings, shares outstanding, etc.).

—Bonds—yields, maturity dates and Moody's ratings.

—Options—exercise prices, expiration dates and underlying stock prices.

Data may be searched for daily, weekly, monthly or between specified starting and ending date periods. Securities are identified by CUSIP numbers, ticker symbols or issuer name.

Cost to use the MicroQuote data base is a combination of "connect time" charges for the system, a per-access fee for each time the data base is used and transaction fees based on the specific program used and amount of information requested.

Further information may be obtained by writing CompuServe.

MICROSTAT

Ecosoft
P. O. Box 68602
Indianapolis, IN 46268

North Star, 32K, BASIC,
2 disk drives recommended

A comprehensive statistics package which features:

—File orientation with complete editing.

—Data Management Subsystem for editing, ranking, lagging and data file transfers.

—Eleven data transformations (linear, reciprocal, etc.).

—Probability distributions and scatterplots, correlations, etc.

Manual and sample data with associated printouts available separately.

Price—$200.00 (Disk)

MULTIPLE REGRESSION ANALYSIS

System Design Lab
121-8th Street Altizer
Huntington, WV 25705

Apple II,
16 K free memory,
Applesoft
ROM

A statistical program which may be used in business, investments, education, or any field where historical data is used to predict future events. Similar to Turf Analysis program from the same company. Includes the Correlation Matrix, Inverted Matrix, the Sum, Mean and Standard Deviation, optional hard copy printout, etc. Fully tested and documented.

Price—$29.95 (Disk), $24.95 (Cassette)

OPTION EVALUATION PACKAGE

TRS-80, Model I,
Level II,
16K for tape version,
32K with disk drive
for disk version

Software Sooner, Inc.
P. O. Box 2338
Normak, OK 73070

Provides programs to compute the theoretical option value and neutral hedge ratio according to the Black and Scholes model and provide for the update and creation of quick access data files.

Program features include:

— Choice of manual or file based data input.

— Choice of using historical volatility or the volatility implied by recent option and underlying stock prices.

— File based data can be selected randomly by ticker symbol or sequentially in alphabetical order.

— Obtain answers to questions such as, "What should the value of the option be if—days from now the stock price is—and the short term interest rate is —?"

— Single query provides values and hedge ratios for all expiration dates for striking prices immediately above and below the stock price.

Includes an initial data tape containing price volatility of underlying stocks, dividends and ex-dividend data, etc. Additional data available.

Price—$69.95

PLOT

Apple II or Apple II Plus,
Disk II

The Basic Business Software Co.
P. O. Box 2032
Salt Lake City, UT 84110

This program will plot a file of X, Y data points using a standard 80 or 132 column printer. The user may select the following options:

— Specify horizontal and vertical axes.

— Title all axes with multiple lines of text.

— Control the scale of the plot.

— Remove the printer distortion.

— Print values on each line of the plot.

— Specify special characters to be used in the plot.

— Control the tick marks and increments.

— Specify the maximum and minimum X and Y values.

— Plot X values on the Y axis and Y values on the X axis.

Includes other options. Users manual included.

Price—$25.00 (Disk)

PORTFOLIO AND TAX RECORDS

Apple II,
36K, Disk II

Rainbow Marketware
3111 Berkshire Rd.
Baltimore, MD 21214

Record keeping program. "Evaluate your portfolio. Record capital gains and dividends. Eliminate paperwork. Coded files protected by your password."

Price—$29.95 (Disk)

PORTFOLIO BOOKKEEPING PACKAGE

TRS-80, Model I,
Level II, 16K for tape version, 32K
for disk. Printer recommended
for maximum usefulness.

Software Sooner, Inc.
P. O. Box 2338
Norman, OK 73070

Package performs three tasks:

—Maintain records of portfolio holdings.

—Provides summary of period to date results in terms of long and short term gains and losses, dividend and interest income, interest expenses and miscellaneous expenses.

—Provides year end listing of individual security transactions for tax preparation uses.

Provision for handling uncommon, complex transactions is included. In addition to seven basic accounts (cash, special cash, other assets, dividend income, interest income, interest expense and other expense), individual security accounts are limited only by the memory capacity of the machine.

Price—$29.95

PORTFOLIO MANAGER *TRS-80, Model I,*
The Software Foundry, Inc. *Level II,*
15 East 10th Street *32K, 1*
New York, NY 10003 *disk drive*

Will keep track of stock holdings in up to 27 portfolios, using the Dow Jones news/retrieval system to obtain prices on a 15 minute delay basis. Graphs, quotes and news available on over 5000 companies.

Price—$75.00 (Disk)

SECURITIES ANALYSIS *TI 99/4 Solid*
Texas Instruments, Inc. *State Software (tm)*
Command Module

A program package designed to provide the serious investor with assistance in evaluation, selection and management of a portfolio. The user is able to:

—Evaluate stock prices based on combined yields from dividends and a change in stock price.

—Compare the value and implied volatility of options.

—Determine expected return from option hedges.

—Compute bond yields to maturity and percent of par market price.

Also provides basic financial calculations such as compound interest, annuities, uneven cash flow and days between dates.

Price—$54.95

SECURITY ANALYSIS Apple II
Dr. George L. Haller *or TRS-80*
1500 Galleon Drive
Naples, FL 33490

Package designed to list and analyze a portfolio of securities by name, number of shares, cost per share, dividend per share and recent quote. User may select one of three alternative presentations:

—Displays the total value of each security and then the total value of the portfolio.

—Lists the name, number of shares, cost, value and gain or loss of each security and a total cost, value and gain or loss for the portfolio.

—Analysis of dividends by displaying for each security the percent of dividend to cost, percent to value and dollar value of the dividend. The same data is then totalled for the users portfolio.

Includes provision for adding date and Dow Jones Average. Easy addition, modification and deletion of data. TRS-80, Model I, Level I, 4K will handle about 35 securities at one pass.

This program is similar to that described by Dr. Haller in the December, 1977 issue of *kilobaud/MICROCOMPUTING*. Also included is a copy of his Golf Handicap program.

Price—$15.00 (Disk), $10.00 (Cassette)

SECURITY CHARTING
Apple II,
Programma International, Inc.
48K, Applesoft,
3400 Wilshire Blvd.
Disk II
Los Angeles, CA 90010

This program is geared toward the stock investor. Stocks may be entered daily or weekly and graphed, in HIRES, on a 4, 9 or 14 day or week moving average.

Price—$79.95 (Disk)

STANDARD & POOR'S
STOCKPAK & PORTFOLIO MANAGEMENT
Radio Shack
TRS-80, Model I,
Available from Radio Shack Stores
Level II, 32K,
Expansion Interface, 2 disk
drives. Printer optional.

This package contains a stand alone portfolio management system and the software required to use Standard and Poor's monthly STOCKPAK Common Stock Data Service (available on a subscription basis). STOCKPAK data (about 30 current items of information on approximately 900 common stocks) is contained on a diskette and in a newsletter received monthly by subscribers.

Features of the system include:

—User may define and manage a personal stock portfolio and apply it against the S & P data base. Areas of analysis include dividend yield, diversification, risk, performance, etc.

—Provides the opportunity to screen a group of companies by means of simple criteria statements. This analysis may focus on the areas of stock purchase or sale, merger, acquisition, option purchase, etc.

—Includes facilities to store and manage any subset of the S & P information in user defined data files, as well as access to and management of the entire monthly data base.

—User is able to format, generate and print a report. Pre-defined report formats may be stored in the system for later use.

—Calculations and functions may be specified by the user.

—Portfolio management is interactive with data base, enabling the user to compare the performance of his stocks against any selected group of stocks in the S & P files.

Annual subscription to the Standard & Poor's STOCKPAK service is approximately $200.00.

Price—$49.95 (Disk)

STATISTICS PAC
Apple II, 32K,
Charles Mann and Associates
Disk II
7594 San Remo Trail
Yucca Valley, CA 92284

Contains a data management system (also available separately) and a battery of programs for curve fitting, probability, general statistics, distribution mathematics and test statistics. Uses the HIRES capabilities of the Apple II to allow for curve fitting of the data using linear, exponential, logarithmic or power relationships. Built-in data base included to produce a complete set of working examples. General statistics element includes LOWRES plots for standard histograms and distribution arrays. Includes sophisticated probability analysis, random number generation routines and distributions. Can handle up to five 100 X 1 matrices containing raw data, grouped data or frequency arrays.

Price—$89.95 (Disk)

STOCK ANALYSIS AND PROJECTION PROGRAM

Edward L. Bates	*TRS-80,*
6010 Benning Drive	*Model, Level II,*
Houston, TX 77096	*16K*

Provides financial report analysis based on historical price data provided in most company annual reports and makes a stock price projection for three future years. Files are saved on tape.

Price—$100.00 (Cassette)

STOCK AND OPTIONS TRADING ANALYSIS

	TRS-80,
Creative Computing Software	*Model I, Level II,*
P. O. Box 789-M	*cassette or disk*
Morristown, NJ 07960	

Package contains four programs:

—*OPGRAPH* presents important indices of both opening and closing call option transactions.

—*OPTION* presents a graph or table (user selected) of profit from any combination of six basic positions.

—*NEWPREM* enables the user to predict the future premiums of an option at whatever time and future stock price the user selects.

—*PORTVAL* enables the user to determine cost, current value per share, total current value and capital gain of a portfolio. May contain long and short stock and long and short option positions.

Extensive documentation includes sample runs and covers possible investment attitudes, the listed option markets, puts, calls and option strategies. The basic strategy used is hedging listed options against common stock.

Price—$99.95

STOCK CONTROL FOR THE INVESTOR

	TRS-80,
Small Business Systems Group	*Model I, Level II,*
6 Carlisle Road	*32K,*
Westford, MA 01886	*3 disk drives*

Keeps track of buys, sells, splits and expenses. Calculates profit and loss for 999 clients, 500 assets, 3000 transactions. Reports include summary or detail of current or closed transactions, client list, year to date dollar volume, asset list.

Price—$225.00 (Disk)

STOCK MARKET

	TRS-80,
John Hoffman	*Model I,*
6725 E. 5th	*Level II,*
Tulsa, OK 74112	*16K*

Game for one to ten players. Buy and sell securities in attempt to become the wealthiest player. Includes margin buying, security conversion and selling short. Players decisions influence market prices.

Price—$7.00 (Cassette), $3.00 (Listing)

STOCK MARKET MONITOR
Galactic Software Div. GS & WS
11520 N. Port Washington Rd.
Mequon, WI 53092

TRS-80,
Model I,
Level II,
16K

A technically based stock monitor for the active trader. Users should be subscribers of *Value Line* or *Moody's*. Constantly compares individual issues to the broad market. Write for more information.

Price—$99.00 (Disk), $89.00 (Cassette)

STOCK MARKET SIMULATION
Ohio Scientific
1333 South Chillicothe Rd.
Aurora, OH 44202

see below

Available in two separate versions for Ohio Scientific computers, SCP-723 for C1P, SCP-722 for C4P and C8P. Contact manufacturer or OSI dealer for further information (Cassette).

STOCK PORTFOLIO
Howard Software Service
7722 Hosford Avenue
Los Angeles, CA 90045

Apple II,
32K,
Applesoft,
Disk II

Records and analyzes price history for individual stocks as well as investor's entire portfolio. Disk based for easy data storage and retrieval.

Price—$19.00 (Disk)

STOCK PORTFOLIO (321012)
Commodore Business Machines, Inc.
950 Rittenhouse Rd.
Norristown, PA 19401

PET, CBM
systems

Contains two programs—STOCK MAINTENANCE and STOCK ANALYSIS. Keep track of all the details, calculate values and rates of return on your stock investments. May be used with CBM printer.

Price—$24.95

STOCK PORTFOLIO MANAGEMENT
Jim Holliday
19 Bryant Road
Turnersville, NJ 08012

TRS-80,
Model I,
Level II, 32K,
1 disk drive

Keeps track of investors portfolio and advises long and short term gains and losses. Calculates break-even points and return on investment, at any time, for an individual stock or the entire portfolio. Write for further information.

Price—$190.00 (Disk)

STOCK PRICE PROJECTIONS
Jim Holliday
19 Bryant Road
Turnersville, NJ 08012

TRS-80,
Model I,
Level II, 16K,
Disk

Projects the price of a stock based on the inflation rate, prime interest rate, company earnings and growth of company earnings. Formula is based on proved statistical techniques.

Price—$12.50 (Disk)

STOCK TRACKER(tm)
H & H Trading Co.
P. O. Box 23546
Pleasant Hill, CA 94523

TRS-80, Model I, Level II,
32K, 2 disk drives.
Apple II or Apple II
Plus, 32K, Applesoft
ROM or language system,
Disk II. Also available, a
CP/M version written in CBASIC.

Based loosely on principles developed by J.E. Granville, this program is designed to improve profits in stocks, options or commodities through enhanced timing of purchases and sales. Signals are geared to short term trading in options, intermediate term trading for stocks and commodities. Requires about two months of basic data (trading date, closing price and sales volume) to begin generating daily trading signals for each security tracked. In addition to buy, sell and hold signals, the system supports short sales and pyramiding.

Stock-Tracker is composed of a series of menu-driven interactive programs and incorporate provisions for correcting input errors not trapped by the system. Eight months one year of data for 15 different securities can be held on one disk, multiple data disks can also be used.

Documentation (available separately) provides detailed information on the use of the system, theory and methodology used, and tips for the novice trader.

Prices—$150.00 (Apple or TRS-80 disk), $350.00 (CP/M version), $15.00 (Software manual only)

TAX INVESTMENT RECORD KEEPING
Texas Instruments, Inc.

Solid State
Software(tm)
Command Module for TI 99/4

No further details have been received as of this writing. Contact your TI dealer or the company for further information on features and availability.

TICKERTEC
Max Ule & Company, Inc.
6 East 43rd Street
New York, NY 10017

TRS-80, Model I,
Level II, 2 disk drives,
North Star Horizon.
TRS-80 Model II.
CP/M compatible systems.

This system is designed to be connected to a dedicated ticker line leased from either the New York Stock Exchange or the American Stock Exchange. In addition to providing real time information direct from the exchange, this system includes provisions to:

—Monitor the last traded price and total volume for selected stocks Number of stocks range from 48 (TRS-80 Version I) to 500 (North Star 65K Version).

—Maintain a price and volume history of current and previous trades of each security monitored, and provides access to this data on user request.

—Monitor holdings separate from indicator or speculation stocks. Securities, maintained in either of the two lists, may be recalled or changed from one list to the other by user command.

—Display selected information or all data received on the exchange ticker line.

—Monitor stocks, in real time, by the use of global limits whose sensitivity can be changed at any time. If a limit is exceeded, an "alert screen" displays the stock symbol and all six normalized parameters.

—Save the information collected during the day on tape or disk. The tape or disk file can then be used to start the system with the previous day's closing information.

Several combinations of options are offered, depending on the version of TICKERTEC selected. The TRS-80 Model I version, for instance, offers a Basic Data Base Retriever which allows access to data on diskette after market close, Portfolio Management System which reports your portfolio position at the close of each trading day and Hard Copy Option which prints the entire ticker tape or selected data.

The TRS-80 Model II, North Star and CP/M versions offer the following options:

—Maintenance of daily high and low for each stock.

—Display up to 600 trades for each stock, up/down tick indicator, full ticker tape or selected stocks.

—Bi-sync protocol interface for linkage to other computers.

—Simultaneous monitoring of both the NYSE and AMEX tickertape lines.

—Automatic page scanning and historic data paging.

—BASIC language routines to access accumulated data.

Prices range from $1000 to over $2500, depending on the configuration and options selected. Contact the distributor for an extensive information packet.

VIDEO GRAPHS
Texas Instruments, Inc.

Solid State Software(tm)
Command Module for
TI 99/4

Offers color and pattern generating capabilities. The user can create fine line drawings, design mosaic patterns or construct pictures. Any pattern generated can be stored for future review or rework. Could also be used to generate stock market graphs and color displays for investment analysis.

Price—$19.95

VISICALC
Personal Software, Inc.
592 Weddell Drive
Sunnyvale, CA 94086

Apple II or Apple II
Plus, 32K, Disk II.
Check with your dealer
for compatibility with other
popular systems.

Applies computer assistance to virtually any problem that can be solved using a calculator, pen and paper and defined in rows and columns. User is provided with an electronic worksheet of up to 63 columns and 254 rows. Any format or form needed can be created by typing in words. Where calculations are necessary, type in a formula. Automatically performs all arithmetic functions, new present value and transcendental functions and displays the results. Any change in numeric data results in an instant display of the new result. Easily allows the user to experiment with numerous data variables and possibilities. Hard copy print of all the information on the worksheet easily obtained.

Extremely versatile program with definite applications for anyone interested in manipulation of numbers.

Price—$150.00 (Disk)

As mentioned in the beginning of this section, the preceeding list does not begin to cover the whole spectrum of commercially available software. Some attempt has been made to limit the list to programs of direct interest to investors. No doubt there are many excellent offerings not listed, and some of the information contained in the listings will be obsolete by the time this reaches your hands. This is an unavoidable state of affairs in a field moving as rapidly as personal computing. New programs are being introduced almost daily, so watch magazine and newsletter new product sections, advertisements and reviews for the latest information.

You may want to refer back to some of the ideas offered in Chapter 6 for evaluating commercial software once you have obtained detailed information on any programs of interest to you. At the risk of being overly repititious, let me again reinforce a basic principle—If you want a program, buy it! Don't steal it!

There are additional sources of programs available to the computer owner interested in investment applications. Books containing programs and program ideas are offered by many publishers, as you will note in Appendix C. Numerous computer oriented periodicals are published, almost all of which feature articles describing and listing programs developed by the author. Some of these programs are released for sale commercially, others may be typed in to your system from the listing published. Users groups often have a library of programs developed by their members, and occasionally members of other user groups across the country. At least one organization of microcomputer owners interested in management of investments publishes a newsletter containing many programs and program ideas (see Appendix B).

There is presently a good selection of software available commercially or through one of the other means just described. We have every reason to expect the future will bring an even more diverse group of sophisticated programs. Constant advances in the state of the art will continue to challenge the abilities of even the most proficient software producers. Many "old favorite" commercial programs are continually being updated to reflect these advances and increase their sales appeal. Others are falling by the wayside, victims of terminal obsolescence.

As the person most directly involved with your investment program, it remains your responsibility to determine whether or not a program is applicable to your particular investment management approach and situation. This is true whether the program is purchased commercially, typed from a published listing or created in your own mind.

Appendix B

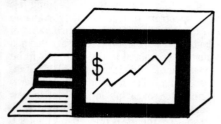

Sources of Information

The primary purpose of the listings in this section is to give you some specific sources of information on the various topics listed. Each of the lists reflects a sampling of sources and is not intended to include every possibility.

In many cases, one source of information is sufficient to obtain many other possibilities. Financial periodicals, for instance, are an excellent way to locate information regarding advisory services, brokerage firms, newsletters, etc. Similarly, computer oriented periodicals feature advertisements and information regarding computer systems, peripherals and software. Reader service "bingo" cards found in such publications offer an easy way to secure a significant amount of information. Somewhat faster results can be obtained by sending an inquiry directly to the advertiser.

COMPUTER MANUFACTURERS

Alpha Micro
17881 Sky Park North
Irvine, CA 92714

APF Electronics, Inc.
1501 Broadway
New York, NY 10036

Apple Computer, Inc.
10260 Bandley Drive
Cupertino, CA 95014

Atari Personal Computers
1265 Borregas Avenue
Sunnyvale, CA 94086

Bally, S-W Distributors, Inc.
5300 B. McDermott Drive
Berkeley, IL 60163

Commodore Business Machines, Inc.
950 Rittenhouse Road
Norristown, PA 19401

Compucolor Corp.
P. O. Box 569
Norcross, GA 30071

Cromeco, Inc.
280 Bernardo Avenue
Mountain View, CA 94040

Exidy
Data Systems Division
390 Java Drive
Sunnyvale, CA 94086

Heath Company
Benton Harbor, MI 49022

Hewlett Packard
1000 N. E. Circle Blvd.
Corvallis, OR 97330

Intertec Data Systems
2300 Broad River Road
Columbia, SC 29210

Mattel Electronics
5150 Rosencrans Avenue
Hawthorne, CA 90250

Midwest
Scientific Instruments, Inc.
220 West Cedar
Olathe, KS 66061

NEC
Information Services, Inc.
5 Militia Drive
Lexington, MA 02173

Nixdorf Personal
Computer Systems, Inc.
168 Middlesex Tpk.
Burlington, MA 01803

North Star Computers, Inc.
1440 Fourth Street
Berkeley, CA 94710

Ohio Scientific
1333 South Chillicothe Road
Aurora, OH 44202

Panasonic
1 Panasonic Way
Secaucus, NJ 07094

Personal Micro Computer, Inc.
475 Ellis Street
Mountain View, CA 94043

Quasar
9401 W. Grant·Avenue
Franklin Park, IL 60131

Quay Corporation
P.O. Box 386
Freehold, NJ 07728

Radio Shack Division
Tandy Corporation
1300 One Tandy Center
Fort Worth, TX 76102

RCA, VIP Customer Service
New Holland Avenue
Lancaster, PA 17604

Sinclair Research, Ltd.
50 Staniford Street
Boston, MA 02114

Smoke Signal Broadcasting
31336 Via Colinas
Westlake Village, CA 91361

Southwest Technical
Products Corporation
219 W. Rhapsody
San Antonio, TX 78216

Texas Instruments, Inc.
Consumer Relations Department
P.O. Box 53 (ATTN: TI-99/4)
Lubbock, TX 79408

Vector Graphics, Inc.
31364 Via Colinas
Westlake Village, CA 91361

COMPUTER ORIENTED PERIODICALS

In each of the listings below, the periodical name will be followed by its specific computer emphasis, if any.

Apple Seed (Apple)
The Software Exchange
6 South Street
Milford, NH 03055

The Apple Shoppe (Apple)
P.O. Box 701
Placentia, CA 92670

BYTE (General)
P.O. Box 590
Martinsville, NJ 08836

CLOAD Magazine, Inc. (TRS-80)
P.O. Box 1267
Goleta, CA 93017

Computer Shopper
(Classified Ads—All)
P.O. Box F20
Titusville, FL 32780

COMPUTRONICS (TRS-80)
50 N. Pasack Road
Spring Valley, NY 10977

Creative Computing (General)
P. O. Box 789-M
Morristown, NJ 07960
Cursor (PET, CBM)
Box 550
Goleta, CA 93017

kilobaud/MICROCOMPUTING
(General)
P. O. Box 997
Farmingdale, NY 11737
MICRO (6502 based computers)
P. O. Box 6502
Chelmsford, MA 01824
MicroMedia Magazine
(Heath H8, H11, H89)
1316 Elmhurst Drive
Garland, TX

NIBBLE (Apple)
Micro-Sparc, Inc.
P. O. Box 325
Lincoln, MA 01733

PEEK(65) (OSI)
62 Southgate Avenue
Annapolis, MD 21401
Personal Computing (General)
1050 Commonwealth Avenue
Boston, MA 02215

Prog/80 (TRS-80)
The Software Exchange
6 South Street
Milford, NH 03055

Recreational Computing
(General)
People's Computer Co.
1263 El Camino Real, Box E
Menlo Park, CA 94025

S-100 Micro Systems
(S-100 bus systems)
P. O. Box 789-M
Morristown, NJ 07960
Softside (TRS-80)
The Software Exchange
6 South Street
Milford, NH 03055
SS-50 Newsletter
(6800 based systems)
P. O. Box 402
Logan, UT 84321
'68' Micro Journal
(6800 based systems)
3018 Hamill Road
Hixson, TN 37343

FINANCIAL, INVESTMENT PERIODICALS

Barron's
200 Burnett Road
Chicopee, MS 01021
Better Investing
1515 East 11 Mile Road
Royal Oak, MI 48067

Chartcraft, Inc.
1 West Avenue
Larchmont, NY 10538

Daily Graphs
P. O. Box 24933
Los Angeles, CA 90024

Finance
5 East Seventy-fifth Street
New York, NY 10021

Financial Weekly
P. O. Box 26565
Richmond, VA 23261
Forbes
70 Fifth Avenue
New York, NY 10011

Money
Time & Life Building
541 N. Fairbanks Ct.
Chicago, IL 60611

Option Charts
Dunn & Hargitt
22 N. Second Street
Lafayette, IN 47902

Stock Guide
Standard & Poors Corp.
25 Broadway
New York, NY 10004

Trendline
25 Broadway
New York, NY 10004
The Wall Street Journal
200 Burnett Road
Chicopee, MS 01021

3 In One
Moore & Schley, Cameron & Co.
Two Broadway
New York, NY 10004

Wall Street Transcript
120 Wall Street
New York, NY 10005

INVESTMENT ADVISORY SERVICES

The Analyst
1106 Main Street
Peekskill, NY 10566
Babson's Reports
Wellesley Hills, MA 02181

Dines Letter
P.O. Box 22
Belvedere, CA 94920
Dow Theory Forecasts, Inc.
P.O. Box 4550, Grand Central Station
New York, NY 10163

Granville Market Letter
Drawer O
Holly Hill, FL 32017
Growth Stock Outlook
P.O. Box 9911
Chevy Chase, MD 20015

Holt Investment Advisory
290 Post Road West
Westport, CT 06880

Indicator Digest
451 Grand Avenue
Palisades Park, NJ 07650
Investor's Intelligence
2 East Avenue
Larchmont, NY 10538
Investment Strategist
333 E. 34th Street
New York, NY 10016

Lang Market Letter
6065 North Kavanagh Ave
Fresno, CA 93711

Professional Tape Reader
P.O. Box 2407
Hollywood, FL 33022

Ruff Times
Target Publishing Co.
P.O. Box 2000
San Ramon, CA 94583

Smart Money
The Hirsch Organization, Inc.
6 Deer Trail
Old Tappan, NJ 07675

United
Business & Investment
210 Newberry Street
Boston, MA 02116

Value Line
Investment Survey
Arnold Bernhard & Co., Inc.
711 Third Avenue
New York, NY 10017

Zweig Forecast
747 Third Avenue
New York, NY 10017

INVESTORS COMPUTER GROUP, SEMINAR

MicroComputer Investors Association
902 Anderson Dr.
Fredricksburg, VA 22401

This group is a nonprofit, professional association of persons who utilize microcomputers to assist in making and managing investments. Publication is *The MicroComputer Investor,* containing contributed articles and programs from members. Send $1.00 for information packet.

MICROSEMINARS
2021 Business Center Drive
Irvine, CA 927515

Seminars conducted by Dr. Alfred Adler, a widely published author of articles and programs dealing with microcomputer investment techniques. Information and guide to investment software on request.

TELECOMPUTING SERVICES

The scope of services offered by these services is being rapidly expanded and modified. If you are interested, write for the latest information and phone connection details.

CompuServe Information Service

CompuServe and Radio Shack have teamed up to offer software and hardware/software packages to access the network. Details from Radio Shack stores.

MicroNET
Personal Computing Division
CompuServe, Inc.
5000 Arlington Centre Blvd.
Columbus, OH 43220

The Source
Telecomputing Corporation of America
1616 Anderson Road
McLean, VA 22102

Additional Reading

Books offering features of special interest may have a short descriptive section following their listing. The publications listed here are but a sampling of the thousands presently offered for investors and a smaller, but rapidly growing number, of computer oriented books.

INVESTORS AND INVESTMENTS

Adler, Bill. *The Wall Street Reader*. World Publishing Co., 1970

Alexander, Jason. *Philosopy for Investors*. San Francisco, CA: Sitnalta Press, 1979

    A collection of 12 essays which originally appeared in 1979 as an institutional advisory service newsletter. Helps the investor to develop consistent investment philosophy and goals.

Amling, Frederick. *Investments*. Englewood Cliffs, NJ:Prentice-Hall, 1974

Ansbacker, Max. *The New Options Market*. New York: Walker, 1978.

Appel, Gerald. *Double Your Money Every Three Years*. Brightwaters, NY: Windsor Books, 1974

Bellemore, Douglas H. and Ritchie, John C. *Investments: Principles and Practice of Analysis*. Cincinnati: SW Publishing, 1974

Bladen, A. *How To Cope With The Developing Financial Crisis*. New York: McGraw-Hill.

    An investment expert's blueprint for financial survival in the 1980's.

Branch, Benjamin. *Fundamentals of Investing*. New York: Wiley, 1976.

Browne, Harry. *New Profits From The Monetary Crisis*. Morrow, 1978.

Clasing, Henry F. *The Dow Jones-Irwin Guide to Put and Call Options*. Homewood, IL: Dow Jones-Irwin, 1977

Cleeton, Claud E. *The Art of Independent Investing*. Englewood Cliffs, NJ:Prentice-Hall, 1976

Cobleigh, Ira U. *Happiness Is a Stock That Doubles In a Year*. New York: Signet, 1976.

    Offers some interesting techniques for identifying stocks likely to experience significant gains.

Cohen, Jerome B. et al. *Guide to Intelligent Investing*. Homewood, IL: Dow Jones-Irwin, 1977.

Craig, Gary H. *Unscrewing the Small Investor*. New York: Van Nostrand, 1976.

Crowell, Richard A. *Stock Market Strategy*. New York: McGraw-Hill, 1977.

Darst, David M. *The Complete Bond Book*. New York: McGraw-Hill, 1975.

Edwards, Robert D. and Magee, John. *Technical Analysis of Stock Trends*. Springfield, MA: John Magee & Associates, 1976.

Emory, Eric S. *When to Sell Stocks*. Homewood, IL: Dow Jones-Irwin, 1978.

Engle, Louis. *How to Buy Stocks*. New York: Bantam Books, 1977.

Fischer, Donald E. and Jorden, Ronald J. *Security Analysis and Portfolio Management*. Englewood Cliffs, NJ: Prentice-Hall, 1979.

Fisher, Philip A. *Conservative Investors Sleep Well*. New York: Harper & Row, 1975.

Gastineau, Gary L. *The Stock Options Manual: New, Revised Edition*. New York: McGraw-Hill, 1980.

A comprehensive guide that should be in the library of serious investors considering the field of stock options.

Graham, Benjamin. *The Intelligent Investor*. New York: Harper & Row, 1973.

George, Wilfred R. *The Profit Box System of Forecasting Stock Prices*. Homewood, IL: Dow Jones-Irwin, 1978.

Granville, Joseph E. *Strategy of Daily Stock Market Timing for Maximum Profits*. Englewood Cliffs, NJ: Prentice-Hall, 1977.

Hallman, G.V. and Rosenbloom, J.S. *Personal Financial Planning: How to Plan For Your Financial Freedom*. New York: McGraw-Hill, 1979.

Revised edition, contains 18 sections to show you how to attain financial independence sooner than you thought possible.

Hardy, C. Colburn, *Dunn & Bradstreet's Guide to $YOUR INVEST-MENTS$* New York: Crowell, 1980.

1980-81 marks the twenty-fifth edtion of this comprehensive book. Look for whichever edition is current when purchasing.

Hardy, C. Colburn. *Investors Guide to Technical Analysis*. New York: McGraw-Hill, 1978.

Hayes, Michael. *Dow Jones-Irwin Guide to Stock Market Cycles*. Homewood, IL: Dow Jones-Irwin, 1977.

Hazard, John W. *Choosing Tomorrow's Growth Stocks Today*. New York: Doubleday, 1968.

Hazard, John W. *Success With Your Investments*. Garden City, NY: Doubleday, 1973.

Heffert, Erick A. *Techniques of Financial Analyses*. Homewood, IL: Dow Jones-Irwin, 1978.

Heller, Robert. *The Naked Investor*. New York: Delacorte, 1977.

Herzfeld, Thomas J. *The Investors Guide to Closed-End Funds: The Herzfeld Hedge*. New York: McGraw-Hill, 1980.

Complete analysis of an investment area many people are overlooking.

Homer, Sidney. *The Great American Bond Market*. Homewood, IL: Dow Jones-Irwin, 1978.

Investors' Intelligence. *Encyclopedia of Stock Market Techniques*. Larchmont, NY: Investors' Intelligence Inc., 1968.

Jessup, Paul F. *Competing for Stock Market Profits.* New York: Wiley, 1974.

Jiler, William. *How Charts Can Help You in the Stock Market.* New York: Trendline, 1976.

Jones, Charles P. et al. *Essentials of Modern Investments.* New York, Wiley, 1977.

Laurance, Michael. *Playboy's Investment Guide.* Chicago: Playboy Press, 1977.

Lenz, Thomas V. *New Uses For the Home Computer in the Stock Market.* Self published by: Thomas V. Lenz, 596 W. Karval Ct., Spring Creek Elso, NV 89801.

This book provides a new insight into cycles and seasonal factors as they affect stock and commodity prices. Gives the user solid tools for measuring and profiting from them.

Loeb, Gerald M. *The Battle For Stock Market Profits.* New York: Simon & Schuster, 1971.

Lohman, Philipp H. *The Art of Investing.* New York: Hawthorne, 1972.

Lorie, James and Hamilton, Mary. *The Stock Market Theories and Evidence.* Homewood, IL: Dow Jones-Irwin, 1973.

Metz, Robert. *Jackpot!.* New York: Simon & Schuster, 1977.

Ney, Richard. *Making It in The Market.* New York: McGraw-Hill, 1975.

Describes Ney's low risk system for stock market investors.

Noddings, Thomas C. *Advanced Investment Strategies.* Homewood IL: Dow Jones-Irwin, 1978.

Noddings, Thomas C. *Guide to Convertible Securities.* Homewood IL: Dow Jones-Irwin, 1976.

Peissner, Robert N. and Peissner, Darryl. *How to Select Undervalued Stocks.* New York: Dutton, 1972.

Porter, Sylvia. *Syliva Porter's New Money Book for the 80's.* Garden City, NY: Doubleday, 1979.

Widely respected work covering numerous aspects of financial management and investments.

Prendergast, Lawrence S. *Uncommon Profits Through Stock Purchase Warrants.* Homewood IL: Dow Jones-Irwin, 1973.

Pring, Martin J. *International Investing Made Easy: Proven Money-Making Strategies With As Little As $5000.* New York: McGraw-Hill, 1979.

As the title implies, a basic strategy for international investing. Includes buy and sell signals for stock and bond markets as well as guidelines for trading in precious metals, currency and financial futures.

Pring, Martin J. *Technical Analysis Explained: An Illustrated Guide For the Investor.* New York: McGraw-Hill, 1980.

Rosenberg, Claude N. *The Common Sense Way to Stock Market Profits.* New York: New American Library, 1978.

Rukeyser, Louis. *How to Make Money In Wall Street.* Garden City, NY: Doubleday, 1974.

Schwed, Fred Jr. *Where Are the Customers' Yachts?.* New York: Simon & Schuster, 1955.

A tongue in cheek look at the field of investing, subtitled *A good hard look at Wall Street.* First printed in 1940, I recently acquired a copy of the edition reprinted for Kingsley, Boye & Southwood, Inc. Well worth the time it takes to find a copy!

Shulman, Morton. *How to Invest Your Money and Profit From Inflation.* New York: Random House, 1980.

Sokoloff, Kiril (ed.) *The Paine Webber Handbook of Stock and Bond Analysis.* New York: McGraw-Hill, 1979.

The first book to offer investors up to the minute, individual coverage of every industry and fixed income security.

Sokoloff, Kiril. *The Thinking Investors Guide to the Stock Market.* New York: McGraw-Hill, 1978.

Thomas, Conrad. *How to Sell Short and Perform Other Wondrous Feats.* Homewood, IL: Dow Jones-Irwin, 1976.

Tobias, Andrew. *The Only Investment Guide You'll Ever Need.* New York: Harcourt, Brace Janovitch, 1978.

Train, John. *The Dance of the Money Bees.* New York: Harper & Row, 1974.

Train, John. *The Money Masters* New York: Harper & Row, 1980.

Describes nine great investors and their willing strategies, then shows you how to apply them.

Tucille, Jerome. *Everything the Beginner Needs to Know to Invest Shrewdly.* New Rochelle, NY: Arlington House, 1978.

Tucille, Jerome. *The Optimist's Guide to Making Money in the 1980s.* New Rochelle, NY: Arlington House, 1979.

United Business Service. *Successful Investing.* New York: Simon & Schuster, 1979.

Wendt, F. C. *Investment Guide to Profits from Rights, Splits and Dividends.* New York: Pilot Books, 1974.

Widdicus, Wilbur W. and Stitzes, Thomas E. *Personal Investing.* Homewood, IL: Dow Jones-Irwin, 1976.

Williamson, Ellen. *Wall Street Made Easy.* Garden City, NY: Doubleday, 1965.

An unconventional guide to profitable investing.

Wiliger, Betty S. *Dollars and ene.* New York: Random House, 1976.

A rather unique primer for the individual investor, helping to protect your money and watch it grow.

Wysong, Perry. *How You Can Use The Wall Street Insiders.* Wilton House, 1971.

Zahorchac, Michael G. *The Art of Low Risk Investing.* New York: Van Nostrand Reinhold, 1977.

Mentioned in the text of this book as the basis for a computer program dealing with moving averages.

Zarb, Frank G. and Kerekes, Gabriel T. et al. *The Stock Market Handbook.* Homewood, IL: Dow Jones-Irwin, 1976.

COMPUTERS AND COMPUTING

Ahl, David H. (ed.) *The Best of Creative Computing, Vol. 1.* Morristown, NJ: Creative Computing Press, 1976.

A collection of over 30 programs from Creative Computing Magazine, including several of interest to investors. Also Volumes 2 and 3 available.

Albrecht, Robert. *My Computer Likes Me When I speak in Basic.* Menlo Park, CA: Dymax, 1972.

A good introduction to BASIC on an elementary level.

Albrecht, R., Finkel, L. and Brown, G. *Basic (2nd ed) : A Self Teaching Guide*. New York: Wiley. 1978.

Most effectively used while sitting at a computer or computer terminal.

Ball, Marion and Chase, Sylvia. *Be a Computer Literate*. Morristown, NJ: Creative Computing Press, 1977.

A rather elementary level introduction to computers and BASIC programming.

Barden, Willam Jr. *How to Buy & Use Minicomputers & Microcomputers*. Indianapolis, IN: Sams, 1976.

Barden, William Jr. *How to Program Microcomputers*. Indianapolis, IN: Sams, 1977.

Explains assembly language programming for microcomputers based on the 8080, 6800 and 6502 microprocessor chips. Includes a number of useful routines.

Barna, Arpad and Porat, Daniel. *Introduction to Microcomputers and Microprocessors*. New York: Wiley, 1976.

Brainerd, W., Goldberg, C. and Gross, J. *Introduction to Computer Programming*. New York: Harper and Row, 1979.

Primarily designed as a college text, also develops concepts helpful in many computer languages.

Brown, Jerald R. *INSTANT (Freeze-Dried Computer Programming in) Basic*. Forest Grove, OR: Dilithium Press, 1977.

Capece, Raymond P. (ed.) *Personal Computing: Hardware and Software Basics*. New York: McGraw-Hill, 1979.

A collection of articles selected from numerous publications. Designed to provide a thorough introduction to computers.

Carlson, Edward H. *All About OSI BASIC-IN-ROM*. Okemis, MI: Edward H. Carlson (3872 Raleigh Dr., 48864).

Chance, David. *Computer Graphics—with 29 ready-to-run programs*. Blue Ridge Summit, PA: TAB Books Inc.

Chmura, Louis J. and Ledgard, Henry F. *COBOL With Style: Programming Proverbs*. Rochelle Park, NJ: Hayden, 1976.

Describes structured programming. Offers 19 guidelines (proverbs) to help write readable and easily modified COBOL programs.

Coan, James S. *Advanced BASIC: Applications and Problems*. Rochelle Park, NJ: Hayden, 1976.

Features a review of basic BASIC concepts, then offers advanced techniques and applications for those who want to extend their expertise. Also helpful to those learning BASIC as a second or third programming language.

Coan, James S. *Basic BASIC*. Rochelle Park, NJ: Hayden, 1978.

Contains over 100 sample programs used to illustrate the concepts of BASIC. Useful as a classroom text, with solutions to some of the problems posed contained in the separate Teacher's Guide.

Dence, Thomas P. *The Fortran Cookbook*. Blue Ridge Summit, PA: TAB Books Inc.

Covers a wide range of FORTRAN programming exercises for the beginning or more advanced programmer.

Donahue, Carroll S. and Enger, Janice K. *PET/CBM Personal Computer Guide*. Berkeley, CA: Osborne/McGraw-Hill.

Dwyer, Thomas and Critchfield. *BASIC and The Personal Computer*. Reading, MA: Addison-Wesley, 1978.

One of the best BASIC texts this author owns. Along with detailed explanations and examples, methods of converting complex functions to relatively simple subroutines are described. Especially helpful in converting programs from one version of BASIC to another.

Dwyer, Thomas and Kaufman, Michael. *A Guided Tour to Computer Programming in BASIC*. Boston: Houghton Mifflin, 1973.

Written primarily for high school age classes, also helpful to beginning programmer.

Editors of 73 Magazine. *The Giant Handbook of Computer Projects*. Blue Ridge Summit, PA: TAB Books Inc.

Contains complete schematics, parts lists and step-by-step instructions.

Editors of 73 Magazine. *The Giant Book of Computer Software*. Blue Ridge Summit, PA: TAB Books Inc.

Design your own computer programs to fit your individual needs. Covers computer languages and writing programs in BASIC, FORTRAN and PASCAL.

Engel, C. W. *Stimulating Simulations, Second Edition*. Rochelle Park, NJ: Hayden, 1979.

Contains 12 simulation programs (games) which may provide a good starting point for further exploration of simulation programming.

Findley, Robert. *6502 Software Gourmet Guide and Cookbook*. Elmwood, CT: Scelbi Publications, 1979.

Findlay, William and Watt, David A. *PASCAL: An Introduction to Methodical Programming*. Potomac, MD: Computer Science Press, 1978.

A textbook intended for first course in programming based on PASCAL. Also provides good introduction for personal computer users.

Freilberger, Stephen and Chew, Paul. *A Consumer's Guide to Personal Computing and Mircoprocessors*. Rochelle Park, NJ: Hayden, 1978.

Covers the basics of microcomputer principles, review of products available and buying tips.

Frenzel, Louis E. *Getting Acquainted With Microcomputers*. Indianapolis, IN: Sams, 1978.

Self-instructional book designed to teach using the Microcomputer Learning Laboratory described.

Frenzel, Louis E. *The Howard W. Sams Crash Course in Microcomputers*. Indianapolis, IN: Sams, 1980.

Self-instructional text divided into a series of 14 learning units. Provides a good basic education in today's microcomputers.

Gilmore, Charles A. *Beginner's Guide to Microprocessors*. Blue Ridge Summit, PA: TAB Books Inc.

Assumes no prior knowledge of the subject. Primarily devoted to coverage of the microprocesor itself.

Graham, Neill. *Artificial Intelligence*. Blue Ridge Summit, PA: TAB Books Inc.

Interesting reading and good background for use of computer logic in your own progams.

Graham, Neill. *Microprocessor Programming for Computer Hobbyists*. Blue Ridge Summit, PA: TAB Books Inc.

Ranges from the very basic concepts to state of the art knowledge needed by working professional programmers.

Gupta, Madan L. *PIMS: Personal Information Management System.* Elmwood, CT: Scelbi Publications, 1979.

Hallmark, Clayton L. *Computerist's Handy Databook/Dictionary.* Blue Ridge Summit, PA: TAB Books Inc.

Haviland, Robert P. *How To Design, Build & Program Your Own Working Computer System.* Blue Ridge Summit, PA: TAB Books Inc.

A complete computer build-it book that covers design, construction, programming and testing. Combines both hardware and software so you can customize your own computer system.

Heiserman, David L. *PASCAL* Blue Ridge Summit, PA: TAB Books Inc.

Illustrates the use of Tiny PASCAL in a TRS-80 system and covers the basics of PASCAL programming.

Hordeski, Michael F. *Illustrated Dictionary of Microcomputer Terminology.* Blue Ridge Summit, PA: TAB Books Inc.

Provides summary information on almost 4000 terms presently used in the microcomputing field.

Irman, D., Zamora, R. and Albrecht, R. *Introduction To TI BASIC.* Rochelle Park, NJ: Hayden, 1980.

Reference work for the Texas Instruments Home Computer. Covers all the basics plus special features found in this unit.

Lancaster, Don. *The Incredible Secret Money Machine.* Indianapolis, IN: Sams, 1978.

In addition to describing a method of setting up your own "money machine" business, Lancaster outlines an interesting approach to investment management. Entertaining reading with an important message.

Ledgard, Henry F. and Chmura, Louis J. *FORTRAN With Style: Programming Proverbs.* Rochelle Park, NJ: Hayden, 1978.

Ledgard, Henry F., Nagin, Paul and Hueras. *PASCAL With Style: Programming Proverbs.* Rochelle Park, J: Hayden, 1979.

Lenz, Thomas V. *New Uses for the Home Computer in the Stock Market.* Self-published by Thomas V. Lenz, 596 W. Karval Ct., Spring Creek Elko, NV 89801. ($19.95).

This book contains 34 programs written in TRS-80 BASIC for use in stock market applications. The writer has experience both as a stock broker and computer programmer.

Lewis, T.G. *How to Profit From Your Personal Computer: Professional, Business and Home Applications.* Rochelle Park, NJ: Hayden, 1978.

Includes many BASIC program examples to illustrate the techniques described of putting your computer to work for you.

Lewis, T.G. *Software Engineering for Micros: the Electrifying Blueprint Speedcode Method.* Rochelle Park, NJ: Hayden, 1979.

Lewis, T.G. *The Mind Appliance: Home Computer Applications.* Rochelle Park, NJ: Hayden, 1978.

Includes dozens of BASIC programs illustrating the ideas offered.

Lewis, William E. *Computer Programming and the Art of Logic.* Rochelle Park, NJ: Hayden, 1980.

Designed to improve your computer programming problem solving techniques.

Libes, Sol. *Small Computer Systems Handbook.* Rochelle Park, NJ: Hayden, 1978.

Oriented more toward the computer hobbyist, this book describes construction and operation of microcomputers.

Lien, David. *Learning Level II*. El Cajon, CA: Compusoft Publishing.
A tutorial for learning Level II Radio Shack TRS-80 BASIC.

Lien, David. *The BASIC Handbook*. El Cajon, CA: Compusoft Publishing.
Covers many versions of BASIC. Explains commands, statements, functions and operators. Offers ideas on how to replace functions your BASIC may lack with subroutines using alternate commands. Excellent reference work.

Lukoff, Herman. *From Dits To Bits: A Personal History of the Electronic Computer*. Portland, OR: Robotics Press.

McCunn, Donald. *Computer Programming for the Complete Idiot*. San Francisco, CA: Design Enterprises of SF (Box 27677, 94127).
Beginners manual for the Radio Shack TRS-80.

McGlynn, Daniel R. *Personal Computing: Home, Professional and Small Business Applications*. New York: Wiley, 1979.

McQuigg, James D. and Harness, Alta M. *Flowcharting*. Boston: Houghton Mifflin, 1970.
Good introduction to this most important programming skill.

Moody, Robert. *The First Book of Microcomputers: The Home Computer Owner's Best Friend*. Rochelle Park, NJ: Hayden, 1978.
Entertaining introduction to the field of personal computing and many home and business applications.

Myers, Glenford. *The Art of Software Testing*. New York: Wiley, 1979.

Nagin, Paul and Ledgard, Henry F. *BASIC With Style: Programming Proverbs*. Rochelle Park, NJ: Hayden, 1978.

NCR Corporation. *NCR Data Communications Concepts*. Indianapolis, IN: Sams, 1971.
Explores the field of data communications, focusing primarily on telephone based systems.

NCR Corporation. *NCR Data Processing Concepts Course*. Indianapolis, IN: Sams, 1974.
General introduction to data processing, computers and logic for those generally interested in learning about computers.

P.G.I. Publishing. *Micro Shopper 80: The New Computers*. Tempee, AZ: P.G.I. Publishing (145 West 12th Place, 85281).

Pennington, Howard C. *TRS-80 Disk and Other Mysteries*. Upland, CA: IJG, Inc. (569 North Mountain Ave., 91786).

Personal Computing. *The Best of Personal Computing*. Boston, MA: Personal Computing Magazine.
Volumes 1 and 2 available. A collection of programs and articles from the magazine. Includes several investment oriented programs.

Poole, L. (ed.) *Practical BASIC Programs*. Berkeley, CA: Osborne/McGraw-Hill.
Contains forty programs designed for useful purposes. Includes write ups, program notes and instructional examples.

Poole, L., Borchers, M. and Donahue, C. *Some Common BASIC Programs*. Berkeley, CA: Osborne/McGraw-Hill.
Includes 76 programs for numerous mathematical and personal applications.

Safford, Edward L. Jr. *The Complete Microcomputer Systems Handbook*. Blue Ridge Summit, PA: TAB Books Inc.

A complete guide to microcomputers—how they operate, how to use them, how to program them and how to troubleshoot and repair them.

Sagan, Hans and Meyer, Carl. *Ten Easy Pieces: Creative Programming For Fun and Profit*. Rochelle Park, NJ: Hayden, 1980.

BASIC instruction through computer games designed to illustrate various programing techniques.

Sawusch, Mark. *1001 Things to do With Personal Computer*. Blue Ridge Summit, PA: TAB Books Inc.

Contains programs, printouts, flowcharts and sufficient information to try the wide range of applications mentioned.

Schindler, M., D.Sc. *Microprocessor Software Design*. Rochelle Park NJ: Hayden, 1980.

An edited compilation of articles from Electronic Design magazine, covers the whole spectrum of software.

Schoman, Kenneth. *The BASIC Workbook: Creative Techniques for Beginning Programmers*. Rochelle Park, NJ: Hayden, 1977.

Uses only twenty key words from BASIC in an active problem solving approach to learning programming.

Simon, David E. *BASIC From The Ground Up*. Rochelle Park, NJ: Hayden, 1978.

Sippl, Charles J. and Sippl, Roger J. *Computer Dictionary and Handbook (3rd Edition)*. Indianapolis, IN: Sams, 1980.

Contains over 22,000 definitions, acronyms and abbreviations. Fourteen appendices covering a wide range of topics. Dictionary also available separately.

Smith, Robert E. *Discovering BASIC: A Problem Solving Approach*. Rochelle Park, NJ: Hayden, 1970.

Soucek, Branko. *Microprocessors and Microcomputers*. New York: Wiley, 1976.

Spencer, Donald D. *Problems For Computer Solution, Second Edition*. Rochelle Park, NJ: Hayden, 1979.

An experimenting and doing approach to learning and refining programming skills.

Spencer, Donald D. *Sixty Challenging Programs With BASIC Solutions, Second Edition*. Rochelle Park, NJ: Hayden, 1979.

Problems designed for those familiar with BASIC are posed, then a program designed to solve the program is described.

Stark, Peter. *Computer Programming Handbook*. Blue Ridge Summit, PA: TAB Books Inc.

Comprehensive work on computer programming and data processing in general.

Steingraber, Jack. *FORTRAN Fundamentals: A Short Course*. Rochelle Park, NJ: Hayden, 1975.

Good introduction to the fundamentals of FORTRAN. Sample problems and solutions are given as illustrations.

Stern, Nancy. *Flowcharting—A Self-Teaching Guide*. New York: Wiley, 1975.

Sternberg, Charles D. *BASIC Computer Programs for the Home*. Rochelle Park, NJ: Hayden, 1979.

Home financial programs, tutorials, etc. Each program well documented and illustrated.

TIS. *Getting Started With Your Challenger 1P*. Los Alamos, NM: TIS (P.O. Box 921, 87544)

TIS. *Understanding Your PET/CBM Volume 1: Basic Programming*. Los Alamos, NM: TIS (P.O. Box 921, 87544).

Tracton, Ken. *Programmers Guide to LISP*. Blue Ridge Summit, PA: TAB Books Inc.

LISP, the popular languages used in artificial intelligence systems, is described and illustrated.

Tracton, Ken. *The Basic Cookbook*. Blue Ridge Summit, PA: TAB Books Inc.

Covers all BASIC commands, statements and functions by definition and demonstration in actual programs.

Tracton, Ken. *The Most Popular Subroutines in BASIC*. Blue Ridge Summit, PA: TAB Books Inc.

A dandy collection of useful subroutines and ideas for integrating them into your own programs.

Tracton, Ken. *57 Practical Programs and Games in BASIC*. Blue Ridge Summit, PA: TAB Books Inc.

Veit, Stanley S. *Using Microcomputers In Business*. Rochelle Park, NJ: Hayden, 1980.

Wadsworth, Nat. *Learn Micro-Computers*. Elmwood, CT: Scelbi Publications, 1978.

A book and cassette tape package designed to "take the mystery out of operation and application of small computers".

Waite, Mitchell. *Computer Graphics Primer*. Indianapolis, IN: Sams, 1979.

Good discussion of the basics of generating and using computer graphic displays.

Waite, Mitchell and Pardee, Michael. *BASIC Programming Primer*. Indianapolis, IN: Sams, 1978.

Waite, Mitchell and Pardee, Michael. *Microcomputer Primer (2nd Edition)*. Indianapolis, IN: Sams, 1980.

Coverage of the field of microcomputers from the very basics to the latest developments.

Waite, Mitchell and Pardee, Michael. *Your Own Computer*. Indianapolis, IN: Sams, 1977.

An introduction for the neophyte interested in home computers.

War, Brice. *Beginner's Guide To Computer Programming*. Blue Ridge Summit, PA: TAB Books Inc.

Begins with program requirements, then builds a language of its own.

Weisbecker, Joe. *Home Computers Can Make Your Rich*. Rochelle Park, NJ: Hayden, 1980.

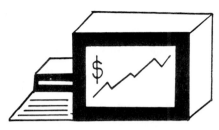

Index